THE TWELVE ZODIAC ANIMALS

十二生肖

研究出版社

PREFACE • • • • • • • • • •

The Twelve Zodiac Animals of China

The *shengxiao*, or animals of the Chinese zodiac, forms a method of numbering the years based on the names of 12 different animals. In sequential order, these animals are the rat, ox, tiger, rabbit, dragon, snake, horse, sheep, monkey, rooster, dog, and pig.

For over three millennia, China has followed the lunar calendar to record time. To count the years, the lunar calendar uses the 10 Heavenly Stems (*jia*, *yi*, *bing*, *ding*, *wu*, *ji*, *geng*, *xin*, *ren*, and *gui*) and the 12 Earthly Branches (*zi*, *chou*, *yin*, *mao*, *chen*, *si*, *wu*, *wei*, *shen*, *you*, *xu*, *hai*). Each person is assigned one of the 12 animals to correspond with, and represent, the Earthly Branch of the year in which he or she was born. The

十二生肖 THE TWELVE

12 animals of the Chinese zodiac thus are used to number the years, record and measure time, and determine each person's zodiac sign.

An essential and deep-rooted part of China's traditional culture, the *shengxiao* has had a profound impact on Chinese people. The *shengxiao* culture permeates every aspect of Chinese social life and is intimately connected with the lives of the Chinese people. The zodiac animals are used to inquire about the age of others, and *shengxiao*-related folktales, customs and even games can be found throughout China. The Chinese zodiac animals also play a prominent role in fortune-telling, and are beautifully illustrated and depicted in works of art and literature. The *shengxiao* has even come to assume a mystical quality. For instance, before a man and woman are married, it is important to first ensure that there is no conflict between their respective zodiac signs. Similarly, when choosing a name, it is also vital to avoid any names that would clash or conflict with the person's zodiac animal. During their time on earth, ancient emperors and the wealthy would use *shengxiao*-illustrated folding screens, precious mirrors, and coins to seek good fortune, and wear zodiac amulets to pray for their well-being. After they passed away, zodiac animal figurines would be sculpted and *shengxiao* frescos would be drawn to accompany them to the afterworld.

The Chinese zodiac and the culture related to it have circulated throughout Chinese society for a very long time. While it is difficult to determine the *shengxiao*'s precise origins, early records related to the zodiac animals are found in the *Classic of Poetry*. China's first anthology of poems, the *Classic of Poetry* comprises some 500 years of poems and songs from the early Western Zhou Dynasty (1046-771 BC) to the mid-Spring and Autumn Period (770-476 BC). In 1975, a set of Qin Dynasty bamboo slips was excavated in Shuihudi of Yunmeng County, Hubei Province. The contents included legal and administrative documents as well as the *Book of Days*, and also dealt with the politics, economy, culture, military affairs and other aspects of social life at that time. One of the essays, entitled *The Robber*, describes the match between a thief's facial features and his zodiac sign. This archaeological discovery further confirmed that the 12 zodiac animals existed as early as the Spring and Autumn Period (770-476 BC). The famous work *Critical Essays*, by materialist philosopher Wang Chong of the Eastern Han Dynasty (25-220), is the most comprehensive document dealing with the 12 zodiac animals discovered to date; the zodiac animals mentioned in the book are identical to the 12 popular zodiac animals in China today.

A paper-cutting of the twelve zodiac animals

ZODIAC ANIMALS

The Zodiac Animals and the Lunar Calendar

The emergence of the 12 zodiac animals has its roots in astronomy and is intimately connected with the Chinese calendar.

China was one of the first countries to devise a calendric system. Its appearance had an important impact on the development of China's economy and culture. From the calendar of the Yellow Emperor (lived in the late clan commune period, about 5500 to 4000 years ago) to the adoption of the western or Gregorian calendar in the late Qing Dynasty (1644-1911), China had witnessed the creation of over 100 calendrical systems — with varying degrees of influence on Chinese culture and civilization.

In Han ethnic areas, the traditional Chinese calendar, also known as the "lunar calendar", is universally adopted. Months are determined by the lunar phases, while the annual cycle is based on the sun. The lunar calendar defines each revolution of the moon around the Earth as one month. The day on which the sun and the moon rise in sync — when the moon cannot be seen from Earth — is set as the first day of each month. The length of each month may be 30 or 29 days depending on the moon phase, with the year consisting of 12 months. Because of the discrepancy between the annual solar cycle and the 12 months as based on the lunar phase cycle, a leap month is added every four years or so. The agricultural calendar, therefore, is a kind of lunisolar calendar.

The lunar calendar uses the Heavenly Stems and Earthly Branches to reckon the years, referred to as the Jia-Zi system. The 10 Heavenly Stems are matched with the 12 Earthly Branches to form 60 different combinations — such as *jia-zi*, *yi-chou*, *bing-yin*, etc.; each cycle, known as one *jia-zi*, thus spans 60 years. From 776 BC to 1911 AD, China used the Heavenly Stems and Earthly Branches continuously to record time, representing the world's longest and most complete chronology. These 60 combinations were further matched with the month (five years per cycle), day (60 days per cycle), and *shichen* or double-hour (120 hours per cycle). (The ancient Chinese employed a unit of time called the *shichen*, equivalent to two modern hours). The Earthly Branches were thus assigned to record the years, months, days, and double-hours. Because there is a one-to-one correspondence between the 12 zodiac animals and the 12 Earthly Branches, the 12 zodiac

THE TWELVE

animals' names were arranged in a fixed sequence by the Southern and Northern Dynasties period (420-589). Each year came to be represented by a specific animal, which serves as the zodiac sign for anyone born in that year. In this way, the following sequence of Chinese zodiac animals (and their corresponding Earthy Branches) evolved: rat (*zi*), ox (*chou*), tiger (*yin*), rabbit (*mao*), dragon (*chen*), snake (*si*), horse (*wu*), sheep (*wei*), monkey (*shen*), rooster (*you*), dog (*xu*), pig (*hai*).

History of the Twelve Zodiac Animals

The culture associated with the 12 zodiac animals has formed gradually over the long course of development of Chinese civilization. As an enduring part of China's folk culture, the zodiac animals have permeated every facet of Chinese society and contain deep psychocultural meaning for the Chinese people. With respect to how these 12 animals came to be chosen, however, opinions have varied widely since ancient times.

An old calendar picture of *shengxiao*

It is generally believed that the 12 animals of the Chinese zodiac were those most inextricably linked with the daily life and social life of the ancient Chinese people.

China has been an agricultural country since ancient times, and the farming and livestock industries have always been major economic pillars of Chinese society. Not only has this agricultural orientation served to direct and foster the development of Chinese society, it has also provided the material foundation on which the Chinese people continue to rely for their existence. China's farming tradition has also led to the emergence of numerous folk beliefs. In the traditional primer text the *Three Character Classic*, it is written: "The horse, the ox, and the sheep; the chicken, the dog, and the pig: these are the six animals which are kept by men." The *liu chu* ("six domestic animals") is an important concept in Chinese farming culture, with auspicious phrases like "the six animals flourish", "timely wind and opportune rain", "a bumper grain harvest", and "may the state be peaceful and the people safe" emerging in the ancient China. The inclusion of these six animals in the Chinese zodiac reflects this significance.

ZODIAC ANIMALS

The tiger, rabbit, monkey, rat, and snake, in contrast, can be said to be the wild animals most familiar to humankind. Stories related to these creatures also abound in Chinese folklore. For instance, in the past, the word "rabbit" (referring to the Jade Rabbit) was used as a pronoun for the moon; other literary and folk references include the Beautiful Monkey King, the Jade Mouse Demon, and the Great Immortal Tiger Power of *Journey to the West*, one of China's four great classic novels; as well as the White Snake and Green Snake in *Madame White Snake*, one of China's four major folktales.

In addition to the abovementioned animals, the Chinese dragon is an extremely important mystical creature in traditional Chinese culture. In Chinese mythology, the dragon is depicted soaring through the sky above, protecting the universe and summoning the wind and rain. Some of the dragon is always half concealed beneath the clouds, giving it an air of enigma and mystery. It is illustrated as a winding, snake-like creature, covered in scales and bearing four pointed claws. Most characteristic is the dragon's long, narrow head, equipped with a pair of shimmering eyes, a protruding mouth, elongated whiskers, and a pair of curved, antler-like horns. Exuding an aura of power and prestige, the dragon's appearance may even instill fear in the faint of heart. China's emperors regarded themselves as "true dragons" and the "sons of heaven", and the utensils they used were also decorated with thepattern of dragon. The dragon was also the chief of the four spiritual beings of ancient China (the dragon, phoenix, *kylin*, and tortoise). Even today, the Chinese people still proudly call themselves the

"Descendants of the Dragon."

There are also scholars who believe that the 12 zodiac animals are related to primitive totem worship, i.e., that the Chinese zodiac signs are derived from early man's worship of the animals of nature.

Sequence of the Twelve Zodiac Animals

With respect to the ordering of the 12 zodiac animals, many different tales have circulated across China. It is said that the first ancestor of the Chinese people — the Yellow Emperor — wanted to select 12 animals to serve as palace bodyguards. This news caused a great sensation among the animal kingdom. The ox was the first one to learn of the emperor's plans, and promptly set out en route to the palace. However, the rat secretly climbed onto the ox's back and as the ox was about to reach

the palace, the rat delivered a vicious bite to the ox's tail. Thrashing around in pain, the ox sent the rat catapulting through the air. The rat, however, came to a landing in front of the palace gate and thus became the first animal to sign up as bodyguard. The ox came in second just behind the rat, followed by the tiger, the rabbit, the dragon, the snake, the horse, the sheep, the monkey, the rooster, the dog, and the pig. According to another version of this story, recruitment and selection were based on each animal's body size. The elephant initially ranked first, but the rat lodged itself in the elephant's trunk, and the elephant had to concede victory to the rat. In an alternate version, the cat was also eager to participate in the selection process, and asked the rat to sign him up. In the end, however, it slipped the rat's mind, and the cat was eliminated from the outset. From then on, the cat and the rat became enemies. These zodiac tales — and countless others which have emerged since antiquity — are the crystallization of the Chinese folk wisdom. While not providing a scientific description, they do embody a very real desire of the Chinese people to explain the selection of the 12 zodiac animals.

A *Luopan*, or *Fengshui* Compass, uesd to determine the precise direction of a structure

In ancient times, China divided the day into 12 parts or *shichen*. Some ancient Chinese scholars relied on the 12 *shichen* to explain the relationship between the Earthly Branches and the zodiac animals. One of the 12 Earthly Branches was assigned to each *shichen* (equivalent to two modern hours) as a way to record time. The *zi*-hour is the period from 11:00pm to 1:00am, the *chou*-hour from 1:00am to 3:00am, and so on. According to this explanation, the ordering of the 12 zodiac animals is based on the time of day during which each animal is most active. (Though the dragon does not exist in real life, it certainly existed in the minds of the ancient Chinese.) The specific sequence is as follows:

ZODIAC ANIMALS

Zi-hour (11:00pm-1:00am): This is the time during which rats are most lively. The *zi*-hour is thus paired with the rat.

Chou-hour (1:00am-3:00am): This is regarded as the time during which the ox begins to plow the soil. As a result, the *chou*-hour is paired with the ox.

Yin-hour (3:00am-5:00am): This period is one of extreme ferocity, as the tiger begins to hunt for its prey. For this reason, the *yin*-hour is paired with the tiger.

Mao-hour (5:00am-7:00am): In ancient Chinese mythology, there is a saying that "the sun holds the crow; the moon holds the rabbit"; the sun is thus known as the "golden crow", while the moon is called the "jade rabbit". During the *mao*-hour, the sun has not yet risen and the moon still hangs in the sky. This time of day is thus paired with the rabbit.

Chen-hour (7:00am-9:00am): In antiquity, the dragon was believed to be the spiritual being responsible for rainfall, and the *chen*-hour was regarded as the most favorable time for the dragon to make rain. This time of day, therefore, is paired with the dragon.

A Master Rabbit toy

The correspondence between the 12 *shichen*, the Earthly Branches and the zodiac animals

十二生肖 THE TWELVE

Si-hour (9:00am-11:00am): By this time, the fog has lifted and sunlight streams down from the sky. As the snake is said to be most lively during this period, the *si*-hour is paired with the snake.

Wu-hour (11:00am-1:00pm): According to the ancient theory of *yin-yang*, this is a period of *yin* and *yang* exchange, during which *yang* (male) energy reaches its limit and *yin* (female) energy is subsequently produced. Horses like to run and frolic during this time. Their hooves soar into the air, representing *yang*, and then hit the ground, representing *yin*. As the horse gallops, it is literally leaping between *yin* and *yang*. The *wu*-hour is thus paired with the horse.

Wei-hour (1:00pm-3:00pm): It is said that the afternoon is the best time for sheep to graze, as it facilitates weight gain. The *wei*-hour is thus paired with the sheep.

Shen-hour (3:00pm-5:00pm): During this period, as the evening draws near, monkeys like to howl, flail their arms, and jump around. The *shen*-hour is thus paired with the monkey. An alternate explanation is that monkeys like to climb up trees by extending their arms; the Chinese word for "extend" (*shen*) is homophonic with the earthly branch *shen*.

You-hour (5:00pm-7:00pm): When the sun sets behind the mountain and dusk falls, the rooster returns to its coop. The *you*-hour is thus paired with the rooster.

Xu-hour (7:00pm-9:00pm): As darkness falls, it is time for dogs to start their "work": guarding the house and keeping watch over the night. For this reason, the *xu*-hour is paired with the dog.

Hai-hour (9:00pm-11:00pm): It is said that if swine are fed at this hour, their body weight increases at the fastest rate. It has also been observed that, as darkness falls and all is quiet, the world breaks into a state of muddled chaos, much as the pig — which eats and sleeps all day long — lives a kind of muddled existence. The *hai*-hour is thus paired with the pig.

A bronze mirror with the pattern of *shengxiao* from the Sui Dynasty

ZODIAC ANIMALS

A Suzhou embroidery of *shengxiao*

In a sense, these explanations reflect the ancient Chinese people's understanding of the world's living creatures and the laws of nature.

Another explanation is based on the Chinese concept of *yin-yang*. Under this scenario, each of the 12 animals was placed into the *yin* or *yang* category, in an alternating fashion, depending on whether the animal has an odd or even number of toes. In ancient times, it was believed that the Earthly Branches *chou*, *mao*, *si*, *wei*, *you* and *hai* belonged to the *yin* class. These Earthy Branches were thus symbolized by, and matched with, animals whose bodies have an even number of toes. For example, the ox, rabbit, sheep, rooster, and pig all have four claws. Since snakes have no feet, they were also grouped into the "even" category. (An alternate reason is that the snake's tongue is divided into two prongs.) The Earthly Branches *zi*, *yin*, *chen*, *wu*, *shen*, and *xu* were regarded as belonging to the *yang* class. These Earthly Branches were thus represented by, and paired with, animals whose bodies have an odd number of digits. The tiger, dragon, horse, monkey, and dog all have five toes. The rat is the most special case: it has four digits on its forelimbs and five on its hind limbs. The first half of the *zi*-hour is the previous night's *yin*, while the second half is the new day's *yang*. According to this scenario, the rat is most capable of symbolizing the Earthly Branch *zi* and was thus chosen as the head of the zodiac animals.

The Zodiac Animals of China: Culture and Beliefs

The Chinese zodiac animals were originally a set of symbols used to reckon the years. They were initially a part of the ancient astronomical calendar, and later became universally adopted across China to form a zodiac calendar. Thereafter, the 12 zodiac animals gradually fused with the concepts of *yin-yang* theory, the Five Elements, Taoism and Buddhism, to become part of the folk religion of China. From the moment of birth onward, each person has his or her own zodiac animal sign, which plays a mysterious role in every aspect of life — illness and aging, weddings and funerals — and even factors into diet selection and the interpretation of dreams.

--------------- *Benmingnian*: The Year of One's Own Zodiac Sign ---------------

An essential part of China's zodiac belief system is the concept of *benmingnian*. A person's

benmingnian refers to any year coinciding with that person's own zodiac animal sign. Since the zodiac animals rotate on a 12-year cycle, people encounter their *benmingnian* once every 12 years. In this way, each person has a *benmingnian* at the age of 12, 24, 36, 48, 60, and so on.

In traditional Chinese culture, year of one's own zodiac sign is often perceived as an inauspicious time. There is a folk saying that "in one's *benmingnian*, great fortune or great calamity awaits"; as a result, the *benmingnian* is also known as the "hurdle year". The taboo associated with this make-or-break year has also influenced the behavior of the Chinese people. For example, when people meet with a *benmingnian*, they should take steps to improve their luck and deflect ill fortune. One of the most common customs is to "hang red" (or "bind red"), i.e., to wear red-colored garments (such as

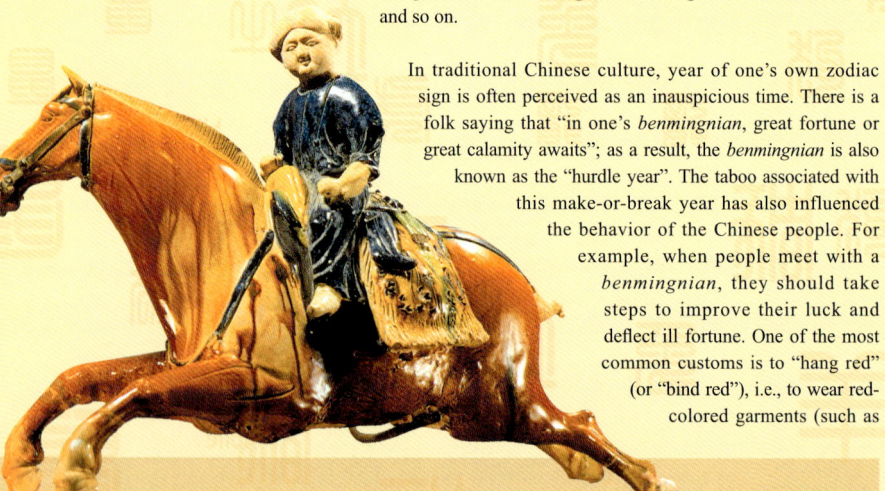

A colored clay sculpture from the Tang Dynasty

underwear, a belt, or a silk ribbon) during the year of one's zodiac sign. Some people also wear auspicious ornaments carried on red string. "Hanging red" to ward off evil and avert disaster is still popular across China today. This custom derives from the worship of red within the traditional culture of the Chinese Han people. Since ancient times, the Chinese formed an indissoluble bond with the color red: the walls and pillars of emperors' palaces were painted red, and the emperor would annotate or amend memorials to the throne using red ink. For the wealthy, red is a symbol of wealth and prosperity. For the common people, it represents jubilance and good fortune. As a result, people believe that, in one's *benmingnian*, only by dressing in red attire and wearing red-colored adornments can potential disaster be thwarted and good fortune renewed.

A stage performance of twelve zodiac animals

ZODIAC ANIMALS

---------- Folk Customs ----------

The zodiac animals, an important component of Chinese folk beliefs and practices, have penetrated virtually every realm of China's culture. The zodiac's cultural significance often manifests itself in an array of folk habits and customs throughout China.

When choosing a name, Chinese characters are also chosen such that their structure matches the person's zodiac sign. In order to summon good luck and circumvent ill fortune, Chinese characters which embody the personality, habitat and other characteristics of a person's zodiac animal are selected. This practice began in antiquity and has since spread far and wide. In the past, for example, as soon as there was any mention of tigers, people would think of sayings like "the tiger roars over the mountain and forest" or "one mountain cannot accommodate two tigers." As the mountain was regarded as the tiger's habitat, people born in the Year of the Tiger should ideally have the symbol for "mountain" embedded in their names. Monkeys, in contrast, like to jump around in trees foraging for food. As a result, it is preferable that people born in the Year of the Monkey have the symbol for

"wood" in their name.

In ancient times, people placed a lot of emphasis on marriage. If a boy's parents wanted a daughter-in-law, they would first ask the prospective bride's parents for her "eight-character horoscope", i.e., choose two Chinese characters each to represent the girl's year, month, date and time of birth. This information would then be given to the fortune teller to determine, based on certain calculations, whether it was compatible with the boy's horoscope. A complete set of theory and standards associated with the eight-character horoscope, as pertains to the zodiac animals, was used to determine whether a marriage was destined to be blissful or whether a boy and girl were meant to be together. Notions regarding the inter-compatibility of different zodiac signs are reflected in folk expressions, including "The Pig and the Monkey shed tears together", "The Rooster and the Monkey won't make it to the end", and "If a Snake coils around a Rabbit, their wealth will keep piling up." Of course, whether a marriage is likely to be harmonious or not depends on man and woman's respective personalities, their attitudes towards marriage, and many other factors; no scientific basis exists for the Chinese zodiac-based notions of marriage and relationships.

THE TWELVE

A paper-cutting of *shengxiao*

Many fascinating customs dealing with the Chinese zodiac animals have also flourished among China's folk culture. Ox plowing, for instance, was one of the most important farming methods in ancient times. Thus, at the arrival of the Beginning of Spring (the first of the 24 solar terms, generally occurring on February 4th of the Gregorian calendar), the "Whip the Spring Ox" ritual would be performed. In this ritual, a "Spring Ox" would be sculpted using clay and placed near the front gate of the village. With whip in hand, the village chief would then strike the Spring Ox three times, to respectively symbolize "a peaceful state and a safe populace", "a bumper grain harvest" and "timely wind and opportune rain." This ritual to usher in the spring expresses the Chinese people's love of this season and also reflects their ardent wishes for the new year. The Beginning of Spring is thus also known as "Whip Spring", a contraction of "Whip the Spring Ox."

The Mystical Culture of the Zodiac Animals

The 12 zodiac animals were originally used as a concept of time. However, the ancient Chinese were influenced by philosophical concepts, such as "the unity of heaven and man" and "*yin-yang* and the Five Elements". As a result, the zodiac animals gradually acquired a space-partitioning function, endowing them with a mystical quality.

The ancient Chinese believed that the universe was the aggregate of space and time, of all that exists in the cosmos, and that *yin-yang* and the Five Elements were the essence of the universe. Thus, people regarded all of creation as being associated with the Five-Element framework of Metal, Wood, Water, Fire, and Earth. Despite the contents of the universe being greatly variegated, they were thought to have a unified structural order: *yin-yang* and the Five Elements. "*yin-yang*" originally referred to the presence or absence of sunlight: "*Yin* sees the clouds but not the sun; as the clouds break, *yang* sees the sun." During the Spring and Autumn Period and the Warring States Period, Chinese ideologists used this concept to explain the effect of the interaction between the mutual antagonism and reciprocal transformation of nature's matter (or its properties) with *yin-yang* interaction on the creation and development of everything in the universe. The cycle of the Five Elements — as well as their mutual affinity or antagonism — reveals the interactive structural relations between things. According to this revolving model, changes in *yin* and *yang* energy act as an internal momentum to impel the sequential

ZODIAC ANIMALS

revolution of the Five Elements. As a structural framework, the Five Elements also provide an ordered cycle for transformations of *yin* and *yang*. Changes in *yin-yang* and the Five Elements form the basis for all of human activity. If people transgress the laws of change of *yin-yang* and the Five Elements, it is believed that catastrophe will ensue. This traditional philosophy served as a guiding force in ancient China, and was gradually integrated into the Chinese zodiac culture.

After popular beliefs about zodiac animals first emerged, they spread far and wide within Chinese folk culture as the art of fortune telling flourished. As the Heavenly Stems and Earthly Branches possess attributes of the Five Elements, the zodiac animals, too, incorporate the traits of these elements. Each zodiac animal sign, in addition to being characterized by one of the Five Elements, is also endowed with concepts such as color and orientation.

Folk superstition holds that the Five Elements are mutually governing and bearing a major influence over one's entire life. People can utilize the different Elements for coordination purposes to ensure that their lives and careers accord with their desires. The zodiac animals are classified into *yin* and *yang* categories to correspond with the Five Elements. This leads to the formation of an art of fortune telling in which the zodiac animal signs are believed to determine a person's fate. Beliefs about the impact of a person's zodiac sign on his or her personality also emerge in folk culture. However, even if two people share the same zodiac sign, their personalities and fates will differ if they were born at different times of day (i.e., during different *shichen*).

The Zodiac Animals and Buddhist Culture

Buddhism originated in India and, according to official records, was introduced to China during the reign of Emperor Ming (58-75) of the Han Dynasty. Historical records indicate that, in the seventh Yongping year (64), Emperor Ming of Han dispatched an envoy to the Western Regions to seek the power

of Buddha. In 67, they returned to the capital Luoyang (in today's Henan Province) with the Indian monks Kasyapa Matanga and Dharmaraksa, bringing back Buddhist scripture as well as a statue of Buddha. At the same time, China's first Buddhist temple, "White Horse Temple", was built at Luoyang. After Buddhism was introduced to China, it gradually interacted and fused with Han culture, developing its own unique characteristics in culture, architecture, sculpture arts, and other areas.

There is no lack of records in Buddhist culture dealing with the zodiac animals. In one Buddhist account, similar to the story of the Yellow Emperor mentioned above, the Tathagata Buddha selected 12 animals to serve as his guards. In addition, it is recorded in Buddhist scripture that the Medicine Buddha — the founder of the Pure Color-Glazed World of the East — had 12 protective deities, also known as his 12 Divine Generals, corresponding one-to-one with the 12 Earthly Branches. It is said that the Divine Generals worked in shifts, during the 12 *shichen* of each day and the 12 months of each year, to guard over the sacred land of Buddha. The images of these 12 Divine Generals are also said to be related to the 12 zodiac animals popular in China: the Buddhist crown worn by each Divine General is adorned with the image of that General's zodiac animal sign. It has also been said that each of the 12 Divine Generals had its own animal used for riding, constituting the 12 animals of the Chinese zodiac.

In esoteric Buddhism, there are eight Buddhas or Bodhisattvas, known as *Benmingfo* or the "Eight Great Protectors," who bless and protect the 12 zodiac animals. If people offer sacrifices to the spiritual protector which corresponds to their own zodiac animal sign, or wear an adornment of the animal's likeness, they can transform latent adversity into bountiful blessings, achieve success in their career, and ensure the health and happiness of their family.

The Zodiac Animals and Taoist Culture

Taoism is a religion indigenous to China. Its teachings are tightly linked with China's indigenous culture and deeply rooted in Chinese soil. Taoism possesses an unequivocal Chinese quality, and has had a deep impact on every aspect of Chinese culture. At the core of Taoism's theology are *yin-yang* and the Five Elements, which formed the basis for the religion's elevated impact on and fusion with the zodiac culture. A notable illustration is the treasured Bronze Sheep at the "Green Sheep Temple" in Chengdu, Sichuan Province. The Green Sheep Temple has two bronze sheep statues, with bodies measuring 90 cm

ZODIAC ANIMALS

long and 60 cm high. One of the sheep is particularly strange in form; it has refined craftsmanship, and a lifelike appearance, but has only one horn. The incarnation of the 12 zodiac animals, this "sheep", in fact, a rat's ears, an ox's nose, a tiger's paws, a rabbit's back, a dragon's horn, a snake's tail, a horse's mouth, a goat's beard, a monkey's neck, a rooster's eyes, a dog's belly, and a pig's thighs. Combining the images of each of the 12 zodiac animals into a single body, it is therefore known as the "Zodiac Sheep." Tradition has it that this statue was among the personal possessions of Prime Minister Jia Sidao of the Southern Song Dynasty (1127-1279).

The numerous gods and deities of Taoism are also intimately connected with the Chinese zodiac animals. Famous examples include the 28 lunar mansions, the 60 *jia-zi* deities and the Six *Ding* and Six *Jia* Divine Generals.

The stellar deities hold a high position in Taoism. In particular, the 28 lunar mansions have long and deep ties with the 12 zodiac animals. In ancient China, the mansions were used to differentiate the constellations for celestial observation. The ancient Chinese customarily divided the stars of the sky into the Three Enclosures and the 28 lunar mansions. The Three Enclosures refer to the "Purple Forbidden Enclosure", the "Supreme Palace Enclosure", and the "Heavenly Market Enclosure"; their main purpose was to classify and name the stars near the north celestial pole. The 28 lunar mansions refer to a ring of dispersed constellations revolving around the ecliptic or celestial equator, similar to the 12 signs of the western zodiac. The mansions can be divided into four categories, with each category containing seven mansions; each mansion has its own spiritual protector to watch over it. The name of each mansion is comprised of three Chinese characters: the first character is the mansion's constellational name; the second character is derived from one of the seven luminaries (the Sun, the Moon, and the Five Elements); and the last character is the name of one of several creatures. In addition to the 12 zodiac animals, one additional creature was added for each of the zodiac animals based on similarity or resemblance. For example, the *jiao* (similar to the dragon) and the leopard (a relative of the tiger) were both added to the list. Since the 12 Earthly Branches associated with the 12 zodiac animals also indicate direction or orientation, one animal was also added for each of the cardinal directions (*zi*, *wu*, *mao*, and *you*, respectively indicating north, south, east, and west). Consequently, there are 28 animals altogether — bearing a one-to-one correspondence with the 28 lunar mansions.

As mentioned, the Chinese lunar calendar uses the Heavenly Stems and Earthly Branches to record the years. The 10 Heavenly Stems are matched with the 12 Earthly Branches to form one *jia-zi* or 60-year cycle. In Taoism,

THE TWELVE

there are 60 deities who serve as Taisui or Stellar God, who preside over the human world administering fortune and evil in one-year shifts. Collectively, they are known as the 60 *Taisui* of the *Jia-Zi*. Each of the 60 deities has its own unique name and appearance, and bears a conspicuous sign of its zodiac sign. For instance, the *jia-zi* deity (General Jin Bian), born in the Year of the Rat, carries a peach; the *gui-hai* deity (General Yu Cheng), born in the Year of the Pig, wears a scholarly robe; etc. The year in which a person is born is known as his or her *yuanchen*. It was an old custom to worship the constellation deity of the *yuanchen* and pray for good luck and the fulfillment of one's wishes. This practice was known as *shunxing*. In the Yuanchen Palace, located in Beijing's well-known White Cloud Temple, offerings are made to statues of the 60 *jia-zi* deities.

In Old Beijing, the eighth day of the first lunar month was a day of "stellar deference", during which the sovereigns of stars would get together. This day also came to be known as the day when the stars "descended to earth." On this day, sacrifices should thus be offered to the stellar sovereigns in order to solicit their blessing and protection. To pray for good fortune and the fulfillment of their wishes, people often went to the Yuanchen Palace on this day. After locating their zodiac's spiritual protector, they would burn incense in front of its statue and offer their respects. This custom has carried on to the present day.

The "Six *Ding* and Six *Jia*" actually refer to the Six *Ding* Deities and Six *Jia* Deities — the protective deities of Taoism. According to the *Tao Ching* (one of two parts of the *Tao Te Ching*), these deities were originally the generals of Emperor Zhenwu. They frequently collaborated with the 28 mansions and the 36 heavenly generals to create wind and thunder and to govern the world of demons and deities. Taoist priests could use books of spells to summon the deities and ask them to expel evil spirits. Each of these 12 deities also has its own unique name. In many paintings and sculptures, they are represented symbolically to depict the zodiac animals.

The Chinese Zodiac and the Western Zodiac

The ancient Chinese divided the stellar sky into 28 unequal regions, known as the 28 lunar mansions. To explain the rotation of the solar periods and the motion of the sun, moon, and Five Elements (metal, wood, water, fire, and earth), the region near the ecliptic was divided into 12 equal celestial partitions. Each partition was represented by certain constellations of the 28 lunar mansions. However, since the 12 celestial partitions were divided equally while the 28 lunar mansions vary in size, the boundaries of the celestial partitions were not fully consistent with those of the constellations. The ancient Chinese created the celestial partitions with two main purposes in mind. First, they were used to indicate the position of the sun during each of the four seasons to describe the rotation of the solar periods. Second, they were used to indicate the position reached by Jupiter (the "Year Star") each year, and thus to record the years.

ZODIAC ANIMALS

In ancient Western astrology, the band of the celestial sphere extending eight degrees to either side of the ecliptic was known as the zodiac; it was believed that the stellar paths of the sun, moon and stars traversed this region. The zodiac was divided into 12 equal sections, known as the 12 zodiac constellations (or signs). The purpose for making this division was similar to that of ancient China's 12 celestial partitions, although the boundaries are somewhat different.

After Western astronomy was introduced to China, the ancient Chinese once used the names of the 12 celestial partitions to translate the 12 zodiac constellations into Chinese. Since the 12 Earthly Branches correspond one-to-one with both the 12 celestial partitions and the 12 zodiac animals, the 12 zodiac animals thus bear a relation with the 12 Western zodiac signs as well. However, the Western zodiac signs and the zodiac animals of China differ in their original meaning. In Western fortune telling, fate is reckoned based on month; people born in the same month, even if born in different years, are said to share a similar fate. The ancient Chinese, in contrast, believed that people born in the same year shared a similar destiny, even if they were born in different months.

The Han Dynasty round eaves-tile ornament with the patterns of the dragon and tiger

CONTENTS

THE *ZI* RAT NIPS THE WORLD 022

- Zodiac Animal File 027
- The Rat and Personality 028
- The Rat and Blood Type 029
- The Rat and Fortune 030
  - Lifetime Fortune: Overview 030
  - Fortune and the Five Elements 031
  - Fortune by the Year 032
- The Rat and the Western Zodiac 035
- *Fengshui* and the Rat 038
- Interpreting Rat Dreams 039
- Health Secrets 039

THE *CHOU* OX OPENS THE EARTH 040

- Zodiac Animal File 047
- The Ox and Personality 047
- The Ox and Blood Type 048
- The Ox and Fortune 049
  - Lifetime Fortune: Overview 049
  - Fortune and the Five Elements 050
  - Fortune by the Year 051
- The Ox and the Western Zodiac 054
- *Fengshui* and the Ox 057
- Interpreting Ox Dreams 057
- Health Secrets 057

THE *YIN* TIGER WHISTLES THROUGH THE WIND 058

- Zodiac Animal File 065
- The Tiger and Personality 066
- The Tiger and Blood Type 067
- The Tiger and Fortune 068
  - Lifetime Fortune: Overview 068
  - Fortune and the Five Elements 069
  - Fortune by the Year 070
- The Tiger and the Western Zodiac 072
- *Fengshui* and the Tiger 074
- Interpreting Tiger Dreams 075
- Health Secrets 075

THE *MAO* RABBIT PLAYS WITH THE MOON 076

- Zodiac Animal File 083
- The Rabblit and Personality 084
- The Rabblit and Blood Type 084
- The Rabblit and Fortune 085
  - Lifetime Fortune: Overview 085
  - Fortune and the Five Elements 086
  - Fortune by the Year 088
- The Rabblit and the Western Zodiac 090
- *Fengshui* and the Rabblit 092
- Interpreting Rabblit Dreams 093
- Health Secrets 093

THE *CHEN* DRAGON DARTS ACROSS THE SKY 094

- Zodiac Animal File 102
- The Dragon and Personality 102
- The Dragon and Blood Type 103
- The Dragon and Fortune 104
  - Lifetime Fortune: Overview 104
  - Fortune and the Five Elements 104
  - Fortune by the Year 105
- The Dragon and the Western Zodiac 108
- *Fengshui* and the Dragon 110
- Interpreting Dragon Dreams 111
- Health Secrets 111

THE *SI* SNAKE ABOVE THE CLOUDS 112

- Zodiac Animal File 119
- The Snake and Personality 120
- The Snake and Blood Type 120
- The Snake and Fortune 121
  - Lifetime Fortune: Overview 121
  - Fortune and the Five Elements 122
  - Fortune by the Year 124
- The Snake and the Western Zodiac 126
- *Fengshui* and the Snake 128
- Interpreting Snake Dreams 129
- Health Secrets 129

THE *WU* HORSE FLIES ABOVE THE SKY ········ 130

Zodiac Animal File ········ 137
The Horse and Personality ········ 138
   The Horse and Blood Type ········ 138
      The Horse and Fortune ········ 139
         • Lifetime Fortune: Overview ········ 139
         • Fortune and the Five Elements ········ 140
         • Fortune by the Year ········ 141
   The Horse and the Western Zodiac ········ 143
Fengshui and the Horse ········ 146
Interpreting Horse Dreams ········ 146
Health Secrets ········ 147

THE *WEI* SHEEP CREATES PROSPERITY AND PEACE ········ 148

Zodiac Animal File ········ 155
The Sheep and Personality ········ 156
The Sheep and Blood Type ········ 156
   The Sheep and Fortune ········ 157
         • Lifetime Fortune: Overview ········ 157
         • Fortune and the Five Elements ········ 158
         • Fortune by the Year ········ 159
   The Sheep and the Western Zodiac ········ 161
Fengshui and the Sheep ········ 163
Interpreting Sheep Dreams ········ 163
Health Secrets ········ 163

THE *SHEN* MONKEY HAS SPECIAL PROWESS ········ 164

Zodiac Animal File ········ 171
The Monkey and Personality ········ 171
The Monkey and Blood Type ········ 172
   The Monkey and Fortune ········ 173
         • Lifetime Fortune: Overview ········ 173
         • Fortune and the Five Elements ········ 173
         • Fortune by the Year ········ 175
   The Monkey and the Western Zodiac ········ 177
Fengshui and the Monkey ········ 180
Interpreting Monkey Dreams ········ 181
Health Secrets ········ 181

THE AUSPICIOUS *YOU* ROOSTER ……… 182

- Zodiac Animal File ……… 189
  - The Rooster and Personality ……… 189
  - The Rooster and Blood Type ……… 190
  - The Rooster and Fortune ……… 192
    - Lifetime Fortune: Overview ……… 192
    - Fortune and the Five Elements ……… 193
    - Fortune by the Year ……… 194
  - The Rooster and the Western Zodiac ……… 196
  - *Fengshui* and the Rooster ……… 198
  - Interpreting Rooster Dreams ……… 199
  - Health Secrets ……… 199

THE *XU* DOG BRINGS PROSPEROUS WEALTH ……… 200

- Zodiac Animal File ……… 207
  - The Dog and Personality ……… 208
  - The Dog and Blood Type ……… 208
  - The Dog and Fortune ……… 209
    - Lifetime Fortune: Overview ……… 209
    - Fortune and the Five Elements ……… 210
    - Fortune by the Year ……… 212
  - The Dog and the Western Zodiac ……… 214
  - *Fengshui* and the Dog ……… 216
  - Interpreting Dog Dreams ……… 217
  - Health Secrets ……… 217

THE *HAI* PIG DELIVERS THE LUCK ……… 218

- Zodiac Animal File ……… 225
  - The Pig and Personality ……… 226
  - The Pig and Blood Type ……… 226
  - The Pig and Fortune ……… 227
    - Lifetime Fortune: Overview ……… 227
    - Fortune and the Five Elements ……… 228
    - Fortune by the Year ……… 230
  - The Pig and the Western Zodiac ……… 232
  - *Fengshui* and the Pig ……… 235
  - Interpreting Pig Dreams ……… 235
  - Health Secrets ……… 235

APPENDIX ……… 236
EPILOGUE ……… 238

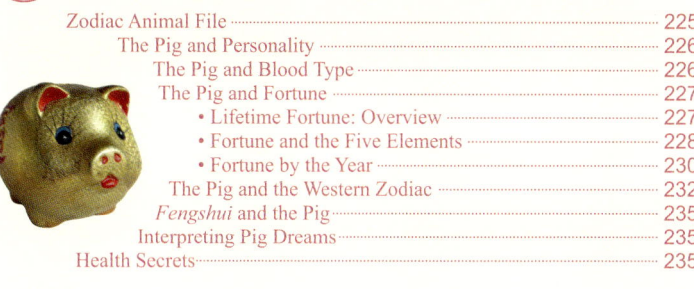

THE TWELVE
ZODIAC ANIMALS

PART 1
THE *ZI* RAT NIPS THE WORLD

【 RAT 】

THE ZI RAT NIPS THE WORLD

Of the 12 zodiac animals, the rat is the smallest in size but occupies the first position ahead of all the others. Of all the fables regarding the sequence of the zodiac animals, those dealing with the rat are most prevalent. In addition to the above mentioned story of the rat biting the ox's tail, there is another one: after the 12 animals were chosen, the rat was placed in the terminal position on account of it being the smallest in size. However, the rat was unwilling to comply and demanded that he and the ox go into the streets together and let the people make the final decision. The ox thought it was sure of success, and swaggeringly took the lead. But since the ox was already seen frequently in their everyday lives, people looked upon it disapprovingly. The rat then made its appearance. It leapt up suddenly onto the ox's back, and people called out in shock, "Look, what a big rat!" In this way, the rat was able to rob the ox of the first position in the hierarchy. There are many other fables similar to this one, but all of them portray the rat as sly, clever and lucky.

In Chinese myths and fables, the rat combines both *yin* and *yang*. Its forepaws symbolize the *yang* of today, while its hind paws represent the *yin* of yesterday. It has also been said that the rat created the world. According to Chinese mythology, during the time of antiquity when the universe was still unformed and the world was in a state of chaos, the rat nipped open a slit in the chaos as the *zi*-hour arrived, thereby creating a separation between heaven and earth. For such distinguished merit, the rat

naturally deserved to be ranked as the head of the 12 zodiac animals. This fable also reflects the Chinese people's awareness of the rat's "nipping" instinct.

The appraisal given to the rat in ancient China is a mixed review of praise and blame. On the one hand, the rat steals food and grain, destroys farmland, gnaws and nips books and clothing, and spreads bubonic plague. In the slash-and-burn agriculture of ancient society, the rat can even be called a great nuisance. On the other hand, the rat's sly and clever disposition and its tenacious vitality are frequently used for analogy, bringing countless pleasure to the people.

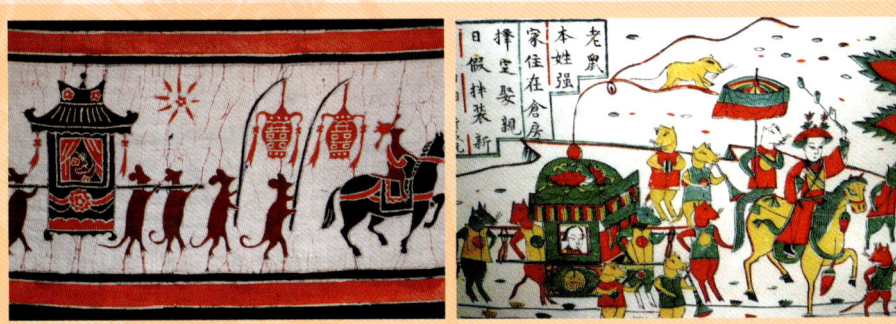

A wax printing (left) and a wooden board New Year's painting (right) of the rat marrying off a daughter

In Chinese mythology, grain is said to have originated from plants which grew naturally on earth, and humanity did not need to sow seeds or engage in cultivation. To prevent people from forming the evil habit of indolence, the Jade Emperor sent a deity to descend to earth with a sack. The deity was told to load it with all the grain seeds and thus starve humankind as a warning. However, just as the deity was ready to ascend to heaven, a rat sneaked into the sack and gnawed off one of its corners. The seeds of grain scattered down onto the earth and the people were saved from starvation. This fable endowed the rat with the positive reputation of "sewing seeds" and, in many parts of China, the rat is aptly known as the "Grain God" or "God of the Granary."

In the past, there was a custom in southern China of "feeding the rat" on the 15th day of the first lunar month. On this day, the rat is said to have started to move. The people would boil meat gruel in a big cauldron and place it where the rat appeared and disappeared frequently. If the rat ate the meat gruel, it would thus no longer eat the silkworms or the crops.

THE ZI RAT NIPS THE WORLD

The Chinese people's use of the term "Granary Filling Festival" to refer to the 25th day of the first lunar month is also related to the rat. Rats would frequently steal food and grain and store them ingeniously in holes underground, filling the people with a sense of awe. Hence, on the day of the Granary Filling Festival, each family would fill up the granary for sacrifice, hoping that the "God of the Granary" would eat little grain. In some places, the people steamed rat-shaped flour desserts, and placed them around the granary. In Chinese mythology, it is said that "the rat marries off a daughter" on this day. The people have to feed the cat until it is full, turn off the lights, and go to sleep early in order to avoid disrupting these marital plans and provoking the rat's retaliation. "The rat marries off a daughter" has also become a traditional theme in Spring Festival paintings, paper-cuttings and brocades. The rat bridegroom, rat bride, rat wedding attendants and rat guests are depicted wearing red unlined upper garments and green trousers, swaggering together like a troop. With its resemblance to human activity, this depiction is at once both grand and comical.

Because the rat has a strong reproductive capacity and vitality, it is also known as the God of *Zi*. The God of *Zi* symbolizes both the earthly branch *zi* (including the *zi-*hour) and the son (also called *zi* in Chinese), which is worshiped when praying for the flourishing offspring of one's family.

By all standards, the rat is a clever little animal. An old children's song passed on through the ages describes the lovable rat: "The little rat leaps onto the lamp stand and steals the oil to drink, but cannot get down." The rat's image is also frequently seen in Chinese literary works. In the *Classic of Poetry*, the earliest existing collection of Chinese poetry, there are

several poems and songs about the rat. *The Large Rat of the Odes of Wei* is one such song: "Large rat, large rat, please do not eat my millet. I have served you well for so many years, but you show no concern for me." In this song, the large rat refers generally to insatiably greedy and indolent exploiters. In the classic Chinese novel *Journey to the West*, there is also a story about the rat, in which the rat spirit in the abyss compels Monk Tang to get married. In *Strange Stories from a Chinese Studio*, written by Qing Dynasty author Pu Songling (1640-1715), there is a chapter called A Qian, which tells the love story of a man who fell in love with a rat. In this tale, a merchant named Xi Shan found a girl to be his younger brother's wife; this girl's name was A Qian. In reality, she was a rat spirit and was good at accumulating millet. After their marriage, the family's grain kept increasing incessantly. Without a doubt, this was good news for a family doing business, and everyone was ecstatic. However, when Xi Shan and others learned that A Qian came from the mean and lowly rat race — a race so horrible that its name could not even be uttered — A Qian immediately suffered threats and discrimination, and was compelled to leave. Shortly thereafter, the Xi family's conditions deteriorated and became poorer with each passing day. They had no choice but to call A Qian back to their home and treat her with as much kindness and consideration as before. Through this imaginary tale, Pu Songling reflects the misunderstandings and disputes of marriage due to family status in feudal society. In the story,

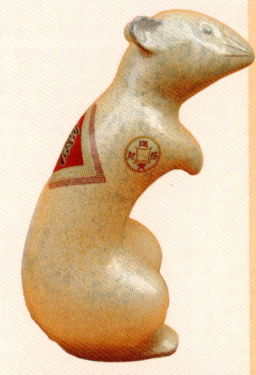

A paper-cutting of the rat offering luck

A Qian was good at accumulating the millet, which was the rat's natural disposition. In the *Three Heroes and Five Gallants*, a Chinese novel dealing with legal cases and chivalry, each of the five gallants adopted "Rat" as his nickname. The story caused great commotion in Dongjing (present-day Kaifeng, Henan Province) and enjoyed great popularity.

ZODIAC ANIMAL FILE

Earthly Branch: *Zi*
Years of Birth: 2020, 2008, 1996, 1984, 1972, 1960, 1948, 1936, 1924, 1912, 1900…
Five Elements: *Zi* belongs to Water
Five Constant Virtues: Water belongs to Wisdom

THE ZI RAT NIPS THE WORLD

Auspicious Directions: southeast, northeast
Auspicious Colors: blue, gold, green
Lucky Numbers: 2, 3
Lucky Flowers: lily, African violet, lily of the valley
Lucky Gemstones: kyanite, black agate, aquamarine, turquoise
Spiritual Protector: Sahasra-bhuja Sahasra-netra (Thousand-Armed, Thousand-Eyed Avalokiteshvara)
Choosing a name: For individuals born in the Year of the Rat, it is appropriate to select characters with the radicals for rice (米), bean (豆), or fish (鱼),

signifying wealth, longevity, and prosperous offspring; characters containing the radicals for grass (艹), metal (金) or jade (玉), which embody dexterity, honesty, and integrity; characters with the radicals for person (亻), wood (木), or moon (月), which signify altruism and the appearance of auspicious persons in one's life; or characters with the field (田) radical, representing kindness towards others and a life of leisure.

THE RAT AND PERSONALITY

Strengths:
The Rat's assets include a high level of alertness, the ability to react quickly, as well as a sharp wit and strong intellect. People born in the Year of the Rat are understanding and sympathetic; cheerful and bubbly; and highly likeable. With a combination of wit and wisdom, they tend to be enterprising and creative. They are also self-reliant and good at seizing opportunities.

Weaknesses:
The Rat's limitations include a lack of aspiration, courage and insight. People born in the Year of the Rat tend to have few opinions of their own, and can be stubborn-minded

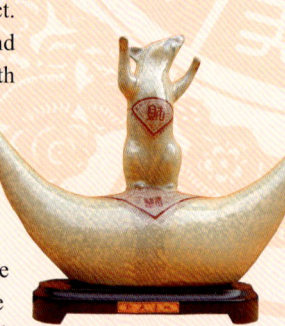

A New Year ornament: a rat riding on a Chinese ingot

THE TWELVE ZODIAC ANIMALS

at times. Despite their good nature, they are sometimes impolite, and often criticize others or fuss over small details. They can also be overly profit-seeking.

THE RAT AND BLOOD TYPE

Blood Type A:
Rats with blood type A appreciate grandiose style but do not like to show off. They tend to be pensive and thoughtful, and have an impressive ability to adapt to changing conditions. Having a large group of friends also enables them to stay well-informed. With agile, precise thinking and the ability to detect the omissions and oversights of others, they make excellent supervisors. Rats of this blood type often keep their emotions veiled.

Blood Type B:
Rats with blood type B are up on the latest fashions and possess strong foresight. They remain calm during

An engraving of the rat marrying off a daughter

a crisis, expressing their ideas as appropriate. Able to sympathize with others, they always help other people to the best of their ability. Rats of this blood type are good at saving money through planning and strict budgeting. They tend to place a lot of emphasis on friendship, and their innocence may cause them to trust others too easily. They can also be garrulous at times.

Blood Type O:
Rats with blood type O are tough and resilient, shrewd and sociable, and able to draw support from others to better themselves. They are also quiet, gentle and good-natured. Most rats of this blood type have a fairly keen memory, and enjoy exploring problems in everyday life. They have a childlike innocence and are romantic by nature.

Blood Type AB:
Rats with blood type AB have a graceful bearing, and are elegant and personable. Always careful and thoughtful in their

THE ZI RAT NIPS THE WORLD

affairs, they're unlikely to risk it all on a gamble. Rats of this blood type care about their family and get along easily with others. They're generous with their friends, but can be quite stingy with those whom they dislike.

THE RAT AND FORTUNE

Lifetime Fortune: Overview

People born in the Year of the Rat tend to have good fate. They will, however, encounter some instability in their lives, with surprises and sudden changes along the way, and a combination of good and ill luck. To prevent potential calamity, Rats should maintain emotional stability at all times and learn to remain calm during a crisis. By middle age, life will proceed according to plan; and, by old age, Rats are destined to achieve wealth, power, and success in all facets of life.

Career:
Lacking an air of authority as well as the ability to command others, the Rat is unsuited to play the role of business leader. Despite this fact, Rats have good prospects for job promotions and pay raises. It is important for Rats not to fall prey to a "the grass is greener on the other side" mentality; giving up on a good opportunity could steer the Rat away from the road to success.

Financial Luck:
Rats have exceptional luck in their finances, with multiple and diverse sources of wealth. They are also adept at investing and establishing their own businesses. In addition, Rats can earn solid returns through joint investments, assuming they protect their own interests and select suitable projects.

Romance:
The Rat's love life tends to be far from ideal. Although Rats get along well with the opposite sex, their behavior is likely to provoke rumors of love affairs. Restraint is needed to ensure that their own sexual desire does not lead to action that damages their reputation beyond repair.

Fortune and the Five Elements

Wood Rat: Born in the Year of *Ren-Zi* (1972, 1912)

Wood Rats possess a strong intellect, artistic creativity, and sharp perceptive skills; rarely do they overlook any details. Despite inferior living conditions, their self-reliance and ability to seize opportunities enable them to carve out a career path. They seek neither fame nor wealth, often preferring to live in the quietude of the countryside. Wood Rats are likely to become officials, bureaucrats, or leaders in the religious community.

Fire Rat: Born in the Year of *Wu-Zi* (2008, 1948)

Fire Rats embody the traits of candor, naiveté and optimism, and tend to be highly responsible and enterprising. They have the potential to become senior officials or leaders, or make it big in the field of science and technology. Nonetheless, Fire Rats are likely to face a life of hardship in which success is difficult to come by; they need to double their efforts and work extra hard to ensure ultimate victory.

A colored statue of Jia-Zi Deity

A colored statue of Ren-Zi Deity

Earth Rat: Born in the Year of *Geng-Zi* (2020, 1960)

Earth Rats often enjoy the support and esteem of their elders, and may leave home to live far away from relatives. Their career plans are often denounced or frowned upon by others. In addition, Earth Rats may face financial turnover difficulties, with no one to lend them a hand. However, their luck will inevitably turn around; in the meantime, they should avoid worrying and try to stay positive.

A colored statue of Wu-Zi Deity

A colored statue of Geng-Zi Deity

Metal Rat: Born in the Year of *Jia-Zi* (1984, 1924)

Metal Rats are usually destined to enjoy riches and honor. Nevertheless, their lives are likely to be both insecure and unstable. They may spend their entire life toiling and running around, and will face inevitable setbacks and disappointments. Metal Rats are also liable to stir up trouble by

THE ZI RAT NIPS THE WORLD

saying the wrong thing, potentially leading to disaster or even their own demise.

Water Rat: Born in the Year of *Bing-Zi* (1996, 1936)

Water Rats are destined to receive the invaluable support of others. Despite being natural-born leaders with high aims and ambitions in life, opportunities rarely present themselves. They also tend to lack staying power, frequently starting a task but rarely seeing it through to completion. Often born into a poor family, it may be suitable for the Water Rat to adopt a new name or pursue a livelihood away from home.

A colored statue of Bing-Zi Deity

Fortune by the Year

A rat engraved on the 12-zodiac-animal screen wall in Beijing's White Cloud Temple

In the Year of the Rat, Rats are likely to be blessed with affluence, promotions to senior positions, and salary raises. If a loved one passes away during the year, there is a chance that the Rat will develop a minor illness. Rats should strive to build good relations with others and avoid being greedy for greatness or success.

In the Year of the Ox, Rats are likely to face stagnant luck and limited positive results. While the Rat's personal gains are few, friends and relatives will meet with good results this year. Although overall turbulence is limited, Rats will still face minor setbacks and negative energy. By spending some time at home to improve their emotional outlook, however, Rats can avoid the onset of ill luck.

In the Year of the Tiger, Rats will see their careers take off. Most Rats are likely to spend the year away from friends and family, rushing about and seeking a fortune away from home. However, they should try to avoid the overzealous pursuit of fame and gain; only by staying within reasonable limits can solid profits be ensured. Health is likely to take a turn for the worse this year, accompanied by disquietude on the family front.

In the Year of the Rabbit, Rats will be blessed with happiness and romance. That being said, the year may be plagued by fallings-out, disputes or misunderstandings

between married couples. It would be an opportune time to establish a business or enhance operational strength. The Rat may experience some physical ailments during the year, and should definitely go for prompt check-ups and treatment.

In the Year of the Dragon, Rats will meet with good wealth-building opportunities, and the success they achieve will put them in a class by themselves. By leading through personal strength and employing their entrepreneurial or investment skills, the Rat is virtually undefeatable. Rats are likely to encounter some despicable lowlifes this year; care should be taken when making new friends — who may actually turn out to be enemies. Rats should also be vigilant against possible lawsuits from the local authorities and should avoid administrative work altogether.

An ornament of the little rat leaping onto the lamp stand

In the Year of the Snake, Rats are bound to face a streak of difficulties and bad luck, including both illness and financial losses. They would be advised to burn incense before Buddha, and avoid chasing fame and fortune. In this way, Rats can convert ill luck into good fortune, prevent potential calamity, and restore and protect their health.

The stone carving of a cat and a rat, Baoding Mountain grottoes, Chongqing

In the Year of the Horse, Rats are likely to have good prospects in their love lives. However, it is important not to let vices, such as drinking or debauchery, destroy their luck. With signs of potential financial difficulties, the Rat should be careful to avoid sudden or unexpected monetary losses. Rats are destined to receive support from others this year, and it would be an opportune time for them to strive forward in their careers.

THE ZI RAT NIPS THE WORLD

In the Year of the Sheep, Rats should avoid gambling large sums of money or drinking to excess. With good people offering their advice and assistance, it is destined to be a year of good fortune for the Rat. Though there may be some vile scoundrels who say mean things behind the Rat's back, these situations can be easily resolved. This is also a year during which the Rat can enjoy a happy family life.

In the Year of the Monkey, Rats are likely to make steady gains in their careers, with wealth and influence remaining stable. Severing ties with friends or associates could spell disaster in the coming year, and should be avoided at all costs. In addition, Rats must not pursue a political career or any other high-publicity work this year. Although they are likely to be busy, it is important that Rats take some time to relax and enjoy a normal life. At the beginning of the year, they should also be vigilant for loathsome troublemakers who may try to spy on them.

In the Year of the Rooster, Rats will reap great benefits from the support of others, and it will be a time to celebrate happiness and longevity. The Rat may also be blessed with a child or grandchild, as well as some financial gains. It is essential, however, that Rats move forward steadily and not let success get to their heads, so as to prevent possible quarrels or the possibility of being harmed by friends.

In the Year of the Dog, Rats will face mediocre financial prospects but see their reputation enhanced. They should exercise moderation in all their activities; buying a few lottery tickets might be a good idea, but large investments should be avoided. Blessed with the kindness of their superiors, Rats should consider pursuing volunteer

Gold rats

A memorial plum-blossom-shaped silver coin with the pattern of rat issued in 2008

or charity-related work. They should also pay more attention to their health and try to exercise during their spare time. Moving to a new residence should be avoided this year.

In the Year of the Pig, Rats will enjoy excellent financial prospects. Nevertheless, it is also a year of instability, as they may face problems relating to travel, immigration, relocation, or career changes. In addition, Rats may find their health taking a turn for the worse and should be careful not to overexert themselves in their pursuit of success.

A dough-modeled rat

THE RAT AND THE WESTERN ZODIAC

Rat-Aries:

Rat-Aries tend to be extremely busy in their work lives but still manage to maintain order; they are also highly gifted in the careers they purse. They reject tardiness or wasting time and often go hand-in-hand with a lack of patience. Rat-Aries are also high in self-confidence and thoroughly enjoy a challenge. In their romantic lives, they meet with little if any frustration, and their attractiveness combined with a strategic approach to love enable them to capture their partner's heart. Early in life, they give off an air of meekness and may even look a bit foolish. By middle age, however, they place a heightened emphasis on feelings while exercising due caution. Rat-Aries are suited to seeking a Gemini or Leo born in the Year of the Dragon or the Ox — or even a Sagittarian born in the Year of the Monkey who is playful — as their companion; Aquarians born in the Year of the Pig or the Dog are also likely to attract the Rat-Aries.

Rat-Taurus:

Rat-Tauruses are tenacious, intelligent, exceedingly talented, and possess a remarkable memory. Not easily swayed by emotion, they remain calm and level-headed in the face of problems and are willing to eat humble pie in order to achieve a personal goal. Despite being cruel and ruthless, they stand ready to protect their loved ones. Rat-Tauruses are steady and committed in

Lanterns in the shape of rats during the Lantern Festival

THE ZI RAT NIPS THE WORLD

their romantic relationships, but are highly possessive and tend to get jealous easily. They place a heightened focus on emotional relations, and are prone to give up on a relationship at the first sign of problems. Rat-Tauruses are most suited to be with Piscees born in the Year of the Ox or the Tiger; Cancers, Virgos or Capricorns born in the Year of the Monkey or the Pig would also make good companions.

Rat-Gemini:

Rat-Geminis are highly gifted, smooth and slick, and make great conversationalists. They are generous and giving by nature, energetic and driven, and given to theatrics in their behavior. One of their shortcomings is a tendency to blame someone else even if they themselves are in the wrong; they are also poor decision makers. Rat-

Small bags in the shape of rat

Geminis are likely to get along well with Aries, Leos, Librans or Aquarians born in the Year of the Dragon or the Monkey; Aries born in the Year of the Ox; and Librans born in the Year of the Tiger.

Rat-Cancer:

Rat-Cancers are naturally intelligent, emotionally changeable, and take the initiative to befriend others. They like to keep up with the latest fashions and reject that which is banal. Possessing creativity and an interest in the arts and writing, they bring surging emotions and an air of mystery to their relationships. Rat-Cancers are suited to seeking a Taurus, Virgo, Scorpio or Pisces as their companion. They also have an affinity with people born in the Year of the Ox, the Monkey and the Horse — especially Aries, Librans and Capricorns born in the Year of the Horse.

Rat-Leo:

Rat-Leos are active and animated, and possess an unusually high level of self-confidence. They live opulently but within reason, and are able to handle

A dough-modeled rat

THE TWELVE ZODIAC ANIMALS

all sorts of challenges. In their romantic affairs, Rat-Leos show generosity and unswerving loyalty to their companions. Geminis, Librans, Capricorns and Sagittarians born in the Year of the Ox or the Dragon tend to make the most suitable partners for Rat-Leos. Aries, Geminis, Librans and Capricorns born in the Year of the Monkey are also good candidates.

Rat-Virgo:

Rat-Virgos are honest, straightforward, selfless and impartial, and possess keen analytical skills. As soon as they fall deeply in love, they may find themselves unable to escape. Radiating with romantic energy, they may even be willing to leave home and settle down elsewhere just to be with the one whom they love. Rat-Virgos tend to be completely immune to external pressures and have the ability to consider matters from multiple points of view. They place a high value on friendship and loyalty, and make excellent listeners.

Rat-Libra:

Rat-Librans are innately gifted and perfectionistic by nature. They are kind and genial, sensitive, highly talkative, and at times childish. The Rat-Libran is greedy but equally generous, adheres strongly to tradition, and makes for an indispensable friend. With respect to romance, Rat-Librans tend to be the conscientious and responsible type, willing to go all out for their significant others. They are likely to be attracted by Geminis, Leos, Sagittarians and Aquarians born in the Year of the Monkey.

Rat-Scorpio:

Rat-Scorpios tend to be sharp-witted, perceptive, chatty, and highly agile. They have an affinity with others, in spite of their acrimonious speech and a tendency to pass judgment. On the romance front, Rat-Scorpions generally wait until they have found that special someone before becoming emotionally committed. With a strong desire to subdue others, they are likely to marry someone who excels at

housekeeping. Rat-Scorpios are likely to get along well with Cancers, Virgos or Pisceses born in the Year of the Ox.

Rat-Sagittarius:

Rat-Sagittarians are self-effacing and conservative, but equally lively and vivacious, and enjoy a variety of social activities. With a sharp wit, clever intellect, and calm disposition, they excel at exploiting opportunities. However, they often lead a life of adventure or

THE ZI RAT NIPS THE WORLD

vagrancy, making it difficult to find a suitable life companion.

Rat-Capricorn:

Rat-Capricorns are driven to succeed and tend to be unmatched in their area of expertise. They are thorough and efficient in their endeavors and highly persuasive. While cautious and reserved, they are also generous, kindhearted, positive and optimistic. Rat-Capricorns often demonstrate innovative thinking and imaginative problem-solving.

Rat-Aquarius:

Rat-Aquarians are intelligent and insightful, with the courage to explore, experiment, and pursue their ideals. While valuing their freedom, they tend also to be unable to endure solitude. Rat-Aquarians are sensitive and get nervous easily; despite being outwardly attractive, they are often highly fragile inside. Their actions are likely to be governed by power, wealth, and desire.

Rat-Pisces:

Rat-Pisceses are intense in personality and incisive in speech. Lacking the ability to get things done on their own, they tend to rely on others. Despite being kind and amicable, they are often snobbish and filled with jealousy. They are also highly self-protective, rarely trusting others and sometimes even engaging in trickery. While they possess group consciousness, Rat-Pisceses are governed by their own selfish motives.

FENGSHUI AND THE RAT

Many people tremble at the mere mention of rats and, in the study of *fengshui*, they are regarded as a malevolent creature. Placing two *fengshui* rats before one's door to face the enemy's home is a method used to inflict harm on others; the victim will suffer from ill luck, such as a mishap or financial losses. However, by pasting a Door God or depiction of the God of the Earth at the entrance of one's residence, or by hanging a *bagua* mirror on the door, the rat's malicious force can be eliminated. Auspicious directions for people born in the Year of the Rat include southeast and northeast. If major pieces of furniture, such as beds, desks or sofas, are aligned in these directions, the cycle of fortune can be enhanced. The directions of south and southwest

The God of Granary in his wedding ceremony

should be avoided. In addition, it would be wise to place an ox sculpture towards the northeast of one's home or wear a chain with an ox pendant. As people born in the Year of the Rat occupy the first position of the zodiac cycle, some financial losses and ill luck are inevitable for them. To improve their fortune, Rats are encouraged to raise brocaded carp at home. Red and white are the essential colors of brocaded carp and, in *fengshui*, the color black has the ability to thwart evil. Brocaded carp are known in *fengshui* as "the fish of wealth and fortune." This kind of carp, therefore, can thwart evil external forces, bring about harmony at home, and ensure a smooth and easy life for the Rat.

 ## INTERPRETING RAT DREAMS

If you dream of a rat, you will soon make many enemies.

If you dream of catching a rat, your enemy is secretly plotting against you.

If you dream of a cat catching a rat, it is a good omen — your enemies will slaughter each other and will perish together.

If you dream of a dead rat, you will be blessed with good fortune.

If you dream of many rats, you will suffer a series of consecutive defeats.

If you dream of a rat digging a hole in your home, your house will be stolen.

 ## HEALTH SECRETS

People born in the Year of the Rat are full of vigor and adapt easily to new situations. Generally speaking, they seldom get sick. However, as soon as they fall ill, recovery may prove difficult. In particular, Rats should watch out for urological, hematologic, and gastrointestinal diseases. Since those born in the Year of the Rat often suffer from a lack of sleep and tend to smoke and drink excessively, it is important for them to maintain a balance between work and rest and not overexert themselves. Rats should also set aside some time for exercise.

THE ZI RAT NIPS THE WORLD

THE TWELVE
ZODIAC ANIMALS

PART 2
THE *CHOU* OX OPENS THE EARTH

【 OX 】

THE *CHOU* OX OPENS THE EARTH

Considering the ox's important production capability in aerial farming society, its ranking of second in the zodiac hierarchy is hardly surprising. According to the Chinese creation legend, the ox was granted this elite position for opening up the earth after the sky had been opened. In Chinese fairytales and legends, there are many versions describing the reason that the rat is listed in the first position. Though specific details may vary, all versions invariably assert that the rat relied on trickery to "steal" first place from the ox. It is for this reason that the ox came to symbolize simplicity and diligence.

Due to the great contribution the ox makes in farming, many ox-related folk customs emerged and became popular. The "Whipping the Spring Ox" ritual, mentioned above, is the most important of them. Many ethnic minorities in China have the custom of "extending regards" to the farm ox. Though different minorities hold the ritual at different times, it is conducted essentially in the same way. After the ox's equipment is removed, the people let the ox rest, wash it, and feed it with good fodder. Some of them read scripture to the Ox King to express gratitude for its hard work in tilling the fields.

In ancient China, there was a solemn ritual called *Sha Xue Wei Meng*, in which blood was kept in the mouth or smeared on the lips. Swearing by the ghosts and gods as well as the

heaven and earth, two people made a solemn oath to each other. The blood they used was taken from the ox's ears. The prominent sacrificial and ritualistic role of the ox is evident from this ritual.

In the past, the ox was used as a means of transportation. According to legend, Lao Tzu (600-470 BC), the founder of Taoism, wrote the classic *Five Thousand Words* (i.e., *Tao Te Ching*) when he passed Hangu Pass (in present-day Lingbao, Henan Province) riding a blue ox, and then disappeared in the distance. In the Chinese fairytale, the

Boju Ge, a bronze ware from the Western Zhou Dynasty decorated with the partten of ox head

A stone ox by the Tousand-Island Lake in Zhejiang Province

A clay sculpture of an ox dragging a drum, a folk custom in Shaanxi Province

An ox engraved on the 12-zodiac-animal screen wall in Beijing's White Cloud Temple

Investiture of the Gods, Huang Feihu, one of the leading roles, rides a mysterious five-colored ox.

Every part of the ox's body is precious. Beef is a good source of protein and crude fiber; milk is often extolled as the optimal food for humans; bezoar (the cow's gallstones) can be made into medicine and used to clarify thinking, eliminate phlegm, relieve convulsion, reduce fever, or detoxify the system; and ox hide can be made into items such as clothes, pants, leather shoes, bags and adornments. In addition, the robust ox horn, in addition to being imitated to make primitive weapons, was used as a bugle to conduct troops in military operations on the battlefield. The ox is praised for its contribution to humanity, and is regarded as a role-model for its diligence and ability to endure hardship. Hence, sayings such as "the ox eats grass but milks in return" and "bowing one's head willingly to be a calf" emerged. In the old days, when people crossed the Yellow River and its valley, they used a raft made out of ox hide to float in the water; the efforts and coordination of several people were necessary to "blow open" the raft. When encountered

THE *CHOU* OX OPENS THE EARTH

by someone who likes to brag or exaggerate, people thus began to call him or her "someone who can blow

open an ox-hide raft by himself or herself." Over time, the phrase "to blow the ox skin" became synonymous with "to boast" or "to exaggerate."

The ox has made outstanding contributions on the battlefield, described in the well-known story *The Fire-Ox Formation*. In the Warring States Period (475-221 BC), Yue Yi, a famous general of the Yan State, led forces to attack the Qi State. The Yan troops won continuous victories and occupied over 70 cities. However, their progress was hampered when they arrived at Jimo (present-day southeast Pingdu County, Shandong Province). Under the lead of the famous general Tian Dan, civilians and soldiers determined to fight to the bitter end. The city was besieged by the Yan troops for three years and still survived. The Qi State sowed discord between the King of Yan and General Yue Yi and, as a result, Yue Yi was transferred to another post. After that, Tian Dan forced the women and elderly to hold the forts so as to confuse the enemies, and quietly requisitioned thousands of oxen. Those oxen were placed on colorful quilts painted with all kinds of strange patterns; two sharp knives were tied on the ox horns; and the ox tails were tied with hemp and reed saturated with fat and oil. At midnight, the oxen were pulled to the city wall which had been chiseled beforehand. The ox herds were terrified at the sight of the burning ox tails, and at once rushed towards the Yan military camps. The deep-sleeping Yan troops woke up with a start, saw numberless monsters rushing towards them with knife-outfitted ox horns and flaming ox tails, and ran around in a panicked fright. The Qi troops took this opportunity to attack and defeated the Yan troops. Heartened by this victory, the Qi troops recaptured the lost

Five Cattles, by a Tang painter Han Huang

The bronze ox head once adorned the Old Summer Palace, or Yuanmingyuan, in Beijing and were stolen by Western armies when they burnt the palace down in 1860.

territories occupied by the Yan troops. Thereafter, Tian Dan and his "Fire-Ox Formation" became known throughout the land, setting a remarkable example in ancient China's military history of how to apply inferior force to overcome a superior power. There are other stories about the Fire-Ox Formation in Chinese folklore. For example, Zhuge Liang's defeat of Xiahou Dun during the Three Kingdoms (220-280); and Yang Liulang's rout over the Liao troops during the Northern Song (960-1126) both relied on this formation. Both of these stories are described in a vivid and dramatic way.

A stone carving of Li Bai on an ox in Jiangyou, Sichuan Province

During the Southern and Northern Dynasties Period (420-589), Shi Le, the tribe leader of the Jie state, also won a smart victory with the help of the ox. After Shi Le occupied Xiangguo (present-day Xingtai, Hebei Province), there were confrontation and conflicts between him and Wang Jun, the Western Jin governor of Youzhou (present-day Beijing). After failing many times in battle, Shi Le wrote a letter one day to Wang Jun pretending to be friendly and sent thousands of oxen as gifts. When Shi Le's troops arrived at Youzhou, they drove the oxen to jam all the roads in the city so that the Western Jin's troops could not be dispatched. Shi Le's troops seized the opportunity to attack and occupied the city of Youzhou, suffering only minor casualties. These victories secured

THE *CHOU* OX OPENS THE EARTH

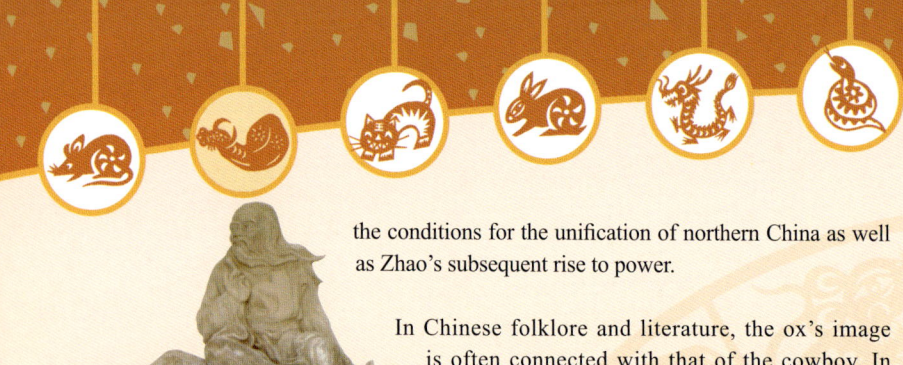

the conditions for the unification of northern China as well as Zhao's subsequent rise to power.

In Chinese folklore and literature, the ox's image is often connected with that of the cowboy. In ancient literature and paintings, the image of a cowboy on the back of an ox reading or fluting at ease was a common creative theme. There are many well-known stories about the ox: Zhu Yuanzhang (1328-1368), the emperor and founder of the Ming Dynasty (1368-1644), read while herding oxen and finally achieved great success; Wang Mian, a famous painter and poet of the Yuan Dynasty (1206-1368), listened to class in secret at private school while herding oxen; the famous Beijing opera *Little Cowherd*, a drama with interesting dialogs and stories, portrays a mischievous and lovely shepherd boy. Finally, the story of *The Cowherd and the Weaving Maid* has practically become a household tale, and is regarded as one of the four major Chinese folktales.

A clay sculpture of Lao Tzu riding on a blue ox

According to Chinese legend, the God of Taurus in heaven was sent down to the temporal world for violating the heavenly rules, and became a cowherd's ox. The cowherd, who treated his ox very kindly, was so poor that no father would allow his daughter to marry him. He and his ox thus depended on each other for life. One day, the ox suddenly started to talk. He instructed the cowherd to go to a pond where the fairies bathed and hide a red-colored garment; in this way, the ox explained, he could find his wife. The cowherd approached the pond and did as the ox told. Upon seeing a mortal man before their eyes, all but one of the fairies flew away and vanished. Only the Weaving Maid remained; she stood still and looked shy and worried, as she could not find her clothes. The cowherd asked the Weaving Maid to be his wife and, in return, he would give back her clothes. The Weaving Maid recognized the ox and, knowing that the ox would not deceive her, accepted the cowherd's marriage proposal. After the two were married, the cowherd tilled the land and the Weaving Maid weaved cloth. They loved each other deeply, lived a happy life, and soon had two lovely children — one son and one daughter. Upon hearing this news, the Goddess flew into a rage and she sent heavenly soldiers to take back the

Weaving Maid. By then, the ox's punishment term had ended and it had to return to heaven. It asked the cowherd to make shoes with its ox hide after it died. By wearing the shoes, the cowherd could go to heaven and be with the Weaving Maid. The cowherd did as the ox instructed, and brought his son and daughter to chase after the Weaving Maid. When they were about to meet, the Goddess plucked off her golden hairpin and waved. Suddenly, a surging galactic river appeared between them. The cowherd and the Weaving Maid were separated, and wept bitter tears on opposite sides of the river. Their love and loyalty moved the magpies into action. Thousands of magpies flew to them and formed a bridge to facilitate the family's reunion. Thereafter, the Goddess had no choice but to permit the family to reunite on the "magpie bridge" on July 7th of every year. That is the origin of the Double-Seven Festival — which is often regarded as China's Valentine's Day.

ZODIAC ANIMAL FILE

Earthly Branch: *Chou*
Years of Birth: 2021, 2009, 1997, 1985, 1973, 1961, 1949, 1937…
Five Elements: *Chou* belongs to Earth
Five Constant Virtues: Earth belongs to Sincerity
Auspicious Directions: southeast, south, north
Auspicious Colors: blue, red, purple
Lucky Numbers: 1, 9
Lucky Flowers: tulip, Chinese evergreen, peach blossom
Lucky Gemstones: red tourmaline (rubellite), rose quartz, topaz
Spiritual Protector: Akasagarbha Bodhisattva (the "boundless space treasury")
Choosing a name: For individuals born in the Year of the Ox, it is appropriate to select characters with the water (氵) radical, which signifies happiness, comfort and familial harmony; or characters with the radicals for person (亻) or wood (木), which embody uprightness, integrity and honesty.

THE OX AND PERSONALITY

Strengths:
The Ox's assets include an earnest and down-to-earth personality, coupled with determination and tenaciousness. People born in the Year of the Ox tend to be careful and attentive. Once they've made a commitment, others can count on them to carry out their duty and see tasks through to completion. Oxen are honest and good-natured, loyal and reliable, possess strong convictions, and are physically robust and energetic.

THE *CHOU* OX OPENS THE EARTH

They are also natural-born leaders. Females of this sign make for good homemakers and wives.

Weaknesses:
The Ox's limitations include being dull and slow, as well as the tendency to haggle over small details. People born in the Year of the Ox lack diplomatic skills, and tend to be strict and serious by nature.

THE OX AND BLOOD TYPE

Blood Type A:
Oxen with blood type A are careful and prudent, stubborn, direct and straightforward, and devoted and steady-going. Although people born in the Year of the Ox may be persistent in their old ways, they do not hurt others. They are earnest and hard-working in their endeavors, putting all their energy into a task once they have committed to it. Oxen of this blood type are good talkers, possess a forthright attitude, and are never pretentious.

Blood Type B:
Oxen with blood type B have a sharp wit, and are enthusiastic, enterprising, courageous and strong-minded. Placing a high value on friendship, they are straightforward in manner and naturally generous with others. They are also honest, kindhearted, thrifty and simple. Although they possess patience and forbearance, they can quite harsh if they lose their temper.

Blood Type O:
Oxen with blood type O have a keen sense of time and a high level of self-restraint. Demonstrating diligence and detailed thinking, they are thorough in their work and can be counted on to keep their word. They are also honest, cultured and refined, polite and well-behaved, and

are not the garrulous or verbose type. However, they are often stubborn and uncompromising, and tend to have limited expressive skills.

Blood Type AB:
Oxen with blood type AB are clever and dexterous, modest and solemn, and both keen-sighted and open-minded. With a quick wit and philosophical outlook, they are flexible in handling matters and adapt easily to changing conditions and new environments. Oxen of this blood type also tend to have a graceful demeanor and cheerful personality, and treat others with courtesy and respect.

THE OX AND FORTUNE

Lifetime Fortune: Overview

People born in the Year of the Ox will be blessed with good luck all around and their lives will radiate with joy. The Ox may be faced with difficulties or encounter the occasional good-for-nothing lowlife. With the support of others, however, the Ox is set to rise swiftly in the world. It is important for Oxen to avoid clinging stubbornly to their own views, but they should not be swayed by others' sweet talk either. The Ox will have a blissful youth, toil hard in middle age, and be blessed with happiness and longevity in old age.

Career:
The Ox is bound to have a thriving career, as diligent efforts lead to success. However, it is important for Oxen to be on guard against despicable scoundrels and learn to adopt a survivalist approach. By exercising due caution, the Ox can overcome any unfavorable conditions which may arise.

A bronze ox inlaid with green kallaites from the Warring States Period

Financial Luck:
The Ox is likely to meet with steady luck in moneymaking, with multiple profit-making opportunities. Income will gradually grow from a stable base, and good luck in investing will further enhance net

THE *CHOU* OX OPENS THE EARTH

earnings. The Ox should feel free to dabble in any investments that seem promising.

Romance:

The Ox has strong emotions, and a clear demarcation between love and hate. The Ox's love life is not always smooth sailing; it is thus important to avoid suspicion and jealousy with partners.

Fortune and the Five Elements

A colored statue of Yi-Chou Deity

Wood Ox: Born in the Year of *Gui-Chou* (1973, 1913)

Wood Oxen are full of energy and highly active by nature. Generally abiding by their principles, they do not hesitate to do what is right or defend others against injustice. They are also good at seizing opportunities, enabling them to succeed in their endeavors; if they decide to go into business, profits will pour in from all sides.

A colored statue of Gui-Chou Deity

Fire Ox: Born in the Year of *Ji-Chou* (2009, 1949)

Fire Oxen are highly intelligent and vivacious, but tend to be easily lured by external temptations. By associating and collaborating with those in positions of power, wealth and material comfort can be attained. Fire Oxen have stable luck over the course of their lives, and are able to balance revenues and expenditures. In addition to earning a basic income, the Fire Ox may also come across some unexpected wealth.

A colored statue of Ji-Chou Deity

Earth Ox: Born in the Year of *Xin-Chou* (2021, 1961)

Earth Oxen are not the scheming or calculating type, and tend to be faithful to others. They usually spend their early life running around and toiling hard. Only in middle and old age are they finally able to enjoy a life of comfort. While Earth Oxen have fairly good luck in finances, they also tend to be big spenders and should seek ways to reduce expenses.

Metal Ox: Born in the Year of *Yi-Chou* (1985, 1925)

Metal Oxen are destined to receive the support of others, fostering successful careers as well as fame and fortune. Their early years are defined by honor and a high salary, followed by a stable career in mid-life and a life of ease and comfort in old age. Due to a lack of money management skills, the Metal Ox may find it difficult to amass

earnings into a large fortune.

Water Ox: Born in the Year of *Ding-Chou* (1997, 1937)

Water Oxen are highly capable, have the ability to endure hardship, and possess a strong sense of justice. They tend to hold to their own ideas and are not easily swayed by others. With the support of friends, the Water Ox stands a good chance of making a fortune.

A colored statue of Xin-Chou Deity

A colored statue of Ding-Chou Deity

Fortune by the Year

In the Year of the Rat, Oxen will meet with good luck all around. By devoting themselves to their work, they can make big accomplishments; it is thus a good year for Oxen to expand their careers. Although they may become slightly ill, they will recover naturally. During the year, potential calamities will be turned into blessings. The Ox may face setbacks around mid-year; however, by withdrawing first and waiting until opportunity arrives before advancing, obstacles will disperse naturally.

In the Year of the Ox, Oxen are likely to experience stagnating luck, minimal profits, and gains in neither fame nor reputation. The Ox is bound to face resistance in getting work done and will have to contend with a continuous flow of minor problems. By continuing to forge ahead, however, the Ox can still make solid gains.

In the Year of the Tiger, Oxen will

THE *CHOU* OX OPENS THE EARTH

experience good luck overall, and a family member is likely to get married or engaged. However, financial prospects are mediocre at best, and the Ox should avoid being too aggressive or bullish. Oxen should also diversify in their business activities and make profits by selling a higher volume at lower margins.

In the Year of the Rabbit, Oxen will face multiple nuisances. They should keep an eye on the health of family members, abstain from visiting sick friends or relatives, and avoid personal involvement in funeral plans. The Ox should also forego having a birthday celebration this year. In this period of less-than-ideal financial luck, turnover is of the essence; large investments must be avoided. By enduring difficulties, calming the mind, and engaging in self-cultivation, the Ox can ensure that the year passes smoothly.

In the Year of the Dragon, Oxen are likely to meet with a combination of blessing and calamity, of good luck and ill fortune. It would be wise to let things take their natural course and not worry about food or clothing; the year will thus pass smoothly and serenely. Despite having a good year of financial luck, a lot of resistance will be encountered. In particular, the Oxen should be cautious about investments made by their spouse or relatives. By collaborating with others, the Ox's luck can be augmented.

In the Year of the Snake, Oxen will meet with flourishing revenues, profitable business ventures, and a plentiful

harvest. It will also be a year of happiness and joy. Carelessly choosing friends, however, may lead to multiple quarrels and disputes during the year.

In the Year of the Horse, Oxen will stumble upon luck in romance. Unfortunately, this may lead to envy and even cause the Ox to be framed by others. Monetary losses and other problems may also evolve. In each case, however, the Ox can defeat ill luck and turn the tables of fortune. Overall luck will improve in the second half of the year.

In the Year of the Sheep, Oxen will be faced with heavy financial outlays, an array of steep challenges, and tremendous pressure in life; many things are likely to go contrary to the Ox's wishes. Nevertheless, luck is destined to arrive by year-end, at which time the Ox will see good

opportunities for investment and profit-making.

In the Year of the Monkey, Oxen will encounter a lot of good luck on the homestead. It will be a year of good fortune, possibly with a wedding in the family or the birth of a child or grandchild. Financial prospects are also excellent, with the chance of large winnings in the lottery. In every respect, this is a year of jubilation for the Ox.

In the Year of the Rooster, Oxen will suffer from ill fortune, with natural disasters and manmade calamities both taking a toll. Faced with meager profits and ailing health, the Ox must make efforts to calm the heart, relax the mind, and pay increased attention to physical wellbeing. By doing good deeds and accumulating virtue, the year is likely to pass without incident.

THE *CHOU* OX OPENS THE EARTH

In the Year of the Dog, Oxen will enjoy a surplus of good fortune and meet with success in their business ventures. Luck is fairly consistent throughout the year, with only minor fluctuations. Through careful calculations and strict budgeting, the Ox can recover from the prior year and invest in new undertakings. However, Oxen must avoid licentiousness at all costs, lest they find themselves on a path of self-destruction.

In the Year of the Pig, Oxen are liable to encounter hardship. Facing barriers in every direction, most or all endeavors are likely to be frustrated, ultimately resulting in financial misfortune. It might be best for the Ox to leave town and seek business opportunities away from home for the year.

THE OX AND THE WESTERN ZODIAC

An ox-shaped bronze lamp from the Eastern Han Dynasty

Ox-Aries:

Ox-Aries are self-reliant and destined to accomplish big things. Though withdrawn and conservative by nature, some of them can be quite talkative as well. They also possess inner strength, are loyal and dependable, and make for good companions.

Ox-Taurus:

Ox-Tauruses are taciturn, unhurried, detail-oriented and cautious, and are predisposed to cherish time. Their hobbies include dancing and singing. To some extent, they may be workaholics, willing to make unremitting efforts to achieve a goal. Although they tend not to focus on externalities, such as clothing or appearance, Ox-Tauruses are themselves highly appealing to others.

A porcelain ox made in Jingdezhen, the Capital of Porcelain in China

A bronze crouching ox treasured in the Museum of Western Xia Imperial Tombs in Ningxia

Ox-Gemini:

Ox-Geminis are naturally pensive and family-oriented. Although they may appear silent and dull on the surface, they are actually quite talkative and humorous. They also have a glib tongue and excel at debating.

Ox-Cancer:

Ox-Cancers have a strong sense of determination, combined with abundant creativity. With natural talent that approaches the realm of perfection, they hate to be defeated. They also dislike others telling them what to do. The Ox-Cancer's thinking is meticulous, deliberated and goal-oriented.

Ox-Leo:

Ox-Leos are stern and do not easily let others get close to them. With strength, courage, and abundant energy, they're always moving forward and are able to surpass obstacle after obstacle to reach their goal. Identifying the crux of the matter at hand enables them to solve problems quickly and efficiently. Always as busy as a bee, the Ox-Leo brims with vivacity and energy.

Ox-Virgo:

Ox-Virgos are defined by their intelligence and sincerity, conservativeness and prudence, and independence and self-reliance. They possess clear judgment and outstanding expressive skills, and demonstrate efficiency, enthusiasm, as well as a high level of energy. Ox-Virgos reveal a level of fortitude, perseverance and stamina matched by few others.

Ox-Libra:

Ox-Librans are gentle and sweet, sharp-witted, and perfectionistic in their pursuits. They dislike commotion and chaos, preferring quiet and tranquil environments instead. Ox-Librans are susceptible to mood swings, rarely attend social events, and tend to rely on their families.

Ox-Scorpio:

Ox-Scorpios are elegant and graceful, humorous and exuberant, and do not give up easily. They tend always to be in a hurry, steadfast and unyielding in the pursuit of fame and gain. With

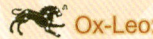

THE CHOU OX OPENS THE EARTH

overbearing dominance, they also enjoy controlling others.

Ox-Sagittarius:
Ox-Sagittarians are energetic and vigorous; ardent and passionate; and aspire after status and privilege. They are notably courageous, often ready to throw caution to the wind. With an alluring charm and positive attitude, Ox-Sagittarians have no trouble achieving success in their professional lives.

Ox-Capricorn:
Ox-Capricorns tend to be a bit slow, but are equally firm and steadfast — seeking perfection and not giving up easily on a plan. They tend to watch their diet, are often conservative-minded, and can be stubborn and indecisive at times. Despite seeming unemotional on the surface, the Ox-Capricorn has a fragile heart.

Ox-Aquarius:
Ox-Aquarians are strong-minded, sharp-witted, hard-working, and able to endure hardship. In addition to being conscientious, responsible and caring of others, they also boast an astonishing memory, fertile imagination, and sharp sense of humor. Coupled with the qualities of agility, vigor, and eloquence, there is nothing the Ox-Aquarian is unable to accomplish.

Ox-Pisces:
Ox-Pisces are modest and unassuming, sensitive and emotional, and yet equally cunning and conniving. They are highly orderly and methodical in their ways and tend to excel at planning. Despite having a shy and timid disposition, Ox-Pisces enjoy good relations with others and are both respected and admired.

A commemorative coin issued in Chinese Ox Year

A wooden carving of ox and *kylin*, which is often seen in old buildings

056 THE TWELVE ZODIAC ANIMALS

FENGSHUI AND THE OX

In the study of *fengshui*, the ox is unquestionably an auspicious creature. By utilizing the ox's habits and characteristics, it is thus possible for *fengshui* ornaments to attract good fortune, improve job prospects, and create wealth. A *fengshui* ox cast of gold will definitely enhance one's career and lead to both success and fortune. Alternatively, a *fengshui* ox made of porcelain or gold-plated copper could be used. It is imperative, however, not to employ a *fengshui* ox constructed of wood.

The dancing of water buffalo performed by minorities in Guizhou Province

This constraint has to do with the Five Elements: *Chou* belongs to the element Earth, which Wood restricts. In terms of the placement of ornaments, north-northeast is the ideal direction, while south-southwest should be avoided.

INTERPRETING OX DREAMS

If you dream of an ox climbing a slope, it is an auspicious sign.

If you dream of leading an ox up a mountain, it is a sign of wealth and honor.

If you dream of an ox brushing against you, your wishes will not come true.

If you dream of an ox leaving its stable, good things will soon happen.

If you dream of riding an ox into town, great happiness awaits you.

HEALTH SECRETS

People born in the Year of the Ox often get so absorbed in carrying out a task that they forget to eat and sleep, and as a result are likely to suffer from gastrointestinal problems. They are easily affected by stress and prone to rapid changes in weight. Oxen should pay special attention to protecting the liver, gallbladder, and digestive organs. They should also try to avoid becoming excessively busy. By going for a walk outside in the fresh air, the Ox can recover strength and improve overall health.

THE *CHOU* OX OPENS THE EARTH

THE TWELVE
ZODIAC ANIMALS

PART 3
THE *YIN* TIGER WHISTLES THROUGH THE WIND

【TIGER】

THE *YIN* TIGER WHISTLES THROUGH THE WIND

The bronze tiger head once adorned the Old Summer Palace

The tiger, regarded as the "king of the beasts" in the old days, is a symbol of power and might be revered for its ferocity and stateliness. In Chinese folk paintings, the tiger in each painting has the Chinese character for "king" on its forehead. There is seemingly a natural relationship between the tiger and the king. It is also said that the Chinese character for "king" is rooted in the stripes on the tiger's forehead. The white tiger is an important concept in ancient Chinese astronomy, geomancy and Taoism.

Among the 12 zodiac animals, the tiger is listed in the third position. In ancient literature, this placement is explained as follows: The sky was opened up during the *zi*-hour (11:00pm-1:00am), the earth was opened up during the *chou*-hour (1:00am-3:00am), and people were born during the *yin*-hour (3:00am-5:00am). Dying is as natural as living, and nothing can kill people more easily than the tiger. The *yin*-hour, which occupies the third position and also represents awe, thus belongs to the tiger.

The ancient Chinese regarded wind as "belonging" to the tiger; wherever a tiger appeared, the wind would howl, causing people to tremble in fear. For this reason, tigers became the totem of many tribes in primitive society. To the present day, many Chinese ethnic minorities still maintain customs of tiger worship. *Meige*, an epic folk poem of the Yi nationality, records that everything in the universe was created or transformed by the tiger: the tiger's bones supported the sky; the tiger's left eye became the sun; its right eye became the moon; its whiskers became the sunshine; the tiger's teeth became the stars; and so on.

In feudal society, the emperor was the sovereign authority and wielded absolute power. People around the emperor had to be cautious at all times, or else they might be beheaded. Consequently, several old sayings emerged, including "to accompany an emperor is to accompany a tiger" and "it is hard to be an official as understrapper of the tiger." The sign for dispatching troops was tiger-like, and was called the "tiger tally". The "tiger tally" was divided into two parts held by the emperor and the commander-in-chief. When the emperor wanted to dispatch troops, he would send an emissary with the "tiger sign" to the army. After checking that the two parts were suited, the commander-in-chief would dispatch the troops. During the Warring States Period (475-221 BC), Lord Xinling of the Wei State stole the "tiger tally" and sent fake military orders to help the Zhao State out of siege. This event, in fact, was part of the basis for Guo Moruo (1892-1978)'s historical play *Tiger Tally*.

An embroidery tiger

THE *YIN* TIGER WHISTLES THROUGH THE WIND

The tiger is also a symbol of prestige. For example, Bao Zheng (999-1062), a famous uncorrupted government official of the Northern Song Dynasty, had a lever-knife shaped like a tiger's head, which he used for killing corrupt officials. In addition, the gang leaders in traditional Chinese dramas and novels typically sit in tiger leather chairs to reveal their sovereign status.

In addition to symbolizing prestige, the tiger is also regarded as valorous and hot-blooded. For this reason, the tiger gradually formed an indissoluble bond with war and combat. In the past, the tiger's head was often drawn at the soldiers' shields to frighten enemies. In ancient times, the "White Tiger Hall" was the place at which military affairs and strategy were deliberated, while the commander-in-chief's tent was known as the "Tiger Tent." The tiger's image is so awe-inspiring that it has been used to symbolize soldiers' bravery and strength, with expressions such as "tiger general", "tiger stateliness", "tiger step", "eye covetously like a tiger", and "tiger's son, bear's waist." Many titles used by ancient officials also contained the word of tiger. During the Three Kingdoms period, Liu Bei (161-223), the emperor of Shuhan, ennobled the five valorous generals as "General of the Five Tigers". Other official positions included the "energetic tiger general" and the "tiger-tooth general". The "White Tiger" was regarded as the god of war. Many famous generals, such as Luo Cheng and Xue Rengui of the Tang Dynasty (618-907), were regarded as the embodiment of tigers coming down to reside in the human

A stone tiger unearthed from the cemetery of Cai Xiang, a famous calligrapher in the 11th century

world. In the famous Battle of Kunyang (in today's Yexian County, Henan Province), Liu Xiu (6 BC-57 AD), Emperor Guangwu of the Eastern Han Dynasty, used tigers to "defeat more with less" on the path to reviving the Han Dynasty. In that battle, Wang Mang established a beast troop made up of tigers, leopards, rhinoceros and elephants. Unfortunately, the beasts were themselves frightened on the battlefield — instead of frightening the enemies — and the troops were left in a state of disorder.

In Chinese legends, people are depicted as believing the tiger to be a very capable animal, which could devour demons and repel the disasters of fire, theft and evil. Tiger paintings were often hung on the wall near the main entrance to frighten the demons and prevent them from entering. The custom of "painting a tiger to thwart evil

A tiger guarding the Supreme Master Cave, a Taoist temple in Chongqing

spirits" is regarded as one of the origins of the Spring Festival paintings. Even in today's China, it is common for children to wear a tiger-head hat and tiger-head shoes, and lay down to sleep on a tiger-head pillow in order to dispel evil. In some places, people present a cloth tiger to friends and relatives as an auspicious gift.

THE *YIN* TIGER WHISTLES THROUGH THE WIND

The tiger culture is a vital component in traditional Chinese culture. Indeed, the multiform beast is virtually everywhere to be found: in poems, literature, paintings, novels, dramas, folk customs, folklore, fairytales, children's songs, New Year paintings, shadow figures, paper-cuttings, sculptures, and cloth toys — just to name a few.

The clay sculpture of a pair of tigers

In *Strange Stories from a Chinese Studio*, there is a chapter entitled the *Zhao Town Tiger* depicting a "humanistic tiger" who was sentenced to look after an old woman by the local officer for killing the old woman's son. Every day, the tiger sent her the freshly killed prey and precious treasures. Oftentimes, he would even sit by the old woman's side and accompany her, showing a devotion which may even have surpassed her own son. After the old woman died, the tiger howled over the grave in sadness. There are many other literary accounts recording such humanistic tigers, including *Lasting Words to Awaken the World* and the saga *Honorable Tigers* written by Wang Youding, a prose master from the early Qing Dynasty (1644-1911).

There is also a children's fairy tale called "The Tiger Learns a Skill". It is said that a long time ago, the tiger possessed no skills whatsoever and asked the cat to serve as his teacher. The cat did thus imparted many important skills, including jumping and pouncing, but withheld the skill of tree-climbing. This decision was made after the cat discovered the tiger's ruffian nature. Indeed, the tiger was preparing to repay the cat's kindness with ingratitude by eating the cat! Fortunately, the cat climbed up a tree nimbly, leaving the tiger frustrated and disappointed. This story captures the irony of those who are unappreciative and know no gratitude. Over the course of Chinese history, the tiger has gained a spot in countless other tales, legends and anecdotes, as well as the names of places and people.

The Queen Mother of the West, an ancient Chinese goddess, with the teeth of a tiger

064 THE TWELVE ZODIAC ANIMALS

The tiger is so fierce that people often turn pale at the mere mention of its name. Those who dare to fight it, therefore, are regarded as heroes. The *Outlaws of the Marsh*, one of the four great classical novels of Chinese literature, depicts the story of *Wu Song Fights the Tiger*. After slaying a tiger with his bare hands, Wu Song, an outlaw at Liangshan Mountain, was beloved by the local government as well as the common people. Li Kui, another outlaw at Liangshan Mountain, was a rash and dutiful son. When a tiger picked up his mother, he killed four big and small tigers at one go, becoming a truly unrivalled hero. Tigers have also been likened to great might and forces of evil; would-be heroes who seek to defeat the tiger, therefore, are by no means rare.

The tiger, combining magnificence with stateliness, is also a subject highly favored by painters. From ancient times up to the present day, countless experts renowned in tiger painting have emerged. Li Guizhen, a painter during the Five Dynasties (907-960), even lived in the remote mountains for a period to observe tigers firsthand. Indeed, after numerous sketches and copies, the tigers he painted had a spectacular unity of form and lifelike spirit.

 ## ZODIAC ANIMAL FILE

Earthly Branch: *Yin*
Years of Birth: 2022, 2010, 1998, 1986, 1974, 1962, 1950, 1938, 1926, 1914…
Five Elements: *Yin* belongs to Wood
Five Constant Virtues: Wood belongs to Benevolence
Auspicious Directions: south, east, southeast
Auspicious Colors: blue, gray, white, orange
Lucky Numbers: 1, 3, 4
Lucky Flowers: florist's cineraria
Lucky Gemstones: black tourmaline, citrine, blue sapphire, turquoise, sodalite
Spiritual Protector: Akasagarbha Bodhisattva

THE *YIN* TIGER WHISTLES THROUGH THE WIND

Choosing a name: For individuals born in the Year of the Tiger, it is appropriate to select characters with the mountain (山) radical, signifying grandeur and dominance, intelligence and courage, as well as happiness, longevity and family prosperity; characters containing the jade (玉) radical, which embodies beauty, giftedness and talent; characters with the radicals for metal (金), wood (木), clothing (衣), or water (氵), which embody geniality, virtue, fame and wealth; or characters with the radicals for moon (月), dog (犭), or horse (马), representing uprightness and selflessness.

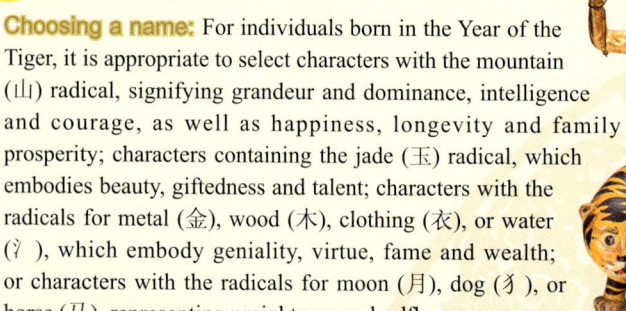

THE TIGER AND PERSONALITY

Strengths:

The Tiger's assets include enthusiasm, courage, resoluteness, and tenacity. People born in the Year of the Tiger like to accept challenges, and they tend to be both positive and proactive. With an honest and upright manner, Tigers gain the trust of others easily. They also possess a high level of self-awareness.

A pair of tiger-head shoes

Weaknesses:

The Tiger's limitations include an obstinate and unyielding nature, rebelliousness, and the tendency to make decisions arbitrarily without consulting others. Though the Tiger has many acquaintances, deep friendships seldom develop. Tigers are willing to do what it takes to achieve a goal, whether by fair means or foul. They possess a bossy and overbearing demeanor, and are unromantic by nature.

THE TIGER AND BLOOD TYPE

Blood Type A:

Tigers with blood type A are enthusiastic and upbeat, daring and down-to-earth, and romantic and charming. They place a high value on friendship, and have a unique disposition which catches the attention of others.

A stone tiger carved in the 10th century

Blood Type B:

Tigers with blood type B are liberal-minded and generous, honest and principled, passionate and romantic, and independent and proactive. They are enterprising and daring, but always stay within reason. Tigers of this blood type treat others with loyalty and warmth, and are prepared to defend others against injustice.

Blood Type O:

Tigers with blood type O are natural-born leaders with a penchant for power. Their intelligence and skills are complemented by a down-to-earth nature and a cautious mind. Tigers of this blood type prefer to adopt a free and open lifestyle. Their greatest pet peeve is people who keep quiet except to argue over petty details.

Blood Type AB:

Tigers with blood type AB are quick-witted and intelligent, vivacious and active,

THE *YIN* TIGER WHISTLES THROUGH THE WIND

romantic and tender, and graceful and charming. Their expressiveness and ability to say the right thing at the right time makes them well-liked by others. They tend to dislike people who mince words, preferring that people communicate with one another in a candid and unrestrained manner.

A relief stone sculpture with the pattern of a tiger (right) from the Han Dynasty

THE TIGER AND FORTUNE

Lifetime Fortune: Overview

People born in the Year of the Tiger are tolerant and staunch, with hearts of heroes. Females of this sign tend to be wise, understanding, chaste and kindhearted. In their youth, Tigers are blessed by good fortune. In middle age, they tend to lack stability, drifting along and facing many changes in their lives. After mid-life, however, they are likely to come across some good opportunities. By old age, some Tigers are able to achieve a high reputation based on strong moral character.

Career:

In general, Tigers are likely to face many obstacles in the early months of each year. They will make great strides in their career starting in March, but should be prepared to hit a low point by year-end. It is important for Tigers to develop habits of modesty and studiousness. They should

also ask for the advice of seniors who have rich practical experience, and show respect and kindness to others.

Financial Luck:
Tigers have mediocre financial luck and are advised against making large investments. They should give full play to their financial skills, and work out a plan to reduce expenses and cash outflows. Tigers should adopt a factual and realistic work style, and make adjustments to their investment plans based on market changes.

Romance:
It is said that "the road to happiness is full of hardships." Tigers should be frank with their other halves, strive to cultivate a mutual understanding, and also spend more time with him or her. Finally, it is essential that Tigers avoid letting impulsive behavior infiltrate their love life.

Fortune and the Five Element

Wood Tiger: Born in the Year of *Geng-Yin* (2010, 1950)
Wood Tigers are sympathetic, loyal and trustworthy. They take pleasure in helping others, and enjoy caring for friends and family. However, they often behave rashly, are liable to fall victim to deception, and tend to lack objectivity in their thinking.

A colored statue of Geng-Yin Deity

Fire Tiger: Born in the Year of *Bing-Yin* (1986, 1926)
Fire Tigers can be counted on to keep their promises and perform work earnestly and diligently. In addition to possessing magnanimity and strong willpower, they also boast a gifted intellect and quick wit. In general, Fire Tigers have good financial luck and can surmount any obstacle in their path, whether illness or some other difficulty.

A colored statue of Bing-Yin Deity

Earth Tiger: Born in the Year of *Wu-Yin* (1998, 1938)
Earth Tigers are highly self-confident, with the tendency to be arrogant and conceited. Nonetheless, they are kindhearted people who take pleasure in helping others. Ambitious by nature, Earth Tigers also have a strong entrepreneurial spirit and innovative mind. With the valuable support of others, they are likely to succeed in all their pursuits.

A colored statue of Wu-Yin Deity

THE *YIN* TIGER WHISTLES THROUGH THE WIND

Metal Tiger: Born in the Year of *Ren-Yin* (2022, 1962)

Metal Tigers are kind and considerate, but also tend to be stubborn, often refusing to accept the advice of others. They enjoy excellent relationships with others, facilitating both financial and career success. To avoid unnecessary losses, however, Metal Tigers must remember not to act impetuously.

Water Tiger: Born in the Year of *Jia-Yin* (1974, 1914)

Water Tigers possess a high scholastic aptitude, often gravitating towards strange and novel things. With high self-esteem and a high opinion of themselves, they tend to be unbending in their ways. Water Tigers are likely to meet with a mixture of good and bad luck over the course of their careers. If they are able to secure the help of friends or a romantic partner, brand-new prospects may emerge on the horizon. The Water Tiger may also wish to pursue small investments, which are likely to generate a return.

A colored statue of Jia-Yin Deity

A colored statue of Ren-Yin Deity

Fortune by the Year

In the Year of the Rat, Tigers will be plagued by multiple setbacks and frequent disasters. To avoid personal injury or financial losses, they should pursue practical and honest work. The Tiger should refrain from gambling, and must avoid becoming a spectator in the physical altercations of others.

In the Year of the Ox, Tigers will be blessed with excellent luck and should not let any opportunities slip away. However, caution should be applied at the beginning of the year. The Tiger is likely to suffer from headaches, but they will ultimately subside without the need for medicine.

In the Year of the Tiger, Tigers will meet with instability, ill fortune, financial losses and emotional upsets. It would be best to avoid attending funerals during the year.

In the Year of the Rabbit, Tigers will have an auspicious year and should strive hard in their endeavors.

With such good luck, the Tiger should seize opportunities and work towards realizing their ideals. It is also a good time to pursue entrepreneurial ventures.

In the Year of the Dragon, Tigers will face turbulent ups and downs. Since accomplishing any task is likely to prove difficult this year, it would be wise to focus instead on retaining current wealth and improving overall stability. The Tiger may also opt to improve career prospects by pursuing work away from home.

In the Year of the Snake, Tigers will face mediocre luck, with multiple expenses but little income. Success is likely to be limited in spite of their hard work. However, even though Tigers will face setbacks in their finances and social life, there are still gains to be made.

In the Year of the Horse, Tigers are destined to have a great year, with opportunities for job promotions, as well as enhanced profits and reputation. With luck on their side, Tigers are likely to succeed in all their endeavors.

It may also be an opportune time to start a business or pursue investments. However, the Tiger must be careful to choose friends and avoid licentious behavior at all costs.

In the Year of the Sheep, Tigers will encounter few major obstacles, despite some financial outflows and minor illnesses. Overall financial prospects are solid. Tigers should avoid making enemies and choose good and honest people as friends. In addition, it would be a good time to meet more people of social standing and solicit their assistance. Tigers should pursue their endeavors with patience and a steady hand.

In the Year of the Monkey, Tigers will face sluggish luck and thus have no choice other than to toil hard and pursue honest endeavors. While the beginning and middle of the year will be particularly arduous, financial gains can be made by year-end.

In the Year of the Rooster, Tigers will enjoy outstanding luck and can turn

THE *YIN* TIGER WHISTLES THROUGH THE WIND

any potential adversity into an auspicious outcome. While the year may see unforeseen mishaps, they are likely to pass without incident. It is important that Tigers exercise moderation and maintain moral integrity in their business pursuits.

In the Year of the Dog, Tigers are destined to be successful in all their endeavors and enjoy a year of prosperity and happiness. The Tiger must take care to avoid becoming mentally exhausted and, when away on business, should avoid prying into others' affairs. By working steadily and watching their health, Tigers can enjoy a worry-free year.

A tiger engraved on the 12-zodiac-animal screen wall in Beijing's White Cloud Temple

In the Year of the Pig, Tigers are likely to face instability. During this time of unpredictability, Tigers should be especially reserved and cautious.

THE TIGER AND THE WESTERN ZODIAC

 Tiger-Aries:
Tiger-Aries are impulsive, and tend to be irrational or childish at times. With a serious and conscientious demeanor, they perform their work efficiently and effectively. Tiger-Aries are independent, naturally gifted, and straightforward in speech.

Tiger-Taurus:
Tiger-Tauruses are down-to-earth, level-headed and steady-going, and show caution and vigilance. They are endowed with wisdom and resourcefulness, and also possess strong leadership skills. The Tiger Taurus's weakness is a tendency to be highly individualistic.

The sculpter of the Group Tiger designed by Han Meilin, a famous modern artist in China

THE TWELVE ZODIAC ANIMALS

Tiger-Gemini:

Tiger-Geminis are cultured and refined, charming and attractive, and possess a quick wit and active mind. However, they tend to be impulsive by nature, and would be advised to exercise self-restraint.

 Tiger-Cancer:

Tiger-Cancers are predisposed to be sensitive, emotional and romantic. As natural risk-takers, they advance boldly and intrepidly in their pursuits. The Tiger-Cancer is always filled with new ideas and has a corresponding propensity to seek out novel things.

 Tiger-Leo:

Tiger-Leos are high in self-esteem, but their arrogance and massive superiority complex tend to make them less approachable. High morale, a strong fighting will and an abundance of energy enables the Tiger-Leo to face life's setbacks and frustrations with optimism and confidence.

Tiger-Virgo:

Tiger-Virgos possess an elevated sense of responsibility; no matter how onerous or tedious the job at hand is, they can be counted on to get it done. They show great enthusiasm and vitality, and excel at offering their input and ideas. The Tiger-Virgo has a tendency to pry into the personal affairs of others.

Tiger-Libra:

Tiger-Librans are diligent, hard-working and self-assured, and have the courage to pursue fame and fortune. They are able to handle any task with proficiency and manifest their skills in unique ways.

A kite tiger

Tiger-Scorpio:

Tiger-Scorpios are natural challenge seekers who enjoy the respect and endearment of others. However, they are also given to impatience and impulsion, and tend to be carried to extremes.

Tiger-Sagittarius:

Tiger-Sagittarians take pleasure in travel, sightseeing, and exploration. With a great attention to detail, they are easily attracted by strange or novel things. The Tiger-Sagittarian is obstinate and childish by nature, and predisposed to have a dual personality.

Tiger-Capricorn:

Tiger-Capricorns seek challenges, aspire to liberty and freedom, and are

THE *YIN* TIGER WHISTLES THROUGH THE WIND

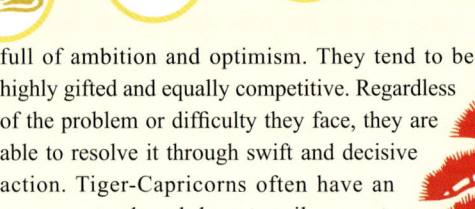

full of ambition and optimism. They tend to be highly gifted and equally competitive. Regardless of the problem or difficulty they face, they are able to resolve it through swift and decisive action. Tiger-Capricorns often have an arrogant streak and do not easily accept others' ideas.

Tiger-Aquarius:
Tiger-Aquarians are highly insightful and frequently engage in deep thought. They like to explore new territory, and gravitate toward excitement and novelty.

Tiger-Pisces:
Tiger-Pisceses are highly generous and giving, taking pleasure in helping others. Despite their charm and high level of self-awareness, they tend to have complex emotions and are often hurt by others.

FENGSHUI AND THE TIGER

The essential nature of tigers is one of brutal violence. For this reason, tigers should not be used as *fengshui* ornaments — except for military or police personnel and others whose style or career correlates with the tiger's aggressiveness. In the study of *fengshui*, tigers are classified as malevolent creatures; as such, their use inside the home is generally deemed inappropriate and unacceptable. Specifically, placing ornamental tigers in the bedroom or the hall opposite the front entrance is absolutely taboo, as it could lead to domestic conflicts and unforeseen mishaps. Entrepreneurs and business owners, too, should avoid

ornaments or paintings of tigers, as the tiger's fierce countenance could instill fear in customers, causing them to flee and negatively impacting business. Finally, ornamental tigers should be avoided in the office, as their presence could cause passersby to feel repressed, and lead to the alienation of coworkers and clients.

INTERPRETING TIGER DREAMS

If you dream of a tiger pouncing on you, you will encounter a series of difficulties.

If you dream of a tiger pouncing on someone else, you are likely to be involved in a car accident, but will ultimately cheat death and survive.

If you dream of shooting a tiger, difficulties will soon be overcome and you will attain success in your career.

If you dream of catching a tiger, your friends may become enemies.

If you dream of a tiger entering your home, you will be promoted at work.

A tiger-shaped steamed bread, which is usually taken as the gift from a grandmother to her one-month-old grandchild in the Yellow River valley

HEALTH SECRETS

People born in the Year of the Tiger tend to lead lives that lack structure and regularity. They may suffer from abnormal eating habits, lack of sleep, and suppressed worries. In addition, they often lack emotional stability, sometimes losing control of their emotions altogether. Tigers would be advised to adjust their outlook so as to reduce pressure and stimulate joyful emotions. They should also try to relax as needed and make any necessary adjustments to their sleep routine and diet.

THE *YIN* TIGER WHISTLES THROUGH THE WIND

THE TWELVE
ZODIAC ANIMALS

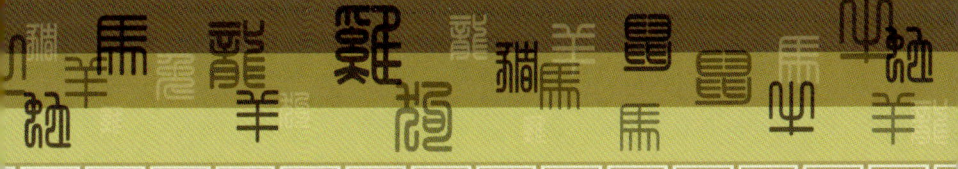

PART 4
THE *MAO* RABBIT PLAYS WITH THE MOON

【RABBIT】

THE *MAO* RABBIT PLAYS WITH THE MOON

Of the 12 zodiac animals, the rabbit is listed in the fourth position. *Mao* was originally used to describe greenery sprouting out of the earth in early spring. Of the day's 12 *shichen*, *mao* represents the period of 5-7am. During this interval, the sun is rising and the moon, also known as the Jade Rabbit in ancient times, still hangs in the sky. *Mao*, therefore, is aptly fitting for the rabbit. It is generally believed that the rabbit's status in Chinese fairy tales about the moon is what determined this match. Some scholars also offer a theory describing why the moon and rabbit are appropriately matched. In ancient Chinese astronomy, the "Morning Star" (i.e., Mercury) was also known as *tu* (rabbit). The Morning Star lies in the north sky, belongs to Water, and represents the essence of the moon. The rabbit therefore represents the moon, and vice versa. Considering the fact that the rabbit was one of the animals used in ancient sacrifice (the others being the ox, the horse, the sheep, the pig, the rooster and the dog), its listing among the 12 zodiac animals is hardly surprising. Its relative placement near the top of the list, however,

must be due to its "connections" with the moon.

In ancient Chinese mythology, the moon was far from vacant. On it were the Guanghan Palace, cassia trees, a goddess named Chang'e, the medicine-pounding Jade Rabbit, a toad, and a lumberman named Wu Gang (who was added during the Tang Dynasty). The moon thus garnered many different appellations, including "Chang'e", "Jade Rabbit" and "Golden Toad." *Chang'e Flying to the Moon* is a fairytale well-known throughout China. In antiquity, there were said to be 10 suns in the sky at the same time; as a result of the intense heat, the rivers dried up, vegetation withered and died, and human beings became thirsty and exhausted. Houyi, an archer, shot down nine suns with his miraculous powers to save the world. With this feat, he became a legendary hero worshipped by the people and was bestowed an elixir by the Queen Mother. Consumed by curiosity, Houyi's wife Chang'e secretly drank the elixir. In that instant, her body

A relief stone sculpture depicting the fairytale of Chang'e

Chang'e Flying to the Moon, a painting from the Long Corridor in the Summer Palace

THE *MAO* RABBIT PLAYS WITH THE MOON

became as light as air and she floated up the moon. Chang'e's rabbit, upon seeing this spectacle, pounced into her arms and the two lived together in the desolate Guanghan Palace. In folk paintings, there are many images of Chang'e holding a white rabbit. It is also a subject commonly depicted by both ancient and modern writers alike.

The rabbit is deeply adored by all people, and many expressions have been created based on its appearance, character, and habits. For example, a person with bloodshot eyes may be described as having "eyes red like a rabbit's", and the rabbit's short tail is used figuratively to refer to situations which cannot be maintained for long. Other rabbit phrases include "a crafty rabbit has more than one hideout" and "the rabbit does not eat the grass beside the nest." Even in the Chinese martial art of *wushu*, the technique "Rabbit Kicks the Hawk" is inspired by observation and imitation of the rabbit. It is said that when a rabbit is hunted by a hawk, the rabbit would kick the hawk suddenly with its hind legs, sometimes hurting the hawk by this action.

That the rabbit is swift on its toes is common knowledge and also reflected in many Chinese figures of speech, such as "run faster than a rabbit" and "move like a rabbit." There is an ancient legend about a swift horse named the "Red Hare" (literally the "Red Rabbit Horse"), which moved about freely and quickly on the battlefield and was ridden by Guan Yu, a famous general during the Three Kingdoms Period (220-280). The use of "rabbit" to name horses also has

A Master Rabbit toy

THE TWELVE ZODIAC ANIMALS

Commemorative coins issued in Chinese Rabbit Year

its history. It is recorded in *Xiang Ma Jing* (*Classics of Horse Judging*, written by Bo Le according to legend) that the first step in judging a horse is to judge its head. This is because the horse's head is the obvious external representation of a horse's variety, quality, physical fitness, and dental health. According to the shape of the horse's head, the ancient Chinese classified the horse as a "straight head", "rabbit head," "concave head", "wedge-shaped head", etc. The horse with a "rabbit head" is regarded as a good horse. The common people, however, are even more likely to believe the fable of the "Red Rabbit".

According to the "Red Rabbit" fable, there were initially no cassia trees in the human world. The Lunar Lord thus sent the Jade Rabbit to plant cassia trees. The Golden Crow, the underling of the Solar Lord, went privately to the human world to romantically pursue the Jade Rabbit. The Golden Crow asked the Red Rabbit — who was of the same clan as the Jade Rabbit — to serve as matchmaker. Unexpectedly, however, the Red Rabbit fell in love with the Jade Rabbit and decided to marry her. Upon hearing this news, the Golden Crow crashed the wedding ceremony, provoked a fight, and spawned an all-out war in the human world. When the Jade Emperor of Heaven learned of this event, he sent soldiers to take back the Jade Rabbit and Golden Crow, and transformed the Red Rabbit into a horse called the "Red Hare". This story is recounted in the Beijing Opera *Tian Xiang Qing Jie*.

In the past, a performance of the play *Tian Xiang Qing Jie* at the royal palace was essential during each year's Mid-Autumn Festival. Wang Yaoqing (1881-1954), a reputable Beijing Opera performing artist, used to play the leading role of the Jade Rabbit. The Mid-Autumn Festival is one of the most important traditional festivals in China. Activities are held which involve admiring and worshipping the moon, eating moon cake, and holding a family reunion. The rabbit, which is closely connected

THE *MAO* RABBIT PLAYS WITH THE MOON

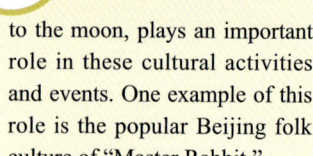

to the moon, plays an important role in these cultural activities and events. One example of this role is the popular Beijing folk culture of "Master Rabbit."

In old times, Master Rabbit was a favorite toy of Beijing children during the Mid-Autumn Festival. Many different clay or paper-pulp based models of the Jade Rabbit, who was endowed with its own personality and worshipped as a god in *Chang'e Flying to the Moon*, were also made. A larger Master Rabbit stood about three feet high, while smaller versions measured only three inches. The toy rabbit had a rosy face and wore a golden helmet; its body was covered in armor, and it carried a signal flag or umbrella-shaped shield on its back. Riding atop a lion, tiger, deer or elephant, the Master Rabbit held a mortar and pestle in its hands, giving the appearance of pounding medicine. Each year, as the Mid-Autumn Festival drew near, peddlers selling Master Rabbit could be seen throughout beijing. There is even a legend about the Master Rabbit. One year, as a dreadful pestilence was raging in Beijing, Chang'e sent the Jade Rabbit down to earth to cure the sick people. The Jade Rabbit went door-to-door curing the ill. The people offered her many different gifts to show their gratitude, but the Jade Rabbit was only willing to accept clothing. She wore different dresses in different places and frequently changed the animal she rode — which included, among others, the lion, the tiger, and deer. After ridding the capital of pestilence, she returned to the Moon Palace. In appreciation of the good luck and happiness she brought, people would mold her image with clay and worship her with offers of fruit, vegetables and beans on August 15th of the lunar calendar. Because the Jade Rabbit wore different dresses and rode different animals, clay sculptures of Master Rabbit also vary in appearance.

A glazed vase with the pattern of rabbit from the Yuan Dynasty

Throughout China, there are all kinds of customs

082 THE TWELVE ZODIAC ANIMALS

and expressions related to the rabbit. In ancient China, for instance, it was customary to "hang the rabbit head" on the first day of the lunar new year. On that day, a steamed "flour rabbit head", New Year's banner and mask were hung above the door to repress evil and thwart disaster. A custom used to educate the children was to give them a "rabbit painting." In the painting, six children sit around a table. On the table, an adult holds an auspicious painting of a rabbit. Each child who received this painting was said to be blessed with a tranquil and successful life.

In Chinese literature, the primary role of the rabbit is to represent or speak for the moon. In children's songs, however, rabbits are simply portrayed as lovely and innocent. The following lyrics from one such song capture this essence: "The little rabbit is oh-so-white; its two little ears spring upright. Radishes and veggies are a delight; jumping and scampering, what a cute sight!" These rhymes are easy to sing and effectively describe the rabbit's habits and vivacious energy. The following lyrics, in contrast, were used in the past to educate children on safety: "'Good little rabbit, please open the door — hurry now, and let me in.' 'No, I won't open the door. Before my mom's back, no one comes in.'"

Earthly Branch: *Mao*
Years of Birth: 2023, 2011, 1999, 1987, 1975, 1963, 1951, 1939...
Five Elements: *Mao* belongs to Wood
Five Constant Virtues: Wood belongs to Benevolence
Auspicious Directions: northeast, south
Auspicious Colors: red, pink, purple, blue
Lucky Numbers: 3, 4, 9
Lucky Flowers: snapdragon, hosta, nerve plant (fittonia)
Lucky Gemstones: furquoise, aquamarine, green phantom, emerald
Spiritual Protector: Manjusri Bodhisattva
Choosing a name: For individuals born in the Year of the Rabbit, it is appropriate to select characters with the moon (月) radical, signifying beauty, aptitude, geniality and integrity; characters containing the radicals for enter (入) or roof (宀), which embody friendship and trustworthiness; characters with the radicals for metal (金), white (白), jade (玉), or bean (豆), which embody thriftiness, diligence and discipline, as well as riches and honor; or characters with the dog (犭) radical, representing kindness, benevolence, and flourishing offspring.

THE *MAO* RABBIT PLAYS WITH THE MOON

THE RABBIT AND PERSONALITY

Strengths:
The Rabbit's assets include attention to detail, courage and determination, as well as a gentle and considerate demeanor. Kindhearted, loyal and honest by nature, Rabbits are sympathetic towards others and always ready to lend a helping hand. They are also level-headed, cautious and prudent, and incisive in speech.

Weaknesses:
The Rabbit's limitations include a lack of decisiveness, and the inability to investigate matters thoroughly. Rabbits tend to be outwardly obsequious while being stubborn inside. They are also inclined to try to escape reality.

THE RABBIT AND BLOOD TYPE

Blood Type A:
Rabbits with blood type A are kind and virtuous, clever and dexterous, and watchful and alert. They do not easily expose their inner feelings, but are more than willing to help carry the burden or emotional distress of others.

Blood Type B:
Rabbits with blood type B are strong-minded, perceptive and clever, humorous and vivacious, and look forward to a blissful life. They are also enthusiastic and cordial, gentle and elegant, and honest and gentle. Rabbits of this blood type often lack the ability to express themselves effectively.

Blood Type O:
Rabbits with blood type O excel at planning and like to do things according to

plan. They have strong discrimination skills, excellent team spirit and willpower, and are able to cater to others when necessary. With a clear demarcation between love and hate, they may sometimes say or do something offensive to others.

Blood Type AB:

Rabbits with blood type AB are clever and refined, highly likeable, and possess a strong scholastic aptitude. They speak and act with prudence and reason, and have strong self-protection awareness. They also value peace and tranquility.

 THE RABBIT AND FORTUNE

Lifetime Fortune: Overview

People born in the Year of the Rabbit are gentle and softhearted, kind and

THE *MAO RABBIT* PLAYS WITH THE MOON

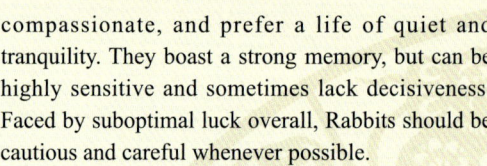

compassionate, and prefer a life of quiet and tranquility. They boast a strong memory, but can be highly sensitive and sometimes lack decisiveness. Faced by suboptimal luck overall, Rabbits should be cautious and careful whenever possible.

Career:

Rabbits are highly creative and innovative, but rarely able to attain a high level of growth or development in their careers. They should be careful to pursue legal business endeavors and comply with regulations and standard procedure in their work.

Financial Luck:

Rabbits tend to face mediocre financial luck. They should expand their career gradually, and avoid being fooled by others' tricks and deceptions. The Rabbit also needs to be careful in borrowing funds from others, as carelessness in this respect could lead to potential disaster.

Romance:

Rabbits have fragile hearts, and it is inevitable that rifts and conflicts will appear in their romantic relationships.

Fortune and the Five Elements

Wood Rabbit: Born in the Year of *Xin-Mao* (2011, 1951)

Wood Rabbits are highly gifted, bright and cheerful, and make loyal and committed romantic partners. They tend, however, to be emotional and selfish. Even in the face of turnover difficulties or the inability to make ends meet, the Wood Rabbit is likely to meet an auspicious person or encounter new opportunities to generate wealth, compensating for previous losses.

A colored statue of Xin-Mao Deity

THE TWELVE ZODIAC ANIMALS

Fire Rabbit: Born in the Year of *Ding-Mao* (1987, 1927)

Fire Rabbits tend to be broadminded and earnest in their endeavors. They also possess unique vision and foresight, and are good at discovering and utilizing the talents of others. By staying composed and level-headed, opportunities can be seized as they present themselves. During emotional lows, Fire Rabbits need to learn to control their speech and maintain reason.

Earth Rabbit: Born in the Year of *Ji-Mao* (1999, 1939)

Earth Rabbits exemplify candor, forthrightness, care and sincerity, but tend to be arrogant and overly ambitious. Because they lack financial management skills, they need to live within their income to avoid potential economic difficulties. In addition, Earth Rabbits should think twice before borrowing or lending money at random.

A colored statue of Ding-Mao Deity

Metal Rabbit: Born in the Year of *Gui-Mao* (2023, 1963)

Metal Rabbits are kindhearted, cheerful, enthusiastic and proactive by nature. They tend to be highly conservative and lack long-term planning skills. With a strong imagination, Metal Rabbits gravitate toward novel and unusual things. A series of unexpected incidents may likely precipitate major financial losses; senseless social engagements and expenditures should thus be avoided.

A colored statue of Ji-Mao Deity

A colored statue of Yi-Mao Deity

A colored statue of Gui-Mao Deity

Water Rabbit: Born in the Year of *Yi-Mao* (1975, 1915)

Water Rabbits have the ability to adapt to different environments. However, they often have weak principles and are easily influenced by others. In addition, they tend to suffer from a negative attitude, passivity in handling problems, and a lack of independence. Water Rabbits are also hedonistic by nature, preferring to live a life of ease and comfort. With little sense of urgency, they muddle along and rarely apply full effort to their work.

THE *MAO* RABBIT PLAYS WITH THE MOON

Fortune by the Year

In the Year of the Rat, Rabbits will see their lucky star shining brightly and meet with good luck in all their endeavors. After some setbacks around the middle of the year, everything will proceed smoothly by year-end. The Rabbit should seize the opportunity to make a fortune this year.

In the Year of the Ox, Rabbits are likely to face some obstacles. However, by seizing opportunities as they emerge, the Rabbit can achieve career success, with calamity and blessing canceling each other out.

In the Year of the Tiger, Rabbits are prone to develop some minor illnesses. They should pay increased attention to health and avoid traveling far away from home. Luck is likely to pick up again following the Winter Solstice.

In the Year of the Rabbit, Rabbits will see luck on their sides, and can expect to enjoy brisk business as well as rising fame and wealth. Though growth may be sluggish early in the year, rare opportunities will present themselves, which the Rabbit should seize

and exploit to build up the family fortune.

In the Year of the Dragon, Rabbits should "retreat to advance." Whether at the beginning or end of the year, it would be best to wait for the right opportunity before making a move. As it is not an ideal year for Rabbits to seek financial gains, they should be exceedingly cautious. When traveling away from home, they should also avoid prying into others' affairs to prevent new problems from cropping up unexpectedly.

In the Year of the Snake, Rabbits are likely to suffer setbacks in their careers, become mentally exhausted, and face some financial losses. However, they should be sure to seize profit-making

opportunities which will appear in the second half of the year.

In the Year of the Horse, Rabbits will inevitably face a string of small annoyances and frustrations. They would be advised to avoid gambling and other licentious behavior.

In the Year of the Sheep, Rabbits will enjoy good opportunities for career success, but there will be multiple barriers to profit-making. Despite it being a tiring and laborious year, few positive results will be achieved. Rabbits should be sure to manage the household with diligence and thrift. They should also regularly strive to meet people of high social standing, so that their support can be obtained when needed.

A painting from the 10th century depicting bamboo, sparrows and a pair of rabbits

In the Year of the Monkey, Rabbits are likely to be plagued by multiple health problems and just barely manage to survive. Although it is bound to be a rough year, the Rabbit will ultimately make it through safe and sound.

In the Year of the Rooster, Rabbits should be on guard against lowlife rascals. Disaster will inevitably befall during the year, and the Rabbit should be mentally prepared, stay strong, and rely on family and friends as a support system. Peace and tranquility will prevail by year-end.

A rabbit engraved on the 12-zodiac-animal screen wall in Beijing's White Cloud Temple

In the Year of the Dog, Rabbits will have a year of good luck and solid profit-making opportunities. They should pursue their career wholeheartedly, be content with their economic status, and show increased care for subordinates. In this way, the Rabbit can generate the factors favorable for success.

THE *MAO* RABBIT PLAYS WITH THE MOON

In the Year of the Pig, Rabbits should pay special attention to disasters or human destruction which may ensue from unforeseen incidents. They should also focus on managing relations between relatives, friends and neighbors.

THE RABBIT AND THE WESTERN ZODIAC

Rabbit-Aries:
Rabbit-Aries brim with intelligence and wisdom. They tend to be humorous in conversation, refined in their demeanor, and extremely caring of others. Rabbit-Aries are also predisposed to enjoy gourmet cuisine.

Rabbit-Taurus:
Rabbit-Tauruses are highly imaginative, artistically innovative, and easy to satisfy. They enjoy the occasional chat with friends, but mostly prefer to stay at home and are often able to achieve success through their own ability. The Rabbit-Taurus are unlikely to attract much attention from others.

Rabbit-Gemini:
Rabbit-Geminis are clever and sharp-witted, possess keen observational skills, and speak with fervor and assurance. They consider matters thoroughly, show meticulous planning, and have an affinity with others.

Rabbit-Cancer:
Rabbit-Cancers are family-oriented and love their family above and beyond all else. They maintain integrity at all times, have a strong sense of honor, and attach importance to trustworthiness. In general, Rabbit-Cancers rarely lose their temper. During festivals or celebrations, however, their malicious side tends to surface.

Rabbit-Leo:
Rabbit-Leos are quick-witted, agile,

A bronze *Zhi* (goblet) with the pattern of rabbit from the Western Zhou Dynasty

♎ Rabbit-Libra:

Rabbit-Librans are highly suspicious by nature and unlikely to place their trust in others. With a tendency to handle affairs in a subconscious manner, many golden opportunities are likely to be missed. Rabbit-Librans have a perfectionist tendency and are inclined to pursue excellence.

♏ Rabbit-Scorpio:

Rabbit-Scorpios are eloquent and humorous, level-headed and self-restrained, and highly respected by others. They tend to speak and act with discretion, and place conviction in their own positions and opinions. They also possess strong financial management skills.

♐ Rabbit-Sagittarius:

Rabbit-Sagittarians are high in self-awareness but tend to suffer from gloomy spirits. They seek the adoration of others and often worry about how other people perceive them. At times, their aloof ways may result in alienation from others.

generous and refined. They are also highly insightful, modest and discreet, never imposing their own will on others.

♑ Rabbit-Capricorn:

Rabbit-Capricorns are lively and extroverted, and extremely ambitious and serious. While endowed with natural intelligence and talents, they are often poor at adapting to changing conditions and may get flustered when faced with abruptly occurring incidents.

🐰 Rabbit-Virgo:

Rabbit-Virgos tend to place strict demands on themselves, with their mind fixed on accomplishing the task at hand. They are strict adherents to tradition, do not like to be disturbed by others, and often prefer to live alone.

THE *MAO* RABBIT PLAYS WITH THE MOON

A stone carving unearthed from a tomb of a Tang-Dynasty princess

Rabbit-Aquarius:

Rabbit-Aquarians are filled with curiosity, and take delight in probing and exploring in the pursuit of knowledge. With erudition and versatility, a positive and optimistic outlook, and intuitive insight, Rabbit-Aquarians are methodical and brilliant in all their endeavors.

Rabbit-Pisces:

Rabbit-Pisces are humorous and witty, thrifty and guileless, and kind and polite. They take good care of their family, and are always willing to offer patient guidance to others. Cautious and reserved by nature, Rabbit-Pisces are sometimes lacking in social skills.

FENGSHUI AND THE RABBIT

Rabbits are both clean and gentle. In the study of *fengshui*, they are thus regarded as auspicious creatures. The use of *fengshui* rabbits is an easy and effective way to halt evil spirits. When selecting a *fengshui* rabbit, wood is considered the best material, followed by porcelain; gold and jade, however, should be avoided. In terms of orientation, the earthly branch *Mao* is classified under East in fengshui; ornamental rabbits, therefore, can be aptly placed in an east or southeast position; a western position should be avoided, as this direction belongs to Metal, which repels Wood. In addition,

the rabbit should be placed such that it faces the left side of the entrance gate, known as the "green dragon position"; this can contribute to enhancing one's relations with others. Placement on the right-hand side (the "white tiger position") should be avoided, as this orientation falls under the element Metal, which repels Wood.

INTERPRETING RABBIT DREAMS

If you dream of a rabbit being caught, it is an auspicious sign.

If you dream of a rabbit fleeing after a defeat, good luck will come your way.

If you dream of a human and a rabbit coming to visit you, you need to be careful not to be deceived by others.

If you dream of shooting a rabbit, you will lose all sources of income.

 HEALTH SECRETS

People born in the Year of the Rabbit are not adept at expressing their feelings. When faced with setbacks or pressure, rarely do they tell others about their troubles — instead choosing to keep these negative emotions bottled up. Rabbits should thus pay attention to mental conditions like insomnia and anxiety. By creating a rhythm in daily life, taking it easy once in a while, and not overexerting themselves, health prospects can be improved.

THE *MAO* RABBIT PLAYS WITH THE MOON

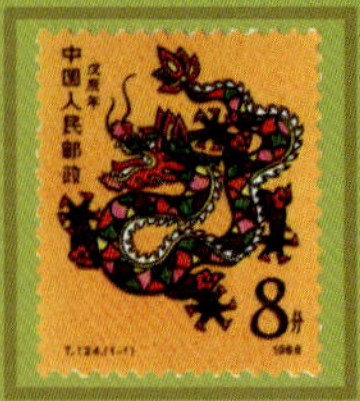

十貳生肖

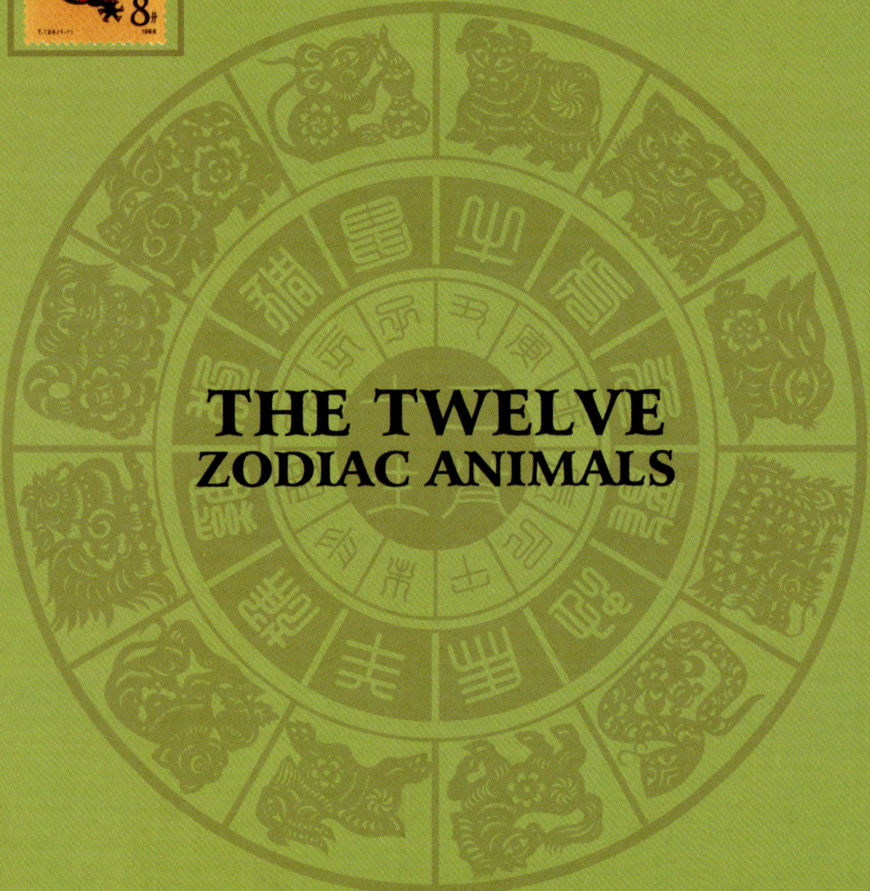

THE TWELVE ZODIAC ANIMALS

PART 5
THE *CHEN* DRAGON DARTS ACROSS THE SKY

【DRAGON】

THE *CHEN* DRAGON DARTS ACROSS THE SKY

The dragon, listed in the fifth position of the 12 zodiac animals, is the only creature which does not exist in the real world. The colorful and dynamic Chinese dragon can be said to be the unique accumulation and distillation of Chinese culture. China's "dragon culture" is founded upon the collective subconscious and, not surprisingly, countless dragon legends have emerged and flourished. To this day, the Chinese still proudly refer to themselves as "Descendants of the Dragon." This usage is even seen in the lyrics of a popular song: "There is a dragon that lives in the East; its name is China. A group of people inhabited the ancient East; they are the descendants of the dragon."

The Chinese dragon is unlike the ferocious winged dragon of Western countries. While the Chinese dragon is depicted in more than one way in the ancient literature, its image is generally the combination of a camel's head, a snake's neck, a deer's antlers, a turtle's eyes, a fish's scales, a tiger's palms, an eagle's claws and an ox's ears. Being the "compound" of so many creatures, the dragon is viewed as the king of the beasts and a virtually all-powerful god. In Chinese legends, the omnipotent dragon can speed across the sky, control the forces of nature, soar above the clouds, and even cruise under water.

A jade carving of dragon boats

The Chinese dragon is known to have derived from totem worship. Opinions on early forms of the dragon, however, have varied widely over the ages. Some people believe that the dragon's prototype was the snake, fish, lizard, or Chinese alligator. Others believe the dragon to be based on a stellar image — that of the seven stars in the east of the 28 Lunar Mansions. Still others regard the early dragon as a depiction of the Tree God, lightning, or even a rainbow. Over the course of history, the ancient Chinese formed an indissoluble bond with the dragon. Not only was the Chinese dragon worshipped, it was also carved and painted everywhere — inside and outside the house, on the body, and on clothing and garments — to transfer its magic power to people. The concept of the dragon that gradually formed in the Chinese consciousness evolved into legends and fairytales and helped the Chinese to establish a "framework" for the universe. The Chinese dragon, therefore, is not only a creature of nature, but a cultural and social phenomenon as well.

A *Ding* (a ritual vessel in ancient China) with the relief of dragons

The dragon is a symbol of power, nobility and dignity in traditional Chinese culture. Many ancient rulers — including the Yellow Emperor, Yan Emperor, Yao Emperor, Shun Emperor and Yu Emperor — are associated with the dragon in ancient texts. The concept of the "divine right of the king", in which the "Son of Heaven" is regarded as a "true dragon", abounded in Chinese feudal society. To a large extent, the use of the dragon's image was limited to the emperor and served as a symbol of imperial power. The emperor

The Dragon Dance, a highlight of Chinese New Year celebrations held in China and Chinatowns around the world

THE *CHEN* DRAGON DARTS ACROSS THE SKY

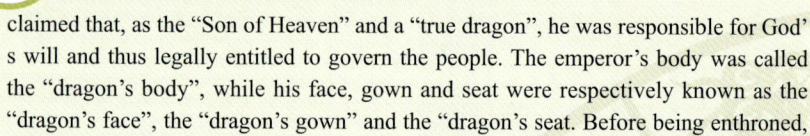

claimed that, as the "Son of Heaven" and a "true dragon", he was responsible for God's will and thus legally entitled to govern the people. The emperor's body was called the "dragon's body", while his face, gown and seat were respectively known as the "dragon's face", the "dragon's gown" and the "dragon's seat. Before being enthroned,

the emperor-to-be was referred to as the "latent dragon", while the enthronement process itself was described by the phrase "the dragon flies". Many imperial possessions, including the emperor's table, bed, boat and carriage, were also labeled with the word "dragon". In almost every aspect of the emperor's daily life, the dragon's image as an ornament was prevalent. The Taihe Hall in Beijing's Forbidden City is recorded to have over 13,000 imprints, ornaments and carvings of dragons. Since the dragon imprints had been prevalent for ages and could not be completely prohibited, the rulers made a compromise. Since the Yuan Dynasty (1206-1368), the rulers of China laid out a "hierarchy" of dragons. The image of the dragon with two horns and five claws was to be used exclusively by the emperor, while images depicting four-clawed or three-clawed dragons were for civilian use. All those who violated this law would bring death upon themselves.

In Chinese culture, the dragon is regarded as an auspicious and spiritual beast associated with heaven and the gods. The lunar mansions were classified into four groups or quadrants. Among them, the eastern group was referred to collectively as the "Blue Dragon". As one of the four immortals guarding Heaven (the others being the White Tiger, Red Bird and Black Tortoise), the Blue Dragon also had the power to dispel evil and regulate *yin* and *yang*. Because the Chinese dragon has the mysterious power of going up to heaven and leaping into the sea, connecting Heaven and Earth, it represents God or immortal and blesses people. When the rulers obey the god's wish and implement open polices, and the common people live a happy life, Chinese dragon will appear in the world, which means an encouragement of the God.

A dragon robe worn by the Emperor

The Chinese dragon is endowed with the ability to control water and rainfall. Fairytales describing this special power are found in *Shan Hai Jing* (literally *Classic of the Mountains and Seas*), one of China's oldest texts. In the olden days, temples at which sacrifices were offered to the dragon king were everywhere to be found. During anomalous weather, such as long periods of drought or rain, the people would visit these temples, burn incense, and pray that the dragon king would regulate rainfall in a way that rendered climatic conditions ideal for raising crops.

The predominance of China's dragon culture is also linked to the religious significance of this creature. In Buddhism, the dragon was listed in the second position among eight immortal protectors. For its special prowess, it was also

An imperial jade seal decorated with dragons

called the "dragon king". Because Taoism is a religion indigenous to China and accords well with the Chinese psyche, the dragon is even more prevalent in Taoist culture as compared to Buddhism. The Taoist dragon has far-reaching supernatural powers, including

THE *CHEN* DRAGON DARTS ACROSS THE SKY

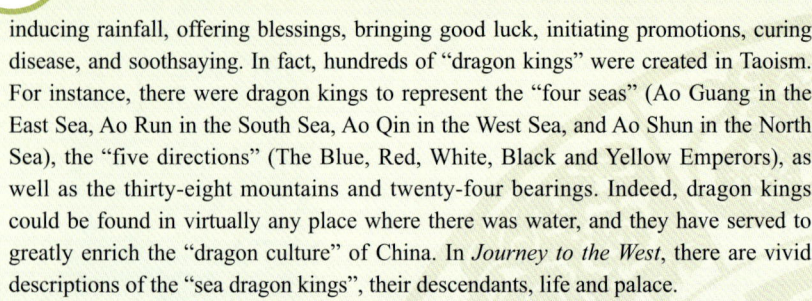

inducing rainfall, offering blessings, bringing good luck, initiating promotions, curing disease, and soothsaying. In fact, hundreds of "dragon kings" were created in Taoism. For instance, there were dragon kings to represent the "four seas" (Ao Guang in the East Sea, Ao Run in the South Sea, Ao Qin in the West Sea, and Ao Shun in the North Sea), the "five directions" (The Blue, Red, White, Black and Yellow Emperors), as well as the thirty-eight mountains and twenty-four bearings. Indeed, dragon kings could be found in virtually any place where there was water, and they have served to greatly enrich the "dragon culture" of China. In *Journey to the West*, there are vivid descriptions of the "sea dragon kings", their descendants, life and palace.

All the imperial porcelains would be decorated with the pattern of dragon in ancient China.

The Chinese dragon also symbolizes a person who possesses integrity, moral character, ability and insight, and who regarded as extraordinary, capable and insightful. For instance, Lao Tzu was likened to a dragon by Confucius; during the Three Kingdoms Period (220-280), the famous Zhuge Liang (181-234) was called a sleeping dragon prior to his leaving the mountains. Cai Yong (133-192), a famous writer and calligrapher of the Eastern Han Dynasty (25-220), was called a drunken dragon for his alcoholism and drunken ways. Gradually, the Chinese word for "dragon" (long) came to be used in names, courtesy names and pseudonyms. Examples include the courtesy-name Zilong for Zhao Yun (?-229), a famous general of the Three Kingdoms period; Feng Menglong (1574-1646), a novelist in the late Ming Dynasty; Yu Chenglong (1617-1684), an honest, morally upright and well-respected government official; and the world-famous martial arts movie stars Li Xiaolong (Bruce Lee) and Cheng Long (Jackie Chan). The Chinese idiom "hoping one's son will become a dragon" expresses parents' aspirations for their children's success. There are also many figures in Chinese literature named or nicknamed with "dragon". In the classic novel, the Outlaw of the Mash the heroes at Liangshan Mountain include the "Cloud-Leaping Dragon", "River-Disturbing Dragon", "Nine-Tattoo Dragon"; "Forest-Exiting Dragon", "Single-Horned Dragon", and "Hole-

Exiting *Jiao* (*Jiao* is another type of Chinese dragon). Among them, the "Nine-Tattoo Dragon", named Shi Jin, received the widest fame for being tattooed with nine dragons.

The dragon's great influence on Chinese society is especially apparent in folk customs. February 2nd of the lunar calendar is one of the most famous festivals for many national minorities of China. On this day, the dragon is said to raise its head. Men are required to shave their heads to beget good luck and have their wishes fulfilled; women are discouraged from doing needlework so as to avoid hurting the dragon's eyes. Many foods have also been named after the dragon. For example, "spring cakes" are called "dragon scales"; noodles are called "dragon whiskers"; boiled dumplings are called

"dragon ears" or "dragon teeth"; and wontons are called "dragon eyes". In addition, dragon lantern dances and dragon boat races are put on during the Lantern Festival and Dragon Boat Festival, respectively. There are countless festivals in Chinese minority nationalities. The Dong nationality of Guizhou Province holds an event every February 2nd called "Eating Dragon Meat". On that day, the entire village kills a single ox and each household in the village is given a piece; this is known as "eating dragon meat."

The colorful dragon culture can be found everywhere in Chinese literature. Long before there had been many descriptions about dragon in the *Classic of Poetry* and the *I Ching* (*Book of Changes*). In *Li Sao*, one of the most famous poems in Chinese history, Qu Yuan (about 340-278BC) also had a fantasy that he could travel in the clouds driving a dragon-drawn carriage. Dragon culture is also the main theme of Chinese drama. Many Chinese dramas are related to the dragon, including *Liu Yi Sending the Letter to Dragon King*, *Zhang Sheng Boils the Sea*, *Chentang Fortress*, *Suo Wu Long* (*Capturing Five Leaders of Wagang Peasant Uprisings*), *Da Long Pao* (*Beating the Dragon's Gown*), and *Long Feng Cheng Xiang*. In drama terminology, there are also many terms related to the dragon, such as *longtao* (utility man), *helong* (closure) and *xiaolongyin*.

THE *CHEN* DRAGON DARTS ACROSS THE SKY

ZODIAC ANIMAL FILE

Earthly Branch: *Chen*
Years of Birth: 2024, 2012, 2000, 1988, 1976, 1964, 1952, 1940…
Five Elements: *Chen* belongs to Earth
Five Constant Virtues: Earth belongs to Sincerity
Auspicious Directions: west, northwest, north
Auspicious Colors: gold, silver, grayish white
Lucky Numbers: 1, 6, 7
Lucky Flowers: bleeding heart vine, summer snapdragon
Lucky Gemstones: red tourmaline (rubellite), topaz, amber
Spiritual Protector: Samantabhadra Bodhisattva
Choosing a name: For individuals born in the Year of the Dragon, it is appropriate to select characters with the water (氵) radical, signifying honor, fortune, prosperity and good luck; characters with the radicals for metal (金), jade (玉), white (白), or red (赤), which embody profound learning as well as happiness, longevity and family prosperity; characters with the moon (月) radical, which embodies geniality, virtue, kindness and benevolence; or characters with the radicals for fish (鱼), wine (酉), or person (亻), representing diligence, thriftiness and solid career prospects.

A bronze ink-stone box decorated with five dragons

A wood carving of dragons

THE DRAGON AND PERSONALITY

A jade carving of dragon from the Hongshan Culture of the Neolithic Age

Strengths:
The Dragon's assets include extreme vigor and youthful spirit, as well as a high level of self-awareness. People born in the Year of the Dragon are never willing to give up or admit defeat. They are always candid and open, never sowing discord or stirring up troubles between others. Dragons do not fear difficulty and try to do everything to perfection. Females of this zodiac sign are straightforward, generous, understanding and sympathetic, while males possess levels of wisdom and audacity unmatched by others.

Weaknesses:
The Dragon's limitations include narrow-mindedness, an arrogant

personality, and a lack of perseverance and fortitude. People born in the Year of the Dragon are perfectionists who crave greatness and success, and are emotionally unpredictable. In addition, they may be unable to endure setbacks and ordeals at times.

THE DRAGON AND BLOOD TYPE

Blood Type A:
Dragons with blood type A are extroverted and energetic, cheerful and upbeat, and calm and rational. They are good conversationalists, who speak and act gracefully and naturally. Although they carry out tasks swiftly and vigorously, strictness may be lacking. They demonstrate original foresight, and are both adept and hard-working.

setbacks that come their way.

Blood Type B:
Dragons with blood type B are cheerful and energetic, resolute and swift, and daring to speak out and take action. They have the courage to assume responsibility, as well as the ability to execute tasks and coordinate efficiently. Dragons of this blood type also have strong survival skills and resilience, enabling them to handle any losses or

Blood Type O:
Dragons with blood type O are loyal, decisive, magnanimous, strong-minded, and highly independent. They have a strong sense of responsibility, clear aims and objectives, and tend to consider matters carefully and thoroughly. In addition, they possess the ability to endure sorrow and frustration.

Blood Type AB:
Dragons with blood type AB tend to be popular and enjoy good relations with other people. With a unique and extraordinary style highly appealing to others, they are invariably the life of a party. Their deep insight also enables them to discern any given situation from all sides. Dragons of this blood type are eager to succeed, and do not like to be outdone by others.

THE *CHEN* DRAGON DARTS ACROSS THE SKY

THE DRAGON AND FORTUNE

Lifetime Fortune: Overview

People born in the Year of the Dragon are resolute, vivacious, impatient, and extreme in their behavior. Females of this sign are self-confident and do not get along well with others. They tend to be stubborn in their youth and may encounter defeat; in mid-life, they are likely to meet with mishaps or even suffer a potential disaster.

Career:
Dragons should maintain an earnest and diligent work ethic, and deliberate carefully before engaging in any business activity. They should also avoid taking on new jobs insofar as possible.

Financial Luck:
Dragons are likely to have mediocre financial luck. It is important that they carefully plan any financial disbursements, and pursue business opportunities which match their skills and capabilities. Dragons should also be especially cautious with respect to large investments.

Romance:
People born in the Year of the Dragon tend to have a good and stable love life. Bachelors and bachelorettes will have an easy time finding a marriage partner.

Zhuan Xu (one of legenary rulers in remote China) riding on a dragon

Fortune and the Five Elements

Wood Dragon: Born in the Year of *Wu-Chen* (1988, 1928)
Wood Dragons possess lofty aspirations, strong problem-solving skills and exceptional talent, but still present themselves in a modest, unassuming manner. Their quiet, introverted personality may contribute to the fact that Wood Dragons have poor social skills and few close friends. They also tend to be petty with money.

A colored statue of Jia-Chen Deity

Fire Dragon: Born in the Year of *Jia-Chen* (1964, 1904)

Fire Dragons are charming, attractive and highly likeable, but often have an explosive temper. Their ability to adapt to changing circumstances makes it easy for them to succeed. With an honest and plain-spoken demeanor, Fire Dragons tend to conduct their affairs in a down-to-earth manner. Their naiveté, however, makes them easy prey for swindlers.

A colored statue of Bing-Chen Deity   A colored statue of Wu-Chen Deity

Earth Dragon: Born in the Year of *Bing-Chen* (1976, 1916)

Earth Dragons are sharp-witted, enterprising and ambitious by nature, unwilling to lag behind others. With a strong work ethic, they bring a positive, earnest attitude to every endeavor in which they participate. Earth Dragons also tend to be generous, bighearted, and highly affectionate.

A colored statue of Geng-Chen Deity

Metal Dragon: Born in the Year of *Geng-Chen* (2000, 1940)

Metal Dragons have a forthright and guileless personality. Although they have many creative ideas and plans, the ability to implement them is often lacking. Metal Dragons' ostentatious mannerisms tend to alienate those around them, while heightened emotionality makes it difficult for others to understand them.

A colored statue of Ren-Chen Deity

Water Dragon: Born in the Year of *Ren-Chen* (2012, 1952)

Water Dragons are high in both determination and willpower, but tend to be lacking in vision. They possess keen observational skills and a strong memory. The Water Dragon is destined to have a highly rewarding career and many romantic admirers. Financial luck is also good, with personal income likely to rise year after year.

Fortune by the Year

In the Year of the Rat, Dragons will be blessed with formidable profits. The Dragon can take advantage of brisk business and bring in impressive earnings. The beginning

THE *CHEN* DRAGON DARTS ACROSS THE SKY

of the year will be marked with joy and the year-end with surpluses. However, the Dragon should take steps to prevent unexpected mishaps during the year.

In the Year of the Ox, Dragons are destined for a blissful and auspicious year. The Dragon may wish to consider making a large business investment, assuming thorough research has been done in advance. As year-end approaches, fortune should be sought in the northwest to ensure tranquility in the coming year.

In the Year of the Tiger, Dragons will face a year of ups and downs and running around. However, all the hard work will pay off and profits will be made. It is a good time to make investments and expand business on multiple fronts. Rather than overworking, however, the Dragon should take some time to relax and cultivate inner tranquility.

In the Year of the Rabbit, Dragons may face a series of health problems, and wander from place to place in search of career prospects. Despite the struggle, they are likely to see happiness and small profits by year-end. Although some bad luck will prove unavoidable, the Dragon can pass the year mishap-free by behaving discreetly and abstaining from gambling.

In the Year of the Dragon, Dragons should

106 THE TWELVE ZODIAC ANIMALS

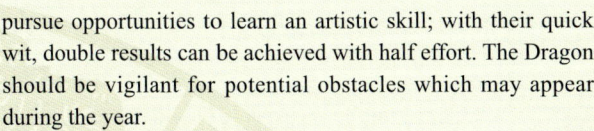

pursue opportunities to learn an artistic skill; with their quick wit, double results can be achieved with half effort. The Dragon should be vigilant for potential obstacles which may appear during the year.

In the Year of the Snake, Dragons will see their lucky star shining brightly in the sky. Bad luck, however, is still likely to emerge from time to time. Male Dragons may sustain unforeseen wounds; they should be extra cautious, stay with others, and avoid solitude.

In the Year of the Horse, Dragons will face a deficit of luck, barriers to success, and a series of minor setbacks. Although luck is bound to turn around by year-end, reckless behavior must be avoided. It is imperative that Dragons avoid becoming envious or jealous of others' riches. Instead, they should keep their cool, wait for luck to improve, and pursue business endeavors as opportunities emerge.

In the Year of the Sheep, Dragons are fated to meet with a combination of joy and sorrow. Rather than acting imprudently, the Dragon should resolve problems with composure and a level head; this will ensure that the year passes without mishap. Although the Dragon is likely to make extra financial gains this year, caution must also be exercised when seeking profits.

In the Year of the Monkey, Dragons will face a mixture of suffering and joy. The best approach would be to plan major undertakings at the start of the year and keep an eye on investments as mid-year approaches. By the end of the year, the Dragon should pursue profits in a prudent manner and be ready for an unexpected windfall.

In the Year of the Rooster, Dragons are destined for success in all they do, and the entire family will be blessed with happiness. Nevertheless, minor financial losses and a series of small health issues are unavoidable, and require the Dragon's inner peace and calmness. It is also an opportune year for Dragons to expand their careers.

In the Year of the Dog, Dragons are bound to make few gains despite hard work and thorough planning. Quarrels and disputes will also prove difficult to avoid.

THE *CHEN* DRAGON DARTS ACROSS THE SKY

In the Year of the Pig, Dragons will meet with universal success and see all their wishes come true. However, it is important that they stay guarded against potential evildoers who may appear at the beginning of the year.

A dragon on the eave

THE DRAGON AND THE WESTERN ZODIAC

Dragon-Aries:
Dragon-Aries are ambitious and strategically-minded, sometimes playing tricks on others. Highly emotional and sensitive themselves, they are able to show sympathy to others. They are also extremely self-confident by nature and tend to be conceited as well.

Dragon-Taurus:
Dragon-Tauruses possess formidable courage and boldness, daring to take risks or pursue challenges never attempted. Despite their active, enterprising and aggressive nature, they are equally sentimental, romantic and tenderhearted.

Dragon-Gemini:
Dragon-Geminis are naturally alluring and unlimited in their potential. While they have an endless stream of novel thoughts and ideas, trivial or tedious tasks often get procrastinated or ignored. Dragon-Geminis are highly enthusiastic and filled with emotion.

Dragon-Cancer:
Dragon-Cancers are filled with emotion, curiosity and life energy. While sensitive and emotional, they are equally bold and enthusiastic, and have a unique appreciation of art. They are also likely to reveal their emotions to others, whether intentionally or inadvertently.

Dragon-Leo:
Dragon-Leos are conservative, reserved, and extremely emotional. Despite a tendency to be conceited and boastful, they have a strong sense of responsibility and are full of sympathy for the weak and feeble.

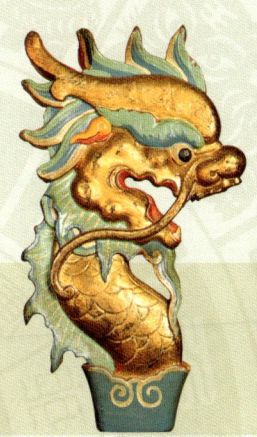

A wood carving of dragon

Dragon-Virgo:
Dragon-Virgos are strong-minded, and enjoy engaging in sports and other forms of competition. Regardless of the situation, they are always able to maintain a cool head and an optimistic, self-assured attitude. However, Dragon-Virgos are also inclined to be hot-tempered and irascible, often making a mountain out of a molehill.

Dragon-Libra:
Dragon-Librans are high in ambition, making unremitting efforts to achieve their goals and refusing to throw in the towel until they succeed. Despite their abundant creativity and foresight, Dragon-Librans tend to lack patience, and are often obsessed with seeking the attention or adoration of others.

Dragon-Scorpio:
Dragon-Scorpios are purposeful and enterprising, courageous and strategic, and prepared to forge ahead even in the face of obstacles. They tend to be serious in demeanor, lacking in humor, and easily swayed by their emotions.

Dragon-Sagittarius:
Dragon-Sagittarians are gregarious, generous, broadminded, and elegant in their comportment. Fearless in the face of danger, they tend to lead rich and colorful lives.

THE *CHEN* DRAGON DARTS ACROSS THE SKY

Dragon-Capricorn:

Dragon-Capricorns are predisposed to being weak and fragile. While they are highly caring and considerate, and enjoy excellent relations with others, they tend to have difficulty expressing their own inner feelings. Dragon-Capricorns are filled with gratitude and always seek to return the kindness of others.

Dragon-Aquarius:

Dragon-Aquarians have a perceptive intellect and excel at planning. They strive for perfection in all their endeavors, but maintain a modest attitude and never show off. Lacking in confidence, they also have the tendency to become anxious or agitated.

A stone small seat decorated with the pattern of dragon

Dragon-Pisces:

Dragon-Pisceses are often arrogant and brusque in their demeanor. Their self-centeredness leads them to do as they please, without taking others' feelings into account. They also enjoy sports activities and often seem unable to sit still.

FENGSHUI AND THE DRAGON

A door panel with the design of Double Dragons Playing with Pearl, a traditional auspicious design in China

The Chinese people worship and adore the dragon more than any other animal. From the expression "hope one's son will turn out a dragon" to the fact that the Chinese regard themselves as "Descendants of the Dragon", the Chinese dragon is clearly regarded as an exalted creature with auspicious powers. To ensure that a *fengshui* dragon can yield its true spiritual force, the first step is to select the appropriate material: gold, jade or porcelain. The ideal orientation for the dragon's placement is east-southeast. At home, a pair of *fengshui* dragons can be positioned on the left-facing wall or on a table facing the main entrance; this can improve a range of unfavorable circumstances which

might arise due to strained relations with others. In addition, financial prospects can be augmented by placing a *fengshui* dragon on top of a fish tank.

 ## INTERPRETING DRAGON DREAMS

If you dream of riding a dragon into the water, you will enjoy a lucrative management position.

If you dream of a dragon sleeping in the water, your wishes will be fulfilled.

If you dream of riding a dragon onto a mountaintop, your wish will come true.

If you dream of a flying dragon, you will be promoted to a more lucrative management position.

If you dream of a dragon and snake entering your home, you will strike it rich.

If you dream of a dragon and snake entering your kitchen stove, you will soon enjoy a management position.

 ## HEALTH SECRETS

People born in the Year of the Dragon are full of vigor and physically robust; only rarely do they suffer from illness. However, as Dragons are extremely active by nature, they are liable to meet with some minor health issues, especially intestinal or digestive problems. Aside from paying increased attention to eating habits, Dragons should avoid turning into workaholics, and try to maintain a balance between work and leisure.

An embroidery dragon

A pottery dragon spraying water

THE *CHEN* DRAGON DARTS ACROSS THE SKY

THE TWELVE
ZODIAC ANIMALS

PART 6
THE *SI* SNAKE ABOVE THE CLOUDS

【 SNAKE 】

THE *SI* SNAKE ABOVE THE CLOUDS

A cloth snake

The snake is an old species on earth. The famous philosopher Han Feizi (about 275-233 BC) of the Warring States Period (475-221 BC) recorded in his works that "During ancient times, there were more beasts than human beings; human beings, therefore, are no stronger than beasts, worms or snakes." In ancient myths and legends, the Chinese ancestors Nüwa and Fuxi are depicted with human heads and snake bodies; these images can be verified from various patterns of Han Dynasty (202 BC-220 AD) relics. Based on this fact, it can be seen that the snake played an important role in the era of totemism.

The snake ranks sixth among the 12 zodiac animals. It is said that during the *si*-hour (9:00-11:00), the mist has lifted and the sun shines brightly. Snakes are extraordinarily active during this period. The *si*-hour is thus matched with the snake. It has also been said that the Chinese character for "*si*" is the pictographic character of the word "worm" and, in Chinese, the word "worm" originally meant "snake." Because the snake ranks after the dragon and the two are similar in appearance, the snake is often called the "little dragon". In term of its figure, the snake most resembles the dragon, hence the saying that "the dragon originates

114 THE TWELVE ZODIAC ANIMALS

A marble carving: a snake on the back of a tortoise. The union of the mythic tortoise and snake was considred to be the Black Warrior who guarding the North in anicnet China.

from the snake." In ancient Chinese texts, the dragon always travels together with the snake. This condition also appears in many idioms and proverbs, such as "the brush moves like a dragon and snake"; "dragons mixed with snakes". The expression "the snake morphed into a dragon, but did not change its pattern" which means that no matter how much something changes in its appearance, the essence remains the same. In this sense, the snake and the dragon refer to the same thing in Chinese. In Chinese mythology, Emperor Gaozu of Han beheaded a white snake and Gongsun Ao beheaded a two-headed snake. Later, the former became emperor and the latter became a famous prime minister. In China, seeing a snake is often considered an auspicious sign, just as is seeing a dragon. However, in ancient Chinese culture, the snake bears a different significance from that of the dragon.

Worship stems from fear. The ancient Chinese ranked the snake as a holy totem and worshipped it. Many places and national minorities in China have retained taboos towards snakes as well as snake-worshipping traditions. For example, in many places it is taboo to refer to a

A paper-cutting of Borrowing an Umbrella, a plot in *Madam White Snake*

A paper-cutting of Travelling on the West Lake, a plot in *Madam White Snake*

THE *SI* SNAKE ABOVE THE CLOUDS

snake by name; instead, the snake should be called a "long worm", "little dragon", or "earth dragon". In Fujian Province, residents will not kill a snake creeping in their houses because they believe the snake to be sent by ancestors to assure the offspring's welfare. If passers-by come across two snakes twisting together, the passers-by should tear off a button and walk away, because it is considered a monstrous crime to watch snakes mating. In some parts of China, a snake's slough is also taboo. There is a proverb "see a snake shed its skin, (and) you will suffer too". In ancient times, the Angde people of Yunnan Province, who believed that the Snake God could protect livestock, had a custom of offering a sacrifice to the Snake God every year.

A paper-cutting with the design of Double Snakes Offering Blessings

In ancient China, people had an innate fear of snakes and viewed them as frightful and mysterious. There are also plentiful of vicious snakes that appear in ancient Chinese myths and legends who repay kindness with ingratitude — similar to the snake in Aesop's Fables, or the one in the *Bible* who seduced Adam and Eve. Snakes stir up trouble and unrest, commit crimes, and are a great nuisance to humans. For

A mural depicts a Chinese idiom Hua She Tian Zu (draw a snake and add feet to it), which means to ruin the effect by adding something superfluous

this reason, many derogatory words concerning the snake have emerged. For example, the expression "snake and scorpion's heart" describes a bad person, and "beautiful lady snake" refers to a woman with an evil heart but a charming appearance. In literary works, however, descriptions of the snake vary significantly, sometimes being depicted as brave, sometimes mysterious, and other times even as humorous. There is a story about a filial snake in *Sou Shen Ji (Stories of Immortals)*. When Dou Wu (a famous chancellor of the Eastern Han Dynasty) was born, his mother also gave birth to a snake. His family sent the snake to the woods. Years later, Dou's mother passed away. The snake crept out from the bushes, kowtowed and wept before the coffin of Dou Wu's mother just like a human being, shedding tears of sorrow. There are other stories about the snake in *Strange Stories from a Chinese Studio* and *Journey to the West*, two very well-known Chinese works of fiction.

The most Chinese famous legend about the snake is *Madam White Snake*, which was extolled as one of China's four major folk legends. It is a love story between a gentleman and a lady snake. Bai Suzhen (the White Snake) and Xiao Qing (the Green Snake), two snake spirits, practiced Buddhism and cultivated themselves into human figures. At West Lake, Bai Suzhen ran into the scholar Xu Xian. The two admired one another, and Xiao Qing made a match between them. To destroy their marriage, Fa Hai, a monk at Jinshan Temple, tricked Bai Suzhen into drinking red orpiment wine. By doing so,

THE *SI* SNAKE ABOVE THE CLOUDS

A commemorative silver coin issued in Chinese Snake Year

fought against Fa Hai to rescue Xu Xian. During the fight, Bai Suzhen performed a magic spell and overflowed Jinshan Temple, causing thousands of people to drown. Bai Suzhen violated the law of heaven and thus was cursed and held in captivity at Lei Feng Tower. Many years later, Bai Suzhen's son, who won the title of Number One Scholar, a title conferred to the one who scored highest on the Imperial Examination, went to the tower, held a memorial ceremony for his mother, and rescued her from imprisonment. *Madam White Snake* is a household story in China. Even to the present day, the story is still popular in operas, movies and television series. The character of Bai Suzhen has become a symbol of a love and freedom while Fa Hai is widely criticized for his cruelty.

In traditional Chinese culture, the snake also symbolizes wealth. In some myths, it is common to see a snake or dragon guarding a cave of treasure. The snake and turtle constitute the Black Tortoise (one of the four symbols of the Chinese constellations), which represents longevity. It protects the northern sky and is often called "the Black Warrior of the North." In traditional culture, especially in astronomy, geomancy and Taoism, the Black Tortoise carries deep significance.

Bai Suzhen lost her human figure and became a monstrous snake, scaring Xu Xian to death. To save Xu Xian's life, Bai Suzhen and Xiao Qing slipped into heaven to steal a magic herbal medicine. However, after Xu Xian came back to life, he was cheated by Fa Hai and brought to Jinshan Temple under house arrest. Bai Suzhen and Xiao Qing went to Jinshan Temple and

Ancient scholars also paid a great deal of attention to the snake. Descriptions of snakes can be found in the *Classic of Poetry* and *Songs of Chu*. Guo Pu (276-324) of the Jin Dynasty wrote a series of songs praising the snake. Monographs about the snake were composed by Fu Xuan (217-278) of the Jin Dynasty, Huang Xidan (1033-1074) of the

Song Dynasty and Zheng Xie (1693-1765) of the Qing Dynasty. Liu Zongyuan (773-819), classed as one of the "Eight Great Prose Masters of the Tang and Song", wrote the well-known essay *Snake Catcher*, comparing poisonous snakes to the heartless rule of government, and concluded that "the ruthlessness of taxation is more poisonous than the snake."

It is fairly common to see the snake used as a metaphor to express ideas in ancient historical, philosophical and military works, and a sea of idioms and proverbs about snakes have thus been created and passed on. In Sun Tzu's famous book *The Art of War*, it is stated that "the skillful tactician may be likened to the *shuai-ran*. Now the *shuai-ran* is a snake that is found in the Chang Mountains. Strike at its head, and you will be attacked by its tail; strike at its tail, and you will be attacked by its head; strike at its middle, and you will be attacked by head and tail both." Sun Tzu imitated the snake in the Chang Mountains and deployed the army in a single-line battle array. Superior in both flexibility and mobility, this "Snake Array" can create a temporary extra-man advantage to help secure victory. The "Snake Array" thus appears frequently in Chinese essays and novels pertaining to military history.

 ZODIAC ANIMAL FILE

An incense burner in the shape of Black Warrior, the union of the tortoise and snake

Earthly Branch: *Si*
Years of Birth: 2025, 2013, 2001, 1989, 1977, 1965, 1953, 1941…
Five Elements: *Si* belongs to Fire
Five Constant Virtues: fire belongs to Propriety
Auspicious Directions: northeast, southwest, south
Auspicious Colors: red, light yellow, black
Lucky Numbers: 2, 8, 9
Lucky Flowers: orchid, cactus
Lucky Gemstones: olivine, malachite, aventurine, red tourmaline (rubellite)
Spiritual Protector: Samantabhadra Bodhisattva

THE *SI* SNAKE ABOVE THE CLOUDS

Choosing a name: For individuals born in the Year of the Snake, it is appropriate to select characters with the grass (艹) radical, signifying joy and prosperity; characters with the radicals for insect (虫) or fish (鱼), which embody wisdom, courage, sincerity and kindness; characters with the radicals for wood (木), grain (禾), field (田), or mountain (山), which connote profound learning; characters with the radicals for metal (金) or jade (玉), which embody diverse skills and talents; or characters with the radicals for moon (月) or earth (土), representing integrity and honesty.

THE SNAKE AND PERSONALITY

Strengths:
The Snake's assets include a high level of adaptability, keen judgment, strong morals, and unparalleled insight. People of this sign are articulate, personable, calm and composed. With the ability to make prompt and resolute decisions, they can achieve quick and decisive victories. Snakes also do not lose their temper easily.

Weaknesses:
The Snake's limitations include a vainglorious nature, an attitude of indifference, and weak individuality. Snakes also tend to be highly possessive, stubborn, and reserved in social relations with others.

THE SNAKE AND BLOOD TYPE

Blood Type A:
Snakes with blood type A tend to be cautious and prudent, and do not easily offend others. With an honest, sincere attitude and a logical mind, they can rise quickly in their profession and often become leaders in the corporate world. Snakes of this blood type have strong emotions and make for good listeners.

Blood Type B:
Snakes with blood type B are sharp, perceptive and astute, earnest and enthusiastic, multi-talented and quick-witted, and highly *adaptable*. They possess extensive knowledge, a strong sense of humor, and a persuasive tongue. Snakes of this blood type place a high value on friendship, but tend to have a hot temper.

Blood Type O:
Snakes with blood type O are keen-sighted and often able to grasp the overall picture. They possess sound judgment and choose their words carefully. They also have a desire to subdue others, and tend to be cunning, profit-oriented and possessive.

Blood Type AB:
Snakes with blood type AB are perceptive, astute and patient by nature. They conduct affairs in a highly rational manner, and make effective use of their time. Snakes of this blood type place emphasis on strategy and efficiency, and enjoy being the center of attention.

THE SNAKE AND FORTUNE

A cloth ornament: Black Warrior

Lifetime Fortune: Overview

People born in the Year of the Snake are extremely sociable, have refined tastes, and are highly regarded by their friends. However, they tend to become envious or suspicious, and often get into arguments with others. Males of this sign may suffer some hardships during their early years, while in middle age they are likely to be seduced by women's charms. As they get older, however, they will gradually find joy and happiness.

Career:
Snakes tend to have excellent luck in their careers, with business opportunities frequently emerging. Projects should be pursued and developed in a steady and gradual fashion. It is crucial that Snakes avoid greed and corruption, and be cautious when collaborating with others or pursuing joint investments.

THE *SI* SNAKE ABOVE THE CLOUDS

Financial Luck:

The Snake is likely to have excellent luck in monetary matters. Work-related social engagements are many and frequent. Though Snakes tend to make money quickly, they also spend it quickly, and should learn to overcome their vanity and avoid pointless expenditures. The fact that Snakes have good financial fortune does not imply that they will necessarily strike it rich in any particular year; a sensible plan is needed to convert latent financial luck to real monetary fortune. By taking this approach, the Snake can create a healthy cycle of economic success.

Romance:

The Snake may have relationship difficulties which are unmentionable or difficult to share with others. In particular, Snakes are likely to be affected by marital discord or misunderstanding in mid-life.

Fortune and the Five Elements

A colored statue of Yi-Si Deity

A colored statue of Ji-Si Deity

Wood Snake: Born in the Year of *Ji-Si* (1989, 1929)

Wood Snakes possess refined tastes and artistic creativity, and seek orderliness in their everyday life. Their easy-going demeanor enables them to make friends easily. However, "Wood Snakes" tend to have a stubborn streak and be lacking in initiative. They may also lack the ability to handle defeat and setbacks.

Fire Snake: Born in the Year of *Yi-Si* (1965, 1905)

Fire Snakes are incredibly vivacious and sociable, and possess exceptional perceptive skills. They are charming, cultured, and highly attractive to others, but do not like to be restrained or controlled and are constantly seeking change. By nature, "Fire Snakes" are impulsive, straightforward and outspoken. Their self-reliance also enables them to achieve success in their career pursuits.

Earth Snake: Born in the Year of *Ding-Si* (1977, 1917)

Earth Snakes are quick-witted, level-headed, and treat others with kindness and care. However, they are likely to be oversensitive and get jealous easily. They are also lacking in patience and perseverance. "Earth Snakes" tend to see themselves in the right and reject the advice of others; this habit should be modified if at all possible.

A colored statue of Ding-Si Deity

Metal Snake: Born in the Year of *Xin-Si* (2001, 1941)

Metal Snakes are courageous and determined, high in self-esteem, and possess a sophisticated, refined style. They demonstrate keen judgment and conduct their affairs in a down-to-earth manner. Commanding the high esteem of others, they enjoy excellent career prospects and are often promoted to senior positions. The Metal Snake is also bound to have many romantic pursuers.

A colored statue of Xin-Si Deity

Water Snake: Born in the Year of *Gui-Si* (2013, 1953)

Water Snakes possess a variety of positive traits: they are diligent, enterprising and quick-witted, positive and optimistic, bold and fearless, and kind, considerate and sociable. The fact that "Water Snakes" suffer from excessive pride, however, may become a barrier to their success.

A colored statue of Gui-Si Deity

THE *SI* SNAKE ABOVE THE CLOUDS

Fortune by the Year

In the Year of the Rat, Snakes will be blessed with great happiness and family celebration. They will achieve positive results in their careers and enjoy strong earnings. Romantic prospects also tend to be excellent this year.

In the Year of the Ox, Snakes may face

unforeseen bodily injuries or other misfortune. They should keep an eye on personal safety, stay at home whenever possible, avoid prying into others' personal affairs, and try to do more good deeds.

In the Year of the Tiger, Snakes will have to contend with a string of endless disputes as well as resistance in their pursuits. However, luck is on ultimately on their side, and they will have unforeseen gains during the year.

In the Year of the Rabbit, Snakes may find themselves running around in pursuit of riches and fame—but to little avail. In spite of their ill fortune, they are blessed with the help of those around them, and good luck will gradually materialize by year-end.

In the Year of the Dragon, Snakes enjoy smooth sailing and success in their endeavors. Minor health problems may arise near year-end, but potential calamity can be thwarted. Dragons will continue to progress in their careers and stand ready to make a fortune.

In the Year of the Snake, Snakes tend to drift along and are likely to face various absurd incidents. Offending the Stellar God near year-end may also result in unavoidable losses or defeat. However, by adjusting to changing circumstances, the Snake can make it through the year unscathed.

In the Year of the Horse, Snakes are beset with bad luck. By devoting time to charitable causes, they can transform crisis into opportunity and

seek triumph in the face of defeat. By year-end, the Snake's efforts will be rewarded and gains will be made.

In the Year of the Sheep, Snakes are likely to see a combination of success and failure. The beginning of the year will be met with some obstacles, but luck will stabilize by mid-year, with gains and losses ultimately canceling each other out.

In the Year of the Monkey, Snakes will be blessed with the support of others, enabling them to attain both fame and wealth. However, despite this good fortune, the Snake is unlikely to find true happiness this year.

In the Year of the Rooster, Snakes will see their careers take off. Despite solid economic prospects overall, the year will also bring frequent financial losses; it would be wise to associate with people of higher status or power. Snakes should also be prepared to deal with good-for-nothing rascals who may appear near year-end.

In the Year of the Dog, Snakes will face a mixture of joy and sadness. There are likely to be opportunities to go out-of-town or overseas. By seizing these opportunities and expanding business away from home, the Snake can definitely make solid gains.

A sculpture of snake in the Garden of Twelve Zodiac Animals in Jiangxi Province

In the Year of the Pig, Snakes will find it difficult to achieve both fame and gain simultaneously. While earnings may be easy to come by, it is imperative not to become excessively greedy. If lucky enough to secure both fame and wealth, the Snake should demonstrate kindness towards others by doing more good deeds; this will ensure the continued flow of affluence.

THE *SI* SNAKE ABOVE THE CLOUDS

THE SNAKE AND THE WESTERN ZODIAC

 Snake-Aries:
Snake-Aries are gifted and talented, highly decisive, and like to engage in deep thought. With strong willpower and a fiery personality, they are well-suited to doing creative work.

 Snake-Taurus:
Snake-Tauruses are naturally indecisive, reserved and cautious, and tend to lack self-confidence. Despite an obstinate personality, they are steady, reliable and serious-minded.

 Snake-Gemini:
Snake-Geminis possess strong intuition and are highly pensive, with the ability to reflect on past events. Despite a lazy demeanor and lack of willpower, they are impelled by an inner force, leading to success in their endeavors.

 Snake-Cancer:
Snake-Cancers are intrepid and forward-looking, able to surmount any obstacle in their path and ultimately improve their fortune. They have a good eye for beauty and are often able to offer good ideas or suggestions. They also tend to be highly active and enjoy frolicking.

 Snake-Leo:
Snake-Leos are self-confident, unyielding in their opinions, and have an inherent love of beauty. Despite being friendly and compassionate, they do not often make contact with others. Snake-Leos have the ability to instill a sense of awe in others.

 Snake-Virgo:
Snake-Virgos possess acute intuition, strong analytical skills, and extraordinary intelligence; nothing is likely to perplex them. Although Snake-Virgos have an introverted personality, they are extremely charming and have many adorers.

 Snake-Libra:
Snake-Librans are rational, cool-headed, and acutely insightful. Gentle and romantic

A square bronze *Yan* (four-legged ritual vessel in ancient China) decorated with the pattern of snake

A pair of jade ornaments with human head and snake body from the Spring and Autumn Period

A bronze *Ding* (a three-legged ritual vessel in ancient China) engraved with the pattern of snake from the Warring States Period

by nature, they have a kind heart and always show thoughtful concern for others. Snake-Librans also excel at planning and budgeting in their daily lives.

Snake-Scorpio:
Snake-Scorpios have heightened sensory perception, enabling them to detect even minor changes. Despite having a tendency to be conceited and arrogant, Snake-Scorpios are extremely sensitive and highly affectionate.

Snake-Sagittarius:
Snake-Sagittarians are highly scrupulous and, in spite of their quiet disposition, possess strong expressive skills. They take pleasure in allaying others' difficulties and worries, and excel at mediating disputes. Although they attract little attention to themselves, Snake-Sagittarians are destined to achieve extraordinary success.

Snake-Capricorn:
Snake-Capricorns are calm and composed, ambitious and intrepid, cultured and refined, and graceful and attractive. Kindhearted and generous by nature, they are readily willing to share their wealth with others.

Snake-Aquarius:
Snake-Aquarians tend to be optimistic, enterprising and brimming with confidence. They take pleasure in travel, adventure and planning, possess a vivid imagination, and are well-versed in the ways of the world.

Snake-Pisces:
Snake-Pisceses tend to be deep and solemn, weary of the world and its banality, and often preferring to live alone. They are loyal, dependable and willing to devote their efforts to the task at hand, but elect not to compete with others. Snake-Pisceses are also elegant and graceful in their demeanor.

THE *SI* SNAKE ABOVE THE CLOUDS

FENGSHUI AND THE SNAKE

At the very mention of snakes, people immediately bring to mind an animal which is cold-blooded, dark and sinister, and potentially deadly. In *fengshui*, the snake is classified as a malevolent creature, which can harm others by emitting a supernatural force of evil. It is thus unadvisable for those born in the Year of the Snake to wear or carry any accessories imprinted with this animal; otherwise, relationships with others are liable to take a turn for the worse.

People born in the Year of the Snake are also advised against having snake drawings or figures in their home; if this advice is not heeded, relations between family members might become distant, or domestic feuds might erupt. Finally, those born in the Year of the Pig should avoid the use of ornamental snakes, as the earthly branches *Si* and *Hai* are mutually conflicting.

A snake engraved on the 12-zodiac-animal screen wall in Beijing's White Cloud Temple

INTERPRETING SNAKE DREAMS

A bronze *You* (a ritual vessel in ancient China) engraved with the pattern of snake and frog from the Spring and Autumn Period

If you dream of being bitten by a snake, you will receive good luck and enjoy a life of affluence.

If you dream of a snake sliding down a hole, your house will be burglarized or possessions will be stolen.

If you dream of a snake fighting with a cat, all suffering will come to an end.

If you dream of a dragon and snake entering through a doorway, money will come your way.

If you dream of a dragon and snake entering your kitchen stove, you will be promoted from your current position.

If you dream of a snake morphing into a dragon, you will be blessed with good luck.

HEALTH SECRETS

People born in the Year of the Snake are physically strong and have a good immune system; as a result, they rarely get sick. Nonetheless, Snakes tend to suffer from poor sleep quality as well as frequent insomnia. They would thus be advised to relax the mind, adjust their emotions, and adopt a more optimistic attitude towards life. By being more broadminded, many problems can be solved with effortless ease.

A snake displayed by vegetables

THE *SI* SNAKE ABOVE THE CLOUDS

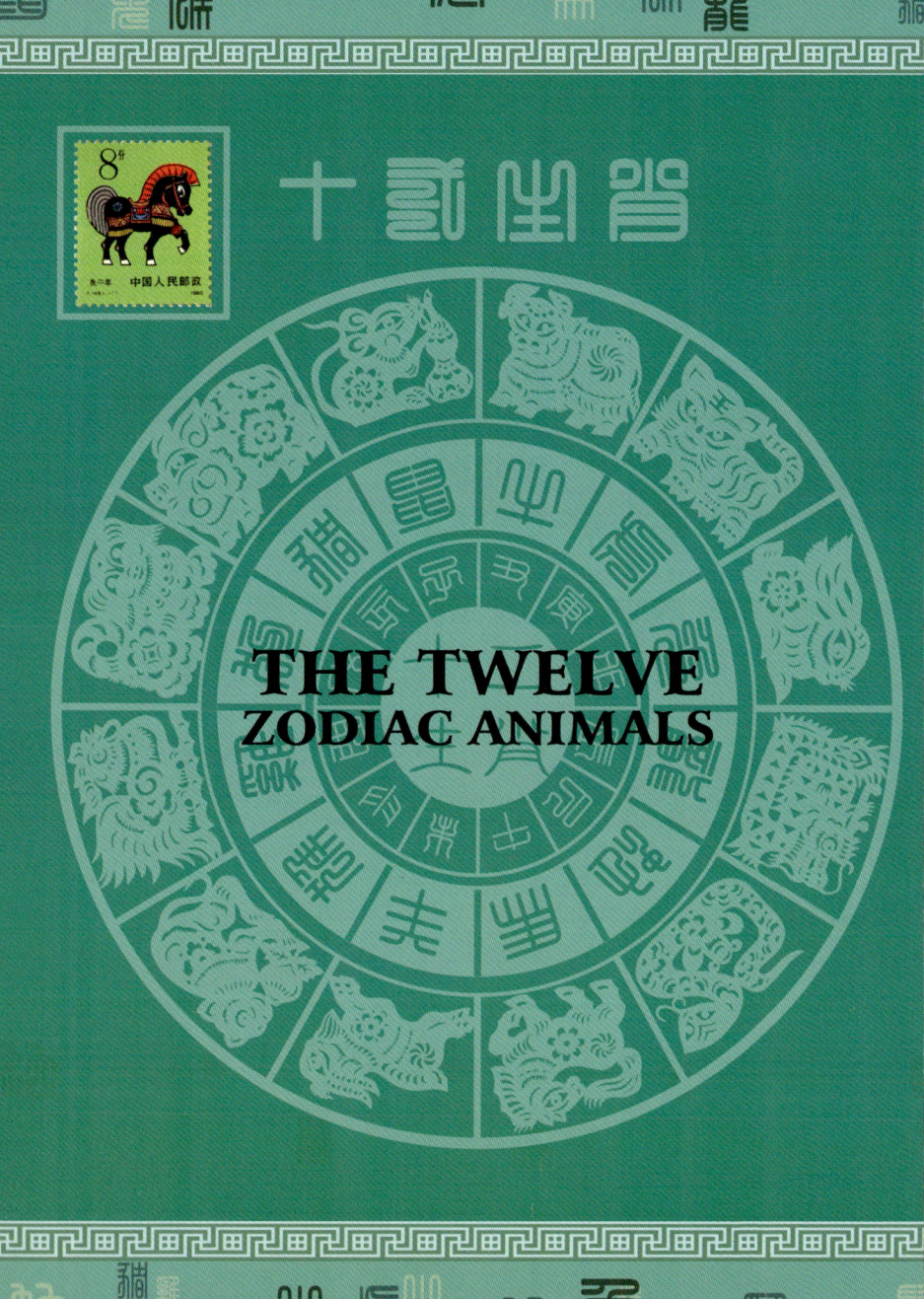

THE TWELVE
ZODIAC ANIMALS

PART 7

THE *WU* HORSE FLIES ABOVE THE SKY

【 HORSE 】

THE *WU* HORSE FLIES ABOVE THE SKY

The ancient Chinese believed that during the *wu*-hour (11:00am-1:00pm), *yang* (masculine) energy reaches its limit and the creation of *yin* (feminine) energy is ready to begin. The *wu*-hour, therefore, is a *yin-yang* exchange period during which horses are highly active. A horse's hooves leaving and returning to the ground are regarded as *yang* and *yin*, respectively. The pairing of *wu* with the horse is first seen in the *Classic of Poetry*: "A lucky day was *geng-wu*; we had selected our horses."

As one of the earliest countries to breed horses, China has a rich horse culture. In ancient China, horses played a vital role in daily life, the economy, and even in art and culture. As a result, the horse possesses important symbolic meaning and enjoys a high status in traditional Chinese culture.

As early as the time of patriarchal society, horses were domesticated by human beings and used as a tool for transport and communication. The horse also played an important role in one of the most crucial events in Chinese history — the introduction of Buddhism to China. Two high-ranking monks from India used horses to transport figures of Buddha and Buddhist scriptures to the Chinese capital of Luoyang.

The horse has also served to enrich the Chinese language. For example, the expression "success arrives with the horse" is used to wish someone quick and effortless success; "the horse and its rider are both fatigued" describes a tiring journey; "the old horse knows its way back home" means

The bronze horse head once adorned the Old Summer Palace

that someone who has a lot of experience should be relatively familiar with the situation; and "spurring on the flying horse to full speed" to express swift action or the acceleration of one's pace. There are also many Chinese proverbs about horses, such as "a good horse is matched with a nice saddle" and "a long journey reveals the horse's endurance; the passing of time reveals a person's heart". The horse is even represented in stories. In the story *Sai Weng Lost His Horse*, there is a line "Sai Weng's loss of a horse is not necessarily unlucky", which means that seeming misfortune may actually turn out to be a blessing.

The horse also carried vital significance in China's ancient political system and system of etiquette. The carriage was

A sculpture on Chamagudao, a pass with the horse as the main means of transportation in Lijiang, Yunnan Province

The Qin Dynasty copper carriage and horses unearthed from the Mausoleum of Qin Shi Huang, Shaanxi Province

invented as early as 4,000 years ago. In the Zhou Dynasty, a strict system of how many horses should be used in a carriage was developed. Carriages were been divided into *jia-yi*, *jia-er*, *jia-san*, *jia-si*, *jia-wu*, *jia-liu* and so on. As to how many horses the emperor's carriage should use is still a matter of controversy in historical research. It is recorded in the *Rites of Zhou* that the emperor's carriage

THE *WU* HORSE FLIES ABOVE THE SKY

The clay red rabbit horse in the Temple of Guan Yu in Jiayu Pass, Gansu Province

Ancient China suffered from frequent wars and the chaos they engendered. Interestingly, horses were involved in almost every war. It can be said that, in ancient China, the horse's main function was to fight in war. No other animal was able to have the great impact on human history that horses did. The horse, therefore, is often found in military expressions, such as "strong soldiers and sturdy horses", "military chaos and disturbed horses", and "golden spears and iron horses". Soldiers regarded dying with a horse skin covering the body as the highest honor. In times of cold weapons, the cavalry was the most fearful power which could greatly strengthen an army's fighting force. The number of war chariots was considered a symbol of a country's strength during

was a *jia-si* (four-horse carriage). However, in another book called *Etiquette and Rituals*, it is recorded that the emperor's carriage was a *jia-liu* (six-horse carriage), while the feudal lord's carriage was a *jia-si*. The former one was verified by a copper carriage unearthed from Emperor Qin's mausoleum; a six-horse carriage unearthed at Luoyang in Henan Province also provided proof of the latter one. Regardless of the specific number of horses, however, the fact remains that the horse was a symbol of nobility in China's system of etiquette. Even to the present day, people still use the expression "fragrant coach and precious horse" to describe abundance and nobility.

A statue of Galloping Horse Treading on a Flying Swallow, the symbol of Top Tourist City of China, standing in Qiqihar, Heilongjiang Province

134 THE TWELVE ZODIAC ANIMALS

the Warring States Period. At that time, the King of Zhao carried out a military reform called "Hu Fu Qi She", which means wearing the clothing of the Hu (an ethnic group in northern China) and also riding and shooting like the Hu. Mongolian cavalry once swept through Europe and Asia. There are also plenty of stories about famous horses and their owners: Xiang Yu (232-202 BC)'s piebald horse committed suicide for him; Liu Bei (161-223)'s *Dilu* horse jumped off a cliff to save him; Guan Yu (162-220)'s Red Rabbit, Cao Cao (155-220)'s *Jueying* and Qin Qiong's *Huangbiao* were all famous horses which achieved great contributions. Tang Dynasty emperor Li Shimin (559-649) bestowed titles upon his six horses and wrote a poem for them. Finally, an even more

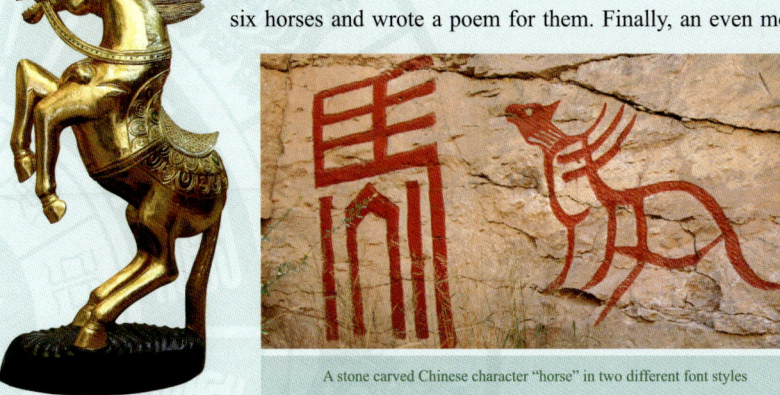

A stone carved Chinese character "horse" in two different font styles

poignant example is that of Emperor Wu of Han Liu Che (156-87 BC), who waged war against Dayuan merely to get a breed of precious horse.

The horse is also a symbol of ability, holiness and achievement. The ancient Chinese often used the term "thousand-mile horse" to represent an outstanding talent, which is reflected in *Zhan Guo Ce* (literally *Strategies of the Warring States*). As the story goes, the King Zhao of Yan, who wanted to revitalize his state, attempted to recruit talents from around the country but was disappointed to see that no one showed up. One of the king's chancellors, Guo Huai, thus told the king, "There was a king who offered a thousand *taels* of gold in exchange for a thousand-mile horse. I, your humble chancellor, spent 500 *taels*, but ended up returning with only the horse's bones." The king lost his temper, but the chancellor added, "Since the whole country knows that Your Majesty spent so much money just for a horse's bones, why be worried that the real thousand-mile horse will not show up on its own?" Sure enough, just as the chancellor had predicted, a great number of thousand-mile horses arrived at the palace. Upon hearing this news, the King of Yan immediately granted Guo Huai a grand villa and gave him royal treatment. Later, Yue Yi, Zou Yan, Ju Xin and other talents set out for the State of

A sculpture of Ouyang Hai (1940-1959), a model of Chinese People's Liberation Army, who spared no effort to push the war-horse in order to save the people's property.

Yan. Under their assistance, the State of Yan finally developed into a strong country and even became one of the Seven Hegemonial among the Warring States.

The horse also appears as the "Sky Horse" and "Dragon Horse" in ancient China. The fact that the horse is the head of the "six domestic animals" clearly demonstrates its importance in the lives of the early Chinese people. Later on, the horse was apotheosized and elevated to become a symbol of spiritual belief. The *I Ching* states, "*qian* is a horse," meaning that the horse is most masculine. The *Classic of Rites* states that "Any horse taller than eight *chi* (equalling to about 2.7 meters) is a dragon. The dragon and horse, therefore, both became spiritual symbols in China. To the present day, the Chinese people still use the phrase "dragon and horse spirit." During the Qin and Han dynasties, there was a legend about a dragon-horse named "River Picture." It is said that in Fu Xi's time, a dragon-horse — an animal with a dragon's head and a horse's body — appeared in the Yellow River. There was a picture that looked like a river on its back, so it was called "River Picture." According to River Picture, Fu Xi developed the Eight Diagrams and created Chinese culture. The *Book of Song* contains a more detailed description of the dragon-horse: "The dragon-horse, which is the spirit of the river, is a royal horse. It is eight *chi* and five *cun* (equalling to about 2.8 meters) tall, and has wings beside its neck. Its roar is one of great misery." In *Journey to the*

West, Tang Seng's white horse was described as the East Dragon King's third prince, is a white horse. We can conclude, therefore, that the dragon-horse's image has penetrated deeply into the Chinese people's consciousness. With respect to the dragon-horse, there is also an explanation in astronomy: It was believed that four stars of the Fang Xiu constellation governed the horses; these stars happen to coincide with the Green Dragon constellation. The dragon and horse thus joined together to become one. A bronze relic known as "Galloping Horse Treading on a Flying Swallow", unearthed in Wuwei (Gansu Province), reveals the brilliance and strength of the horse. National Tourism Administration of People's Republic of China has since designated this image as the symbol of Chinese tourism.

Many folk customs related to horses are popular throughout China and among its different ethnic groups, including horse sacrifices and beliefs about the "Horse Lord". During the Tang Dynasty (618-907), virtually all of the Chinese people — from royal government officials to the commoners — enjoyed playing polo. The Tang Emperor Li Longji frequently played polo with his chancellors in the royal palace. Many historical records also contain descriptions about

A relief of carriage in ancient China

horsemanship, which is especially popular among the nomadic tribes of northern China. In addition to the Horse Racing Festival and Horse Milk Festival, there are many other celebratory events with horse-related themes.

 ZODIAC ANIMAL FILE

Earthly Branch: *Wu*
Years of Birth: 2026, 2014, 2002, 1990, 1978, 1966, 1954, 1942, 1930...
Five Elements: *Wu* belongs to Fire
Five Constant Virtues: Fire belongs to Propriety
Auspicious Directions: northeast, southwest, northwest
Auspicious Colors: dark brown, yellow, purple
Lucky Numbers: 8, 2, 6
Lucky Flowers: giant taro, arrowhead, jasmine
Lucky Gemstones: olivine, aventurine, malachite
Spiritual Protector: Mahasthamaprapta Bodhisattva
Choosing a name: For individuals born in the Year of the Horse, it

THE *WU* HORSE FLIES ABOVE THE SKY

is appropriate to select characters with the radicals for grass (艹) or metal (金), signifying profound learning; characters with the radicals for jade (玉), wood (木), or grain (禾), which embody talent and intellect; characters with the radicals for insect (虫), bean (豆), rice (米), which embody joy and prosperity; or characters with the radicals for person (亻) or moon (月), which represent intelligence and courage.

THE HORSE AND PERSONALITY

Strengths:
The Horse's assets include natural intelligence, a sharp mind, and strong perceptive skills. People of this zodiac sign tend to be cheerful and optimistic, vivacious and bubbly, warm-hearted and romantic, and bold and liberal. Horses enjoy cordial relations with others and have a large circle of friends. Always staying true to their word, they can be counted on to see a task through to completion, even in the face of setbacks. Horses are also eager to defend others against injustice.

Weaknesses:
The Horse's limitations include a hot temper, the tendency to act impetuously, and poor financial management skills. People of this zodiac sign often hold rigidly to their views and are unwilling to accept others' suggestions. They also tend to be vain and to attach too much importance to how others perceive them. Horses are also freewheeling and impulsive by nature.

A wood carving of success arriving with the horse

THE HORSE AND BLOOD TYPE

Blood Type A:
Horses with blood type A are cheerful and confident, kind and amiable, optimistic and forward-looking, and possess high ideals. They consider matters carefully, and carry out tasks thoroughly and with surety. Horses of this blood type possess the qualities of forgiveness and forbearance. They are easy to please, and do not indulge in exaggeration.

Blood Type B:
Horses with blood type B have a sunny personality, living life with enthusiasm and always looking on the bright side. They are courageous, liberal, competent and practical. They also tend to act impetuously at times.

Blood Type O:
Horses with blood type O are guileless and honest, but equally profit-oriented and money-driven. They have strong business and leadership skills, and strive to be practical and efficient in their affairs. Rather than worry about minor gains and losses, they are more concerned with practical interests. However, they tend to be shortsighted, lack patience, and lose their temper at times.

Blood Type AB:
Horses with blood type AB are optimistic and passionate, vivacious and active, and gifted and multi-talented. They have the ability to exercise self-constraint, take initiative, and are good at utilizing the strength of others to improve themselves. Despite being quiet by nature, they are practical in speech. Some of their other qualities include creativity, strong organizational skills, and an aptitude for problem solving. Horses of this blood type are not the type to stir up trouble or cause disputes.

THE HORSE AND FORTUNE

Lifetime Fortune: Overview

People born in the Year of the Horse are boisterous and active by nature. They possess exceptional social skills, which is one of the reasons they enjoy the respect and love of others. Horses are lucky enough to have people in their lives who lead them to success. They also tend to have stable careers and a harmonious family life.

Career:
Horses have a strong entrepreneurial spirit. By seizing business opportunities as they appear, they can get ahead in their career. They also have fairly good financial luck, but should avoid being greedy.

A Tang Dynasty silver kettle with the pattern of a horse holding a cup in the mouth

THE WU HORSE FLIES ABOVE THE SKY

Financial Luck:

People born in the Year of the Horse enjoy a stable financial outlook, with the prospect of creating superior wealth. Because they are well-suited to pursuing business investments, especially those bearing a high return, Horses should feel free to invest liberally and plan their financial portfolio carefully.

Romance:

By letting nature take its course, Horses can enjoy a fulfilling love life. It is important for them to restrain themselves and be more tolerant of their families, so that small matters do not blow up into major incidents. In the event that husband and wife live in different geographical locations, maintaining frequent contact is of paramount importance.

Fortune and the Five Elements

Wood Horse: Born in the Year of *Ren-Wu* (2002, 1942)

Wood Horses have a rich imagination as well as profound ideas and judgments. Their prudence and decisiveness gives them the ability to thoroughly persuade others. Wood Horses tend to be hasty, aggressive and emotional, patience and perseverance are also lacking, with many jobs ending up half-finished. Since Wood Horses are likely to fall behind in their expenses, it would be best for them to avoid joint financial endeavors.

A colored statue of Geng-Wu Deity

A colored statue of Ren-Wu Deity

Fire Horse: Born in the Year of *Wu-Wu* (1978, 1918)

Fire Horses are naturally gifted, active and lively, and bold and enthusiastic. They are also unyielding and never willing to admit defeat. Strong leadership skills enable them to gain the respect and endearment of others and build up harmonious relationships. Although self-control and self-restraint are lacking, the Fire Horse can open the door to success by listening to others' points of view and patiently complying with the wisdom of elders.

A colored statue of Wu-Wu Deity

Earth Horse: Born in the Year of *Geng-Wu* (1990, 1930)

Earth Horses have an optimistic, easy-going personality and a strong sense of responsibility. Despite a rash temperament, they

are highly sociable and kindhearted, possess high morals, and treat others fairly. The Earth Horse is always ready to lend a helping hand, and strives to assist friends to the greatest extent possible.

Metal Horse: Born in the Year of *Jia-Wu* (2014, 1954)

Metal Horses are virtuous and kindhearted, frank and outspoken, and always ready to help others. Although they enjoy popularity among friends, they also tend to stick stubbornly to their own opinions and rarely accept criticism from others. Metal Horses have clear goals and are likely to gain the esteem of their superiors, leading to promotion opportunities.

A colored statue of Jia-Wu Deity

Water Horse: Born in the Year of *Bing-Wu* (1966, 1906)

Water Horses are gentle, easy-going, career-minded, and thorough in their deliberations. They have the ability to put themselves in others' shoes and are also willing to sacrifice their own interests for others. Although Water Horses tend to be impatient and emotional, they are fortunate to have many people who care about them. Throughout their lives, they are likely to receive assistance from members of the opposite sex, and luck is likely to stabilize in old age. Because Water Horses can be emotional and sensitive, however, they tend to be highly indecisive in their love life.

A colored statue of Bing-Wu Deity

Fortune by the Year

In the Year of the Rat, Horses tend to be inundated with quarrels and misfortune. Fortunately, there is always someone to help them through these situations and bring sunshine after the rain.

In the Year of the Ox, Horses will meet with good fortune in all their endeavors and see their wishes fulfilled. However, they are likely to encounter some bad luck midway through the year. It would be best to wait until conditions are favorable before pursuing profits; by waiting patiently for the right opportunity, the Horse can make a fortune and avoid peril.

THE *WU* HORSE FLIES ABOVE THE SKY

In the Year of the Tiger, Horses are beleaguered with poor economic prospects and the likelihood of financial losses. Facing major resistance and tending to drift along, the Horse will have difficulty moving forward. Nevertheless, the year will ultimately pass without major calamity.

In the Year of the Rabbit, Horses will be blessed with all-around success, large financial inflows, and great happiness. Despite having plenty of reason to smile, it is imperative that they not be too greedy. The Horse should also pay extra attention to building and maintaining good relations with others.

In the Year of the Dragon, Horses will see multiple fluctuations in their fortune, with a lot of things going counter to their wishes. Faced with this situation, the Horse should stay determined and focus on one thing at a time.

In the Year of the Snake, Horses may see their health take a turn for the worse. It is also likely to be a time of constant running around and little tranquility. The Horse should try to do more good turns and charitable deeds toward year-end.

In the Year of the Horse, Horses will make advancements in their careers and enjoy strong earnings; there will also be opportunities for promotion. It is an opportune time to expand the business and watch the profits as they pour in. Horses are advised, however, to avoid attending funeral services this year.

In the Year of the Sheep, Horses can celebrate good luck and fortune. Gains will be made near the beginning of the year, paving the way to success by year-end. It will not be all smooth sailing,

however, as the Horse will face inevitable setbacks and resistance near the mid-year point.

In the Year of the Monkey, Horses will see their luck ebb and flow unpredictably. Although most endeavors are likely to meet with success, not everything will go according to the Horse's wishes. Overall, however, it is a year of good fortune.

In the Year of the Rooster, Horses will experience stable luck, and are likely to be blessed with happiness around the middle of the year. There will also be many good chances to bring in earnings. Horses should expand their business, seize opportunities as they emerge, and make efforts to improve their financial management skills.

In the Year of the Dog, Horses are destined to achieve success in their careers, with strong financial prospects and the likelihood of a promotion. Despite setbacks which are likely to materialize, the Horse can ensure victory by monitoring trends as they emerge.

In the Year of the Pig, Horses will inevitably see their luck take a turn for the worse. Only by avoiding potential breakdowns in reputation and wealth is the Horse's fortune likely to turn around. Rather than seeking profits this year, Horses should concentrate on expanding their network and researching potential investments.

A Mongolian mural painting depicting a herdsman and a horse

 ## THE HORSE AND THE WESTERN ZODIAC

Horse-Aries:

Horse-Aries are proactive and purposeful, but tend to have an explosive temper. Fearless in the face of difficulties and challenges, they possess lofty aspirations and make every effort to pursue their ideals. Their practical side also leads them to pursue opportunities as they emerge.

A statue of Zhang Liao (169-222), a general under Cao Cao's command during the Three Kingdoms Period, riding his war horse

THE *WU* HORSE FLIES ABOVE THE SKY

 Horse-Taurus:

Horse-Tauruses are exceptionally gifted, often excelling in music or the arts. They have the ability to make adjustments when faced with difficulties, but have a hard time adapting to new environments. Horse-Tauruses are diligent, down-to-earth, and able to put themselves in others' shoes.

Horse-Gemini:

Horse-Geminis are astute and quick-witted, but tend to lack constancy and be unable to stick to their work. They have an optimistic outlook and cheerful personality, and occasionally like to play practical jokes or do something crazy.

A tri-colored horse from the Tang Dynasty

Wood-carved horses

A painting of *Horse* by Xu Beihong (1895-1953), a famous Chinese painter

Horse-Cancer:

Horse-Cancers are gentle and cordial, noble and romantic, and cautious and prudent. They have a generous and giving nature, and are readily willing to sacrifice themselves for others. Intelligent, diligent, and meticulous in their planning, rarely is there any job that they are incapable of handling.

Horse-Leo:

Horse-Leos fear neither danger nor difficulty, and are inspired to constantly improve and surpass themselves. Once their goal or course of action has been determined, they immediately set to action. Horse-Leos tend to be extremely hard-working, frequently resulting in a heavy mental burden.

Horse-Virgo:
Horse-Virgos are conservative and unassuming, graceful and elegant, and highly gifted. They are self-guided, excel at guiding others, and enjoy good social relationships. They are also likely to be conceited and even a bit opportunistic.

Horse-Libra:
Horse-Librans are elegant, graceful, cultured, and charming. Despite having a tendency to be obstinate and rebellious, they are naturally gregarious, and highly articulate and persuasive.

Horse-Scorpio:
Horse-Scorpios are gifted, multi-talented, and possess the ability to persuade and inspire others. They are able to devote themselves to their career while managing to stay up on the current trends. By adopting a wide range of ideas, they can reach a level of near-perfection in their endeavors. Horse-Scorpios possess acute observational skills, but have a tendency to engage in fantasy.

Horse-Sagittarius:
Horse-Sagittarians are proactive, assiduous, and elegant in demeanor. They demonstrate caring for others and often busy themselves by doing good deeds. Horse-Sagittarians also possess strong organizational and management skills, but are likely to suffer from pressure and anxiety.

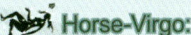

A pottery warrior riding a horse from the Tang Dynasty

Horse-Capricorn:
Horse-Capricorns are naturally kindhearted and blessed with inner peace and calmness. They are positive and conscientious in their endeavors and glad to offer help to others in every possible way. The Horse-Capricorn brims with energy, cherishes time, and is willing to try new things.

Horse-Aquarius:
Horse-Aquarians are quick-witted, clear-headed and hard-working, and possess strong persuasive skills. Filled with vigor and a zest for life, they aspire to freedom and show loving care for others.

A jade carving of an immortal riding a horse

THE WU HORSE FLIES ABOVE THE SKY

Horse-Pisces:

Horse-Pisceses are willing to work hard, but seek no reward for their efforts. They are also willing to go to all lengths to pursue their dreams, but ultimately prefer a life of comfort and are unlikely to wander the world merely to seek a living. Reticent and conservative by nature, they like to engage in deep thought and tend to attract little attention to themselves.

A bas-relief of one of the Six Steeds from the tomb of Emperor Taizong of Tang (reigning from 626 to 649), which were Emperor Taizong's war horses during his military expeditions.

FENGSHUI AND THE HORSE

In the study of *fengshui*, horses are regarded neither as an auspicious creature nor a malevolent one. However, most people view the horse as a lucky and noble animal; the utilization of *fengshui* horses thus seems quite important. Although horses cannot thwart evil forces, they do have the ability to cheer up a desolate heart. Horses can also invigorate financial prospects or a stagnating career. Whether at home or work, the best position for a *fengshui* horse is in the south. The horse's head should also be aligned in this direction to ensure that dreams and aspirations are transformed into reality. In addition, to ensure that one's ideals are fulfilled, it is best to align the horse's head in this direction. With respect to material, gold, jade and copper are all ideal choices; plastic must absolutely be avoided.

INTERPRETING HORSE DREAMS

If you dream of riding a horse, you will soon enjoy both wealth and fame.

If you dream of falling off a horse, it is a sign that you will be demoted and your reputation will be destroyed.

A sculpture of horse in the Garden of Twelve Zodiac Animals in Jiangxi Province

If you dream of buying a horse, you will soon get married.

If you dream of many horses, you will strike it rich.

If you dream of someone giving you a horse, you will become a senior officer in the military.

A snow caving horse in Aer Mountain, Inner Mongolia

 HEALTH SECRETS

People born in the Year of the Horse are physically strong, highly energetic, and seek efficiency in their work. As a result, they tend to be overly wound up and suffer from nervous tension. This can place an increased burden on the cardiac, gastrointestinal and nervous systems, resulting in serious damage over time. Horses should modify their daily routine and habits, and strive to find a balance between work and leisure.

Bathing Horse on the Bank, by Zhao Mengfu (1254-1322), a famous Yuan-Dynasty painter

THE *WU* HORSE FLIES ABOVE THE SKY

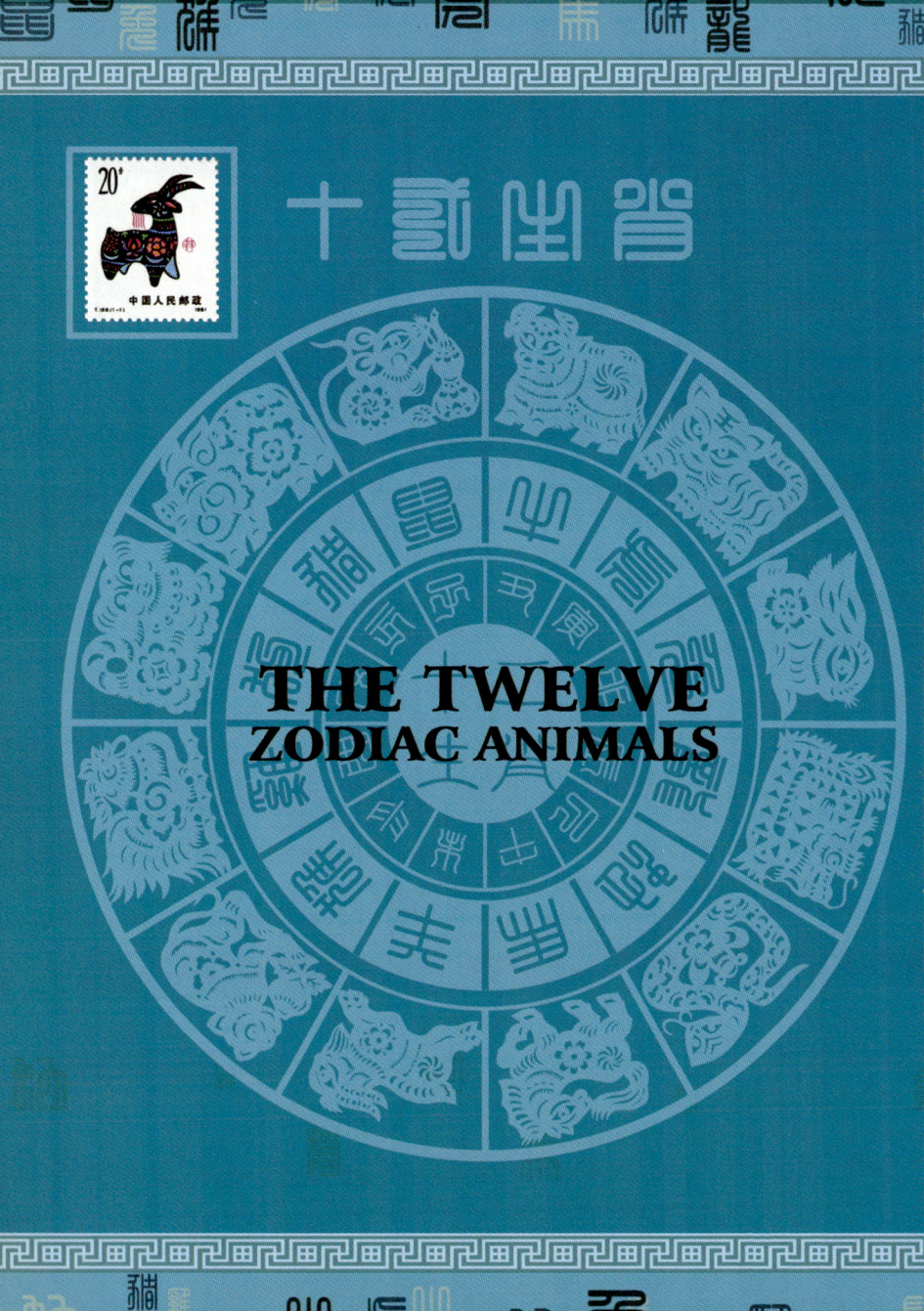

PART 8
THE *WEI* SHEEP CREATES PROSPERITY AND PEACE

【 SHEEP 】

THE *WEI* SHEEP CREATES PROSPERITY AND PEACE

The sheep, which is friendly and non-aggressive, easy to tame, and can satisfy human needs of milk, meat, fur and leather, became one of the earliest animals raised by humankind. As early as the period of matrilineal society, the natives who lived in the grasslands of northern China began to choose places along the river where marshy weeds were luxuriant for shepherding and hunting. From that time on, the sheep gradually became one of the animals with the closest relationship to human beings. Since the dawn of Chinese civilization, sheep formed an indissoluble bond with Chinese culture in almost every realm, including language, food, morality, etiquette, and aesthetics.

Chinese characters represent one of the world's oldest and most extensively used writing systems. The origin and development of Chinese characters are closely tied into Chinese civilization. The rich information embedded in Chinese characters records, reflects and unveils the antediluvian culture of China. The sheep has left many tracks in Chinese characters. For example, the Chinese character for "beauty" combines the characters for "sheep" and "big", meaning that a big sheep is considered beautiful. From this, we can see the ancient Chinese had a tendency toward pragmatism. The Chinese character "fresh" combines the characters for "fish"

THE TWELVE ZODIAC ANIMALS

The stone sculpture of the five mythical sheep in Guangzhou

A blue glazed sheep from the Three Kingdoms Period

and "sheep"; this is because the coastal people of China liked fish, while inland people preferred mutton. There are many Chinese other characters that incorporate the character for "sheep", and the sheep has also entered into many Chinese idioms (including vulgarisms). All of them serve to enrich the Chinese language and culture. Examples of sheep idioms include "a sheep was thrown to the wolves," meaning that someone is in distress and faces certain death; "take precautions after suffering the loss of a sheep", meaning that measures should be taken when something has gone wrong; "steal a sheep in passing", referring to the act of stealing from others when they are not paying attention; and "path like the sheep's intestine", referring to a winding mountain path." Finally, the expression "wool comes from the sheep" means that a favor seems to have been done for someone on the surface, but in fact the benefit is attached to the price.

The sheep also has a close relationship with the ancient decorum. The traditional Chinese character "*yi*" (meaning etiquette), for example, contains the character for "sheep". An explanation for this in the work *Luxuriant Dew of the Spring and Autumn Annals*, attributed to Han Dynasty scholar Dong Zhongshu (179-104 BC), stated that sheep were good-natured, non-aggressive, and patient, thus demonstrating a graceful style of etiquette and well-suited to use in sacrifice and ceremony. Indeed, the sheep has been the most important sacrificial animal throughout Chinese history.

In traditional Chinese culture, the sheep is also a symbol of prosperity and peace. The

THE *WEI* SHEEP CREATES PROSPERITY AND PEACE

A sheep engraved on the 12-zodiac-animal screen wall in Beijing's White Cloud Temple

same pronunciation as *yang* (male energy), the abovementioned idiom — formed mistakenly by substituting "three sheep" in place of "three *yang*" — spread across China over the course of time. The sheep, therefore, symbolizes that good luck and prosperity are about to befall. Paintings that depict the "three sheep creating peace and prosperity" are highly esteemed by the Chinese people.

"In ancient times, the Chinese characters for "sheep" and "luck" were used interchangeably. The sheep is thus endowed the meaning of good luck and is an auspicious symbol. In order to bring good luck, the ancient Chinese would hang a sheep's head on the door at the beginning of the year, present others with a sheep as a social practice, or

idiom "three sheep created prosperity and peace" is based on the original form "three *yang* created prosperity and peace" as seen in the *I Ching*. The Chinese character *tai* (meaning peace and prosperity) is one of the divinatory trigrams in the *I Ching*. The tenth month of the lunar calendar is represented by the divinatory symbol *kun*. *Kun* is pure *yin* (female energy), and when the pure *yin* reaches its extreme, it reverses its course and the opposite *yang* (male energy) appears. The eleventh lunar month is the divinatory *fu* and, in this month, one *yang* is born. The twelfth lunar month is represented by the symbol *lin* and, in this month, two *yang* are born. The first lunar month is represented by the divinatory symbol *tai*, and in this month three *yang* are born. This month also sees the passing of winter and onset of spring; *yin* is declining and *yang* is growing; nature is rejuvenating; and heaven and earth join together to connect the world. Because the Chinese word for "sheep" (*yang*) has the

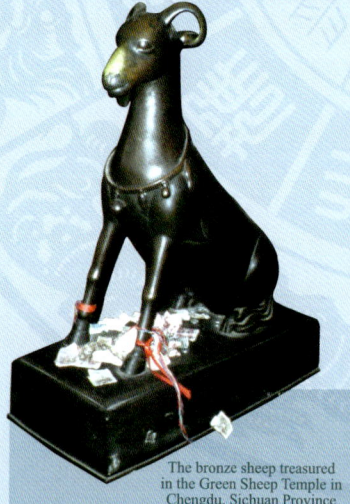

The bronze sheep treasured in the Green Sheep Temple in Chengdu, Sichuan Province

THE TWELVE ZODIAC ANIMALS

offer a sheep as a betrothal gift. Because the lamb kneels down to suck its mother's breast milk and this action is regarded as a show of gratitude to its mother, the sheep is also regarded as a filial and courteous animal.

The real sheep gives a serene, meek and holy impression, while the sheep portrayed in Chinese legends is one of absolute magic. Many stories about the sheep have emerged over the course of Chinese history. Qin Shi Huang (259-210 BC), the first emperor of China, is said to have met with a mythical sheep during his inspection tour; he paid homage to the sheep and established a temple for it. In the Tang Dynasty novel *Liu Yi Zhuan*, all the sheep that the dragon's daughter raised were geniuses that followed the dragon to control rainfall. The jade sheep is not only a lucky omen, but also refers to moon. The city of Guangzhou has another name which originated from a beautiful legend. It is said that, during the Zhou Dynasty, Guangzhou suffered from years of natural disaster and the masses lived in dire poverty. Five fairies rode five five-colored mythical sheep to the city and gave rice to the locals. With rice plants scattered on the fields, the city of Guangzhou met with seasonable weather for crop-raising and a bumper grain harvest. Thereafter, these five mythical sheep turned into stone and remained on the hillside in Guangzhou.

In the minds of the ancient Chinese people, the sheep was always honest and nice. Over the course of time, it thus became a symbol of justice. The *xiezhi*, a Chinese legendary beast, was a mythical sheep with a single horn. It was said that the *xiezhi* was a lamb, had the capability of telling right from wrong, and could determine whether a government official was good. When the *xiezhi* detected a wicked government official, it would knock

A square bronze *Zun* (a ritual vessel in ancient China) decorated with the pattern of sheep at each corner

THE *WEI* SHEEP CREATES PROSPERITY AND PEACE

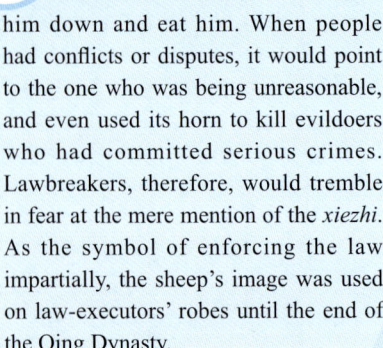

him down and eat him. When people had conflicts or disputes, it would point to the one who was being unreasonable, and even used its horn to kill evildoers who had committed serious crimes. Lawbreakers, therefore, would tremble in fear at the mere mention of the *xiezhi*. As the symbol of enforcing the law impartially, the sheep's image was used on law-executors' robes until the end of the Qing Dynasty.

The sheep is a frequently used subject in traditional Chinese art, and its image is virtually ubiquitous in ancient art. The sheep's image is found in important national treasures, including a bronze *Zun* with four sheep and a bronze *Lei* with three sheep (*Zun* and *Lei* were both ritual vessels in ancient China), both from the Shang Dynasty; a sheep-shaped copper lamp, made during the Han Dynasty; and a tri-colored ceramic sheep, crafted in the Tang Dynasty. As a pleasing and auspicious creature, the sheep is widely used in New Year's paintings, paper-cuttings, sculptures, needlework, and arts and crafts.

Historical customs related to the sheep have been well-maintained among the Chinese people. In rural Shaanxi and Gansu provinces, there is an important annual event known as the "Send Sheep Festival". On July 15 of the lunar calendar, mothers are supposed to model sheep in flour for their married daughters and send them to the daughters' homes. After receiving these "flour sheep", the daughter's husband then carve them with a knife, tie them with silk thread, and hang them in the drawing room. The flour sheep will not be replaced until new ones are received the following year; this symbolizes the new sheep

THE TWELVE ZODIAC ANIMALS

replacing the old sheep, with a surplus of grains every year. The Xibo ethnic group has a folk custom in which a sheep's leg bone is placed on the newlyweds' bed. Both families of the newlyweds are to contest over this bone at the wedding ceremony. If the bridegroom's family gets the bone, it means that the groom is industrious and capable, and that the newlyweds will enjoy a lifetime of happiness. If the bride's family gets the bone, it means that the bride is good at housekeeping and the newlyweds will have a harmonious and prosperous family. There is a popular custom called "respect guests with the sheep's head" prevalent among the Kazakhs in Xinjiang Province. When entertaining guests, the host carries a cooked sheep's head with the sheep's face towards guests to show respect. A horse-riding game called "picking up sheep" is prevalent among China's Kazak, Mongolian, and Tajik ethnic groups, while the Miao nationality celebrates a day known as the "Sheep and Horse Festival."

 ZODIAC ANIMAL FILE

Earthly Branch: *Wei*
Years of Birth: 2027, 2015, 2003, 1991, 1979, 1967, 1955, 1943, 1931…
Five Elements: *Wei* belongs to Earth
Five Constant Virtues: Earth belongs to Sincerity
Auspicious Directions: east, southeast, south
Auspicious Colors: green, red, purple
Lucky Numbers: 3, 9, 4
Lucky Flowers: carnation, primrose (harbinger of spring), fleur-de-lis
Lucky Gemstones: ruby, red coral, red tourmaline (rubellite)
Spiritual Protector: Vairocana
Choosing a name: For individuals born in the Year of the Sheep, it is appropriate to select characters with the radicals for metal (金), white (白), jade (玉), or grass (艹), signifying trustworthiness, loyalty, and profound learning; characters with the radicals

THE *WEI* SHEEP CREATES PROSPERITY AND PEACE

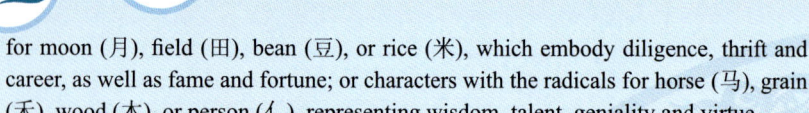

for moon (月), field (田), bean (豆), or rice (米), which embody diligence, thrift and career, as well as fame and fortune; or characters with the radicals for horse (马), grain (禾), wood (木), or person (亻), representing wisdom, talent, geniality and virtue.

THE SHEEP AND PERSONALITY

Strengths:
The Sheep's assets include a gentle demeanor, attention to detail, and strong problem-solving skills. People born in the Year of the Sheep are enterprising, highly driven and courageous individuals who are capable of enduring hardship. They have a strong thirst for knowledge, are cordial and sincere with others, and possess a noble and graceful bearing. Sheep are lovers of nature, and understand the importance of thriftiness. Females of this sign are virtuous and kindhearted, and like to take care of others.

Weaknesses:
The Sheep's limitations include emotional sensitivity, occasional pessimism, and the tendency to be hesitant or indecisive. People born in the Year of the Sheep tend to be resigned to their fate. They are also stubborn, fragile and timid.

THE SHEEP AND BLOOD TYPE

Blood Type A:
Sheep with blood type A are logical thinkers who are capable of seeing the big picture. They are amiable, sociable, and graceful, possess a strong team spirit, and enjoy cooperating with others. Sheep of this blood type are sympathetic, considerate, and show solicitude for others' difficulties.

Blood Type B:
Sheep with blood type B are cheerful, poised and popular with others; capable of accomplishing tasks and solving problems; and good at making friends from all walks of life. They are capable of methodical planning, prefer order and cleanliness in their environment, and excel at performing household duties. Sheep of this blood type are

blood type are able to convey their own style and individuality in a natural way.

Blood Type AB:
Sheep with blood type AB know how to choose the right attire. They are pleasant and likeable; speak with modesty; and enjoys good relations with others. While their personality may change frequently, they remain principled at all times. They are sympathetic towards others and like small animals.

eloquent, sharp-witted speakers, able to sustain reality but never willing to give up.

Blood Type O:
Sheep with blood type O have an extroverted personality but are usually fairly quiet. They do not worry about minor details, but tend to have an irritable temper and be calculating and scheming. Sheep of this

A light in shape of sheep

 THE SHEEP AND FORTUNE

Lifetime Fortune: Overview

People born in the Year of the Sheep often have strong religious beliefs, practice filial piety, and are refined, courteous and warmhearted. They tend to pay attention to their own appearance, and like to lead a life of peace and tranquility.

Career:
Females born in the Year of the Sheep are bound to have a smooth and successful career. Males of this sign should avoid pursuing risky or unstable professions, and adopt a simple and direct approach in their endeavors.

THE *WEI* SHEEP CREATES PROSPERITY AND PEACE

Financial Luck:
Sheep have a fairly stable financial outlook, with few fluctuations in fortune but good prospects for wealth creation.

Romance:
Unmarried women born in the Year of the Sheep tend to have a blessed love life, in which their romantic wishes are fulfilled. Men, on the other hand, may face setbacks; as such, they should try to take is easy and stay optimistic.

Fortune and the Five Elements

A colored statue of Xin-Wei Deity

A colored statue of Gui-Wei Deity

Wood Sheep: Born in the Year of *Gui-Wei* (2003, 1943)
Wood Sheep are kind and genial, honest and virtuous, and full of sympathy for others. They possess high levels of resistance and vitality, and often live alone despite getting along very well with others. Wood Sheep enjoy the esteem of their superiors, leading to promotional opportunities. It is imperative that they take a hands-on approach in all their pursuits and avoid high-risk investments.

A colored statue of Ji-Wei Deity

Fire Sheep: Born in the Year of *Ji-Wei* (1979, 1919)
Fire Sheep are kindhearted, just and upright, and show strong personal loyalty. Their generous nature tends to ensure harmonious relations with friends. They pay little attention to minor gains and losses, but often lack objectivity, and may become sensitive, emotional, and suspicious. After a tiring youth, they will be rewarded with a life of stability and comfort. Although the Fire Sheep's career is one of good luck and smooth sailing, financial prospects are marked by changeability.

Earth Sheep: Born in the Year of *Xin-Wei* (1991, 1931)
Earth Sheep possess a number of positive traits: they are just and upright; honest and innocent; soft and gentle; and graceful and elegant. Always doing their utmost to help

friends, Earth Sheep are in turn blessed throughout their lives with the help of others. They enjoy a smooth and successful career and a destiny of peace and happiness.

Metal Sheep: Born in the Year of *Yi-Wei* (2015, 1955)

Metal Sheep are kindhearted and possess inner strength in spite of a gentle exterior. They are highly conscientious, and prefer to work according to plan in a step-by-step manner. While Metal Sheep are well-suited to become entrepreneurs, they sometimes lack flexibility and adhere rigidly and stubbornly to principles. By specializing in a specific skill or technology, the Metal Sheep is destined to for immeasurable success. The Metal Sheep enjoys solid financial prospects throughout life and stable luck overall.

A colored statue of Y*i*-Wei Deity

Water Sheep: Born in the Year of *Ding-Wei* (1967, 1907)

Water Sheep are highly gifted, with a matching level of self-confidence. They consider others in all they do, are easy to get along with, and never get hung up over personal gains or losses. Nonetheless, they are still bound to suffer upsets now and then. The Water Sheep has excellent career prospects, and is best-suited to work as a researcher or in the field of technology.

A colored statue of Ding-Wei Deity

Hardship is likely to be suffered during youth; however, mid-life will be marked by stability, followed by happiness and comfort in old age. Regardless of gender, the Water Sheep is destined to have a blissful family life.

Fortune by the Year

In the Year of the Rat, Sheep are likely to make career advances and enjoy brisk business. Despite the fact that luck is good, the Sheep should prepare for contingencies and exercise caution toward year-end.

In the Year of the Ox, Sheep will face a combination of good and ill fortune and a series of ups and downs. As there are likely to be frequent quarrels, the Sheep should try to show forbearance and adopt a conciliatory approach.

In the Year of the Tiger, Sheep are destined to enjoy good luck and meet with few obstacles, but need to be on the look-out for vile characters. Despite the fact that overall luck is good, the year is also likely to bring disaster or adversity.

In the Year of the Rabbit, Sheep are blessed with good economic prospects; financial

losses are virtually nonexistent. However, there are likely to be ups and downs in the Sheep's reputation, as well as unforeseen calamity.

In the Year of the Dragon, Sheep will run around busily but ultimately in vain. The Sheep may encounter a major dispute around mid-year, but there is also likely to be an unexpected financial windfall.

In the Year of the Snake, Sheep will see their wishes fulfilled and reign victorious in all their pursuits. However, they must maintain integrity even when counting their profits, or bad return will inevitably follow.

In the Year of the Horse, Sheep will meet with smooth sailing and surefire success in all their pursuits. It is an unusually auspicious year for the Sheep by all measures.

A pair of stone sheep standing in front of an ancient building

The sheep is also common image in brick carving.

In the Year of the Sheep, Sheep are likely to come up against a great deal of frustration, as well as physical discomfort and minor ailments.

In the Year of the Monkey, Sheep will be blessed with great happiness, all-around success, and an absence of conflict and hassle.

In the Year of the Rooster, Sheep are liable to suffer from ill fortune. However, by exercising moderation and restraint, they can ensure that the year passes without incident.

In the Year of the Dog, Sheep are advised to watch over their assets and avoid traveling on business. They should also exercise prudence and caution in all their endeavors.

In the Year of the Pig, Sheep are likely to encounter setbacks in both their social life and career, and see few opportunities for promotion. By year-end, however, some success can be achieved.

THE SHEEP AND THE WESTERN ZODIAC

 Sheep-Aries:
Sheep-Aries are creative, self-supporting, happy and childlike. They place a high value on freedom, but are highly sensitive and tend to get hurt easily. Despite a rebellious streak, they enjoy taking care of their family.

 Sheep-Taurus:
Sheep-Tauruses tend to have a sluggish temperament and be lacking in foresight, but nevertheless are quick-witted, steady and reliable. They lead a cheerful and contented life, and prefer not to argue over trivial details.

 Sheep-Gemini:
Sheep-Geminis tend to have a highly changeable temperament. Perfectionistic by nature, they often become pessimistic or disheartened in the face of reality. Despite being quick-witted, resourceful and artistically gifted, Sheep-Geminis are often highly conflicted inside.

 Sheep-Cancer:
Sheep-Cancers tend to pursue a life of comfort and stability, often leading to their own exhaustion. Sociable and gregarious by nature, they are destined to have a lot of friends, and their keen wit and sense of humor bring smiles and happiness to those around them.

 Sheep-Leo:
Sheep-Leos are inherently smart, clever, and imaginative. Highly driven by nature, there is virtually no task of which they are incapable. They are skilled at self-control and self-protection, and generally ignore the criticisms of others.

 Sheep-Virgo:
Sheep-Virgos are frequently influenced by other people, become anxious or agitated easily, and tend

A sculpture of sheep in the Garden of Twelve Zodiac Animals in Jiangxi Province

A gold ornament of the "three sheep creating peace and prosperity"

to air their grievances and complain a lot. However, they are also meticulous and quick-witted, and able to apply a vivid imagination to their work to produce outstanding results.

THE *WEI* SHEEP CREATES PROSPERITY AND PEACE

Sheep-Libra:

Sheep-Librans are easily offended, like to argue with others, and may act superficially or hastily at times. They are also highly creative, possess a rich imagination, and enjoy cultural activities as well as classical artistic beauty.

Sheep-Scorpio:

Sheep-Scorpios tend to be fragile, but are thorough and meticulous in their work. They have a fascination for anything and everything as well as an affinity for the new and novel, and are able to generate highly creative ideas and plans.

Sheep-Sagittarius:

Sheep-Sagittarians are clear-headed, richly experienced, meticulous in their endeavors, and decisive in their judgment. They are courteous and polite to others, full of vitality always willing to go the extra mile for their family, and have the ability to get things done.

Sheep-Capricorn:

Sheep-Capricorns are determined, resilient, and down-to-earth. Most of their energy is focused on achieving a name for themselves, and at times they may be disingenuous. They also demonstrate flexibility and the ability to adapt to changing circumstances.

Sheep-Aquarius:

Sheep-Aquarians exhibit clear-minded thinking and often have many novel ideas. They are thoughtful, cautious and highly focused, and are able to recognize and rectify their own shortcomings. Though Sheep-Aquarians may behave eccentrically or frivolously at times, they are actually quite conscientious and determined.

Sheep-Pisces:

Sheep-Piscees possess a strong memory and have well-defined goals. Choosing to live according to their own ideology, they tend to reject outmoded conventions and the evil interference or intervention of others. Sheep-Pisces are seemingly oblivious to the trifles of everyday life, and often have difficulty keeping their own affairs in order.

A New Year Picture depicting the "three sheep creating peace and prosperity"

Sheep pouches

FENGSHUI AND THE SHEEP

Sheep tend to give people the impression of being docile, clever, obstinate and steadfast. In the study of *fengshui*, therefore, the sheep does not completely fit the label of being an "auspicious creature." In order to utilize *fengshui* sheep to enhance financial prospects, three entire sheep are required. With respect to material selection, the sheep should be gold or gold-plated; porcelain is also acceptable. It is imperative to avoid using only the sheep's head, as this could engender an evil spirit and lead to illness. The placement of *fengshui* sheep can also enhance a person's patience and determination. The best choice of orientation is the south-southwest of one's workplace or the main hall of one's home; north-northeast locations should be avoided. Because the earthly branches *Chou* and *Wei* are mutually conflicting, people born in the Year of the Ox should avoid the use of *fengshui* sheep.

INTERPRETING SHEEP DREAMS

If a man dreams of a sheep, he will strike it rich.

If a woman dreams of a sheep, she will enjoy a blissful married life with and grow old together with her husband.

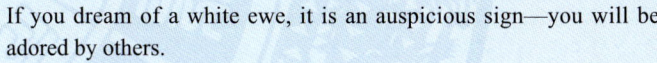

If you dream of a white ewe, it is an auspicious sign—you will be adored by others.

If you dream of trimming a ewe's fleece, you will come into an inheritance.

If you dream of riding a sheep onto the street, you will make a fortune.

HEALTH SECRETS

People born in the Year of the Sheep possess strong vitality, despite a fragile outward appearance. From mid-life onwards, they should pay increased attention to taking care of their health. Sheep are likely to suffer from minor gastrointestinal problems, and thus should adjust their dietary habits as necessary. In addition, Sheep would be advised to reduce their workload and eliminate pressure from their lives as appropriate.

THE *WEI* SHEEP CREATES PROSPERITY AND PEACE

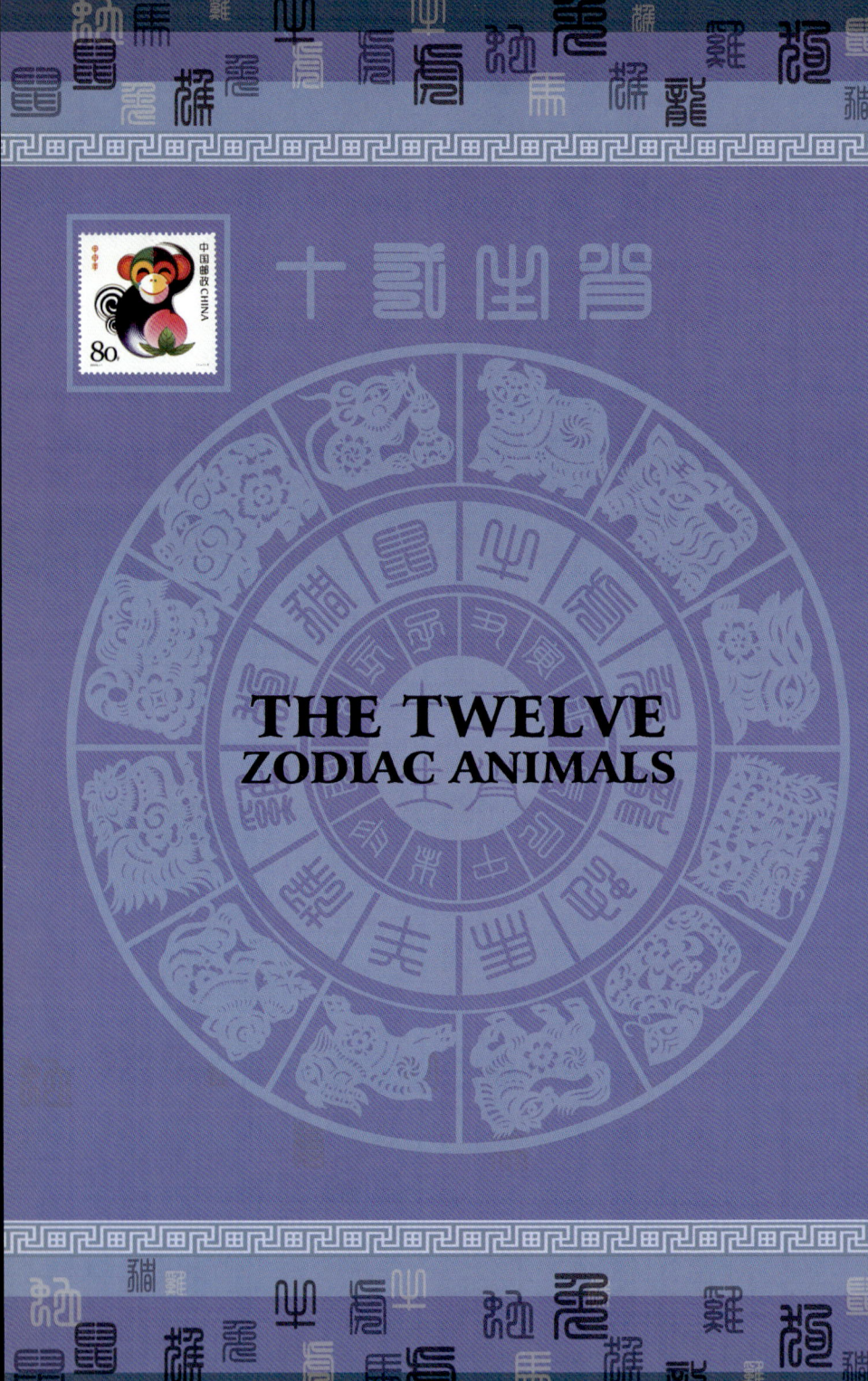

PART 9
THE *SHEN* MONKEY HAS SPECIAL PROWESS

【MONKEY】

THE *SHEH* MONKEY HAS SPECIAL PROWESS

The *shen*-hour refers to the period of time between 3:00pm and 5:00pm. One explanation attributes the pairing of the monkey with *shen* to the fact that monkeys like to howl, extend their arms and jump around at this time of day. Another possible reason is that the Chinese character for the earthly branch *shen* has the same pronunciation as the character for "extend". Finally, some ancient texts record the meaning of *shen* as "ring" (*huan*), which in ancient times was homophonous with the word for "ape", a relative of the monkey. Ultimately, the actual reason why *shen* was paired with the monkey is indeterminable. It is equally difficult to know which specific primate species was originally designated by *shen*; this is because the monkey, as it is known today, was referred to in ancient texts by a variety of names, some of which designated, for example, orangutans or apes. Perhaps the reason that the monkey was selected is because of its unique kinship with humankind.

The bronze monkey head once adorned the Old Summer Palace

In the Chinese language, the word for "monkey" is pronounced as *hou*. The ancient text *Bai Hu Tong Yi* states that the Chinese character for "monkey" was homophonous with the word for "observe". The same text also describes monkeys as standing in high places and looking around to observe whether the trap-

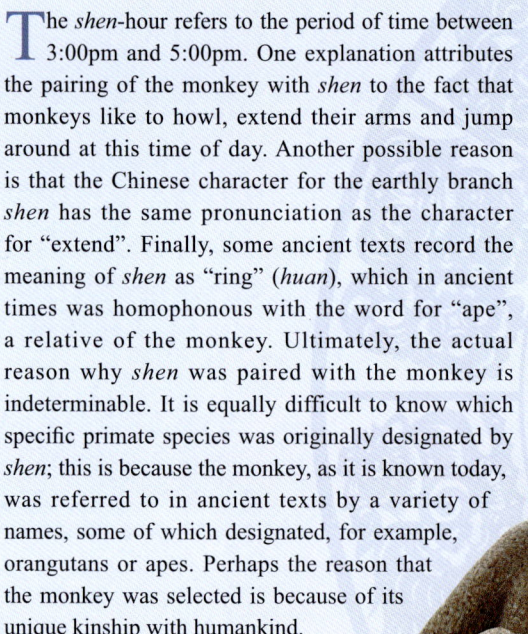

THE TWELVE ZODIAC ANIMALS

A drawing of a baby monkey carried by an older monkey, meaning that a family would be conferred marquis for generations

A golden monkey

setting humans had left. The original meaning of *hou* was "observe". It is apparent, therefore, that the early Chinese people were well aware of the monkey's smart and vigilant nature.

In ancient times, the monkey was regarded as an auspicious creature because it had the same pronunciation with the word "Marquis". As many ancient Chinese people wanted to be promoted Marquis (or above), the monkey thus became a symbol of promotion. For this reason, many lucky patterns related to the monkey were created. For example, a pattern with a bee and monkey meant that someone would be conferred marquis; a pattern with a monkey riding a horse meant that someone would soon be conferred marquis; and a pattern with a baby monkey carried by an older monkey meant that a family would be conferred marquis for generations. These patterns are found on the screens of ancient feudal officials, as well as on sketches, writing sets, household wares, and jade carvings.

A New Year gift: a monkey sending the wish that the money and treasures will be plentiful

In Beijing's White Cloud Temple, there is a monkey-related folk custom known as "Touching the Stone Monkeys". It is said that, at the temple, there are three stone monkeys in different places. If someone finds these monkeys and touches them, he or she will be blessed, preclude disaster, and cure disease. When the spring temple fair is held, people flood in to touch the stone monkeys; the monkeys become smooth and bright from all the touching. This event has become a great spectacle at the White Cloud Temple. In Beijing, there is a famous handicraft known as the "furry monkey". It is composed of the traditional Chinese medicinal ingredients lily magnolia and

THE *SHEN* MONKEY HAS SPECIAL PROWESS

A clay sculpture of "the monkeys holding a birthday peach"

A sculpture of monkey in the Garden of Twelve Zodiac Animals in Jiangxi Province

played an indispensable role in the circus. Monkey tricks were already mentioned among the "hundred palace shows" of the Han Dynasty writings and became prevalent during the Tang Dynasty. It is said that Emperor Zhaozong of the Tang Dynasty, as he fled into exile, took his monkey and tamer with him; this indicates the great degree to which he was consumed by the monkey tricks. After the Song Dynasty (960-1279), monkey tricks cicada slough; lily magnolia is used for the monkey's body and the cicada shell is used for the head and four limbs. There is even a legend about the furry monkey. It is said that, during the Qing Dynasty, a man who worked in a medicinal herb store and was often bullied by an accountant made the furry monkey to satirize the accountant. The furry monkey thus grew popular in society and became a handicraft item. These furry monkeys in all shapes and sizes were lively and lifelike, and could be made using simple materials. The furry monkey reflects the daily life of old Beijing natives, as well as their wit and sense of humor. In addition to the "furry monkey", many other monkey toys — including the "mud monkey", "bamboo monkey" and "cloth monkey" — are welcomed and enjoyed by children across China. The monkey is also an important subject in paper-cuttings and New Year's paintings. Frequently seen images of the monkey include the "monkesy snatch away straw hats", "monkeys fish up the moon", and "monkeys hold birthday peaches".

The monkey is a sympathetic and understanding creature, and one that is highly skilled in the art of imitation. As a result, monkeys have always

flourished in popularity among the people. During the early Ming Dynasty, Prime Minister Hu Weiyong raised over ten monkeys and dressed them in clothing; the monkeys were trained to serve wine and kneel down before the guests. In Chinese society, it was also asserted that raising monkeys could thwart horse illness. Many people who raised horses, therefore, also raised monkeys in their stables. The *Herbalist's Manual*, compiled by Li Shizhen (1519-1593), a physician and pharmacologist of the Ming Dynasty, claimed that "raising female monkeys could immunize against horse illness." This claim was later borrowed by Wu Cheng'en (1500-1582), a novelist of the Ming Dynasty, who created the character of the Monkey King and gave him the official position of *Bimawen* for taking charge of of horses.

The Monkey King, Sun Wukong, may be considered the most famous monkey in Chinese culture. He is the leading role of *Journey to the West*, one of the Four Great Classical Novels of Chinese literature. This novel is based on the story of the Tang Dynasty monk Xuanzang, who sets out on a pilgrimage to the West for Buddhist scripture. In the story, Sun Wukong, Zhu Bajie and Sha Wujing team up to protect Xuanzang, kill the demons and finally arrive in the West to obtain the scripture. Following its release, the novel spread far and wide over the world; enjoying sustained popularity, it has been translated into dozens of languages and adapted for a variety of local operas, movies, television dramas, cartoons and caricatures. As the leading role, the Monkey King is seen throughout the story. He is known to all Chinese and appreciated for his great ability, abhorrence of evil as a deadly foe, and for being fearless, daring, persistent and dauntless.

Today, many idioms and vulgarisms about monkeys still can be heard. No matter how monkey tries to please

It is equally difficult to know which specific primate species was originally designated by *shen*; this is because the monkey, as it is known today, was referred to in ancient texts by a variety of names, some of which designated, for example, orangutans or apes.

THE *SHEN* MONKEY HAS SPECIAL PROWESS

humankind, disparaging or scoffing evaluations of the monkey seem to outnumber those of praise or respect. For example, the phrase "sharp month and monkey cheeks" describes an emaciated appearance; "a monkey in beautiful clothes cannot hide the ugliness inside" is used to mock people who, in order to gain status and authority, become lackeys of the rich and powerful; "play ghost and shake off monkey" is used to describe a child who is terribly naughty; "killing a chicken in front of a monkey" is used to make an example out of someone in order to frighten others. Monkey-related vulgarisms are even more unsparing. For instance, "monkey rides in a sedan chair" means not knowing how to appreciate someone's kindness; "the monkey is reading" refers to someone who gives the false appearance of being refined; "the monkey sweeps the floor" means living in the present and lacking foresight. If a mediocre person is charged with an important mission, he or she is the monkey king among the blind animals. When adherents disperse, the situation is described by the expression "When the tree falls, the monkeys scatter."

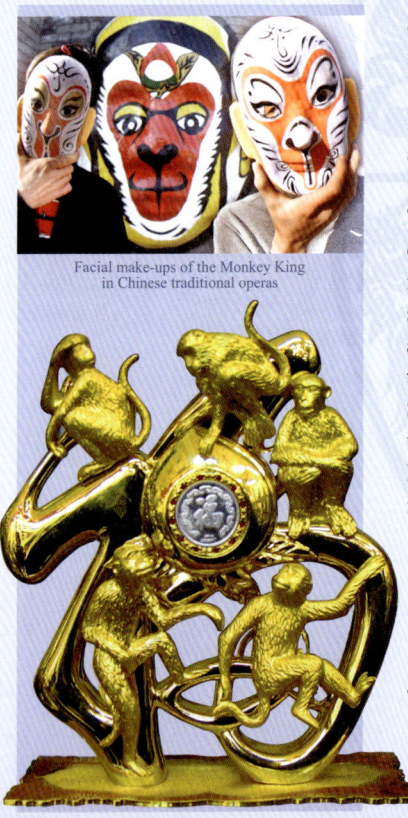

Facial make-ups of the Monkey King in Chinese traditional operas

In addition to its role in language, the active and nimble monkey has been responsible for enriching China's sports events. Hua Tuo, a famous and highly skilled physician of the Eastern Han Dynasty (25-220), imitated animals' postures and created a set of treatments for body-building known as "Five-Animal Exercises"; monkeys, too, were imitated in these exercises. Some of the patterns in the silk paintings unearthed at Mawangdui (in Changsha, Hunan Province) contain images of humans imitating monkeys. The monkey's actions are also absorbed in the Chinese martial arts of wuxingquan, liuhequan and xingyiquan, and many of the skills of these martial art forms are named after the monkey. Additionally, the martial arts of "Monkey Boxing" and "Monkey Stick" are based entirely on imitations of the monkey, demonstrating its speed, agility and alertness.

170 THE TWELVE ZODIAC ANIMALS

ZODIAC ANIMAL FILE

Earthly Branch: *Shen*
Years of Birth: 2028, 2016, 2004, 1992, 1980, 1968, 1956, 1944, 1932…
Five Elements: *Shen* belongs to Metal
Five Constant Virtues: Metal belongs to Righteousness
Auspicious Directions: north, northwest, west
Auspicious Colors: white, gold, blue
Lucky Numbers: 1, 8, 7
Lucky Flowers: chrysanthemum
Lucky Gemstones: topaz, diamond, amber, white pyramid crystal
Spiritual Protector: Vairocana
Choosing a name: For individuals born in the Year of the Monkey, it is appropriate to select characters with the radicals for wood (木) or grain (禾), signifying moral uprightness, comfort and joy, and success and prosperity; characters with the radicals for metal (金), jade (玉), bean (豆), or rice (米), which embody beauty, multiple talents, joy and prosperity; characters with the radicals for field (田), mountain (山), or moon (月), embodying integrity, honesty, fame and wealth; or characters with the radicals for water (氵) or person (亻), representing wisdom and courage.

THE MONKEY AND PERSONALITY

Strengths:
The Monkey's assets include a strong thirst for knowledge, an astonishing memory, and the ability to seize and capitalize on opportunities. People born in the Year of the Monkey are sharp-minded, intelligent, vivacious and active. They are eloquent speakers who possess a very strong desire for self-expression. Monkeys adapt easily to changing environments, and are able to act according to the circumstances. Tenacious and determined by nature, they are never willing to give up or admit defeat.

THE *SHEN* MONKEY HAS SPECIAL PROWESS

Weaknesses:

The Monkey's limitations include self-righteousness and the tendency to boast and exaggerate. People born in the Year of the Monkey are shortsighted, frivolous, vain, and fickle in affection. They also lack staying power and rarely see tasks through to completion.

THE MONKEY AND BLOOD TYPE

Blood Type A:

Monkeys with blood type A are sharp-witted and shrewd, easy-going and amicable, and love to be close to nature. While they tend to be fairly quiet, they are highly sociable and have an optimistic attitude toward life. Male Monkeys of this blood type often possess strong leadership skills and enjoy participating in team sports.

Blood Type B:

Monkeys with blood type B are bright and agile, courageous and enterprising,

A carving of a monkey riding a horse, meaning that someone would soon be conferred marquis

natural and unrestrained, opinionated and insightful, and quick-witted and perceptive. They are rational in their manner, demonstrate strong organizational skills, and have a variety of interests. Monkeys of this blood type also have a cheerful personality, and tend not to worry about minor details.

Blood Type O:

Monkeys with blood type O are resolute and fortitudinous, calm and composed, and calculating and shrewd. They tend to be profit-oriented, emphasizing short-term gains and lacking long-term vision; they also like to receive small benefits and favors from others. Monkeys of this blood type are highly gifted speakers, whose words are filled with wisdom.

Blood Type AB:

Monkeys with blood type AB are inherently gifted, perceptive and insightful; face challenges with courage; and have the ability to subdue others without their

The stone carving of a monkey on a fisherman's back, Baoding Mountain Grottoes, Chongqing

knowing it. They have a knack for maintaining good relations with other people and are unlikely to stir up trouble. However, Monkeys of this blood type should learn to develop greater patience as well as the ability to view situations from a wider angle.

THE MONKEY AND FORTUNE

Lifetime Fortune: Overview

People born in the Year of the Monkey are vivacious and active, clever and multi-talented, and chivalrous and well-mannered. However, they also have a tendency to exaggerate and tell lies. Only by overcoming this flaw can Monkeys achieve success and fortune.

Career:
Monkeys tend to have stable and smooth careers; they possess strong entrepreneurial skills as well as the ability to exploit new business opportunities. With staying power, a strong worth ethic, and plans which are both detailed and realistic, Monkeys are destined to achieve success. Those in the working class are also likely to meet with pay-raise opportunities.

Financial Luck:
Monkeys are likely to have excellent luck in monetary matters, with prospects for large increases in personal income. However, they need to be vigilant against possible financial swindles.

A gold monkey "awakens" the spring

Romance:
Monkeys have deep affection for elder members of their family, but tensions and disputes commonly arise between husband and wife. In addition, extramarital affairs are prevalent among people born in the Year of the Monkey. Singles are likely to become highly emotional, but this tendency can be overcome by finding a romantic partner.

Fortune and the Five Elements

Wood Monkey: Born in the Year of *Geng-Shen* (1980, 1920)
Wood Monkeys possess high ambitions, a sympathetic heart, and a keen sense of

A colored statue of Jia-Shen Deity

A colored statue of Bing-Shen Deity

time. With a strong sense of responsibility and dedication to their work, they always strive to complete every task. The results they achieve are likely to lead to recognition by their superiors and promotional opportunities. Despite a conservative tendency, the Wood Monkey is an enthusiastic and committed romantic partner. Wood Monkeys are also able to weather the occasional marital dispute and enjoy a long and happy marriage.

Fire Monkey: Born in the Year of *Bing-Shen* (2016, 1956)

Fire Monkeys are smart, enthusiastic, bold and daring. Their lofty ideals, strong business mind, and driven nature pave the way to their success. However, they tend to act impetuously at times or bite off more than they can chew, leading to a series of ups and downs in their lives. The Fire Monkey is blessed with a happy family and sound financial prospects. On the whole, career prospects are stable with some upward mobility.

Earth Monkey: Born in the Year of *Wu-Shen* (1968, 1908)

Earth Monkeys are down-to-earth, studious, hard-working, and modest. They have an optimistic and candid personality, and believe in work before play. Youth is likely to be toilsome, but Earth Monkeys can make their way in the world by specializing in a special skill. By establishing a personal business, they have the chance to amass a sizeable fortune. From middle age onwards, life is likely to become comfortable. Financial prospects are good, with the occasional windfall. Earth Monkeys tend to have a weak physical constitution. However, by watching their diet and getting sufficient rest and exercise, health and fitness can be improved.

Metal Monkey: Born in the Year of *Ren-Shen* (1992, 1932)

Metal Monkeys are clever and cunning, eloquent and articulate, valiant and resolute, and tend to be stubborn and hot-headed as well. They are often conceited in their intellect and enjoy playing tricks on others. Only by curbing their frivolous

A colored statue of Wu-Shen Deity

A colored statue of Geng-Shen Deity

and impetuous ways can Metal Monkeys increase their popularity and improve career prospects. It is important to remember, however, that becoming self-supporting is the first step toward making a fortune. The "Metal Monkey" should avoid marrying at a young age, or else they may face an instable marriage filled with ups and downs.

Water Monkey: Born in the Year of *Jia-Shen* (2004, 1944)

Water Monkeys are smart and clever, and possess solid leadership skills. However, they tend to be arrogant and like to show off, eliciting a negative reaction in others. This, in turn, can create a series of barriers in the Water Monkey's career. To improve social and work relations, Water Monkeys should keep their ego in check. As long as they bring their abilities into play, they are bound to achieve enviable success. The Water Monkey also has outstanding luck in romance, getting along well with members of the opposite sex and often receiving their invaluable support. Married life, too, is destined to be blissful and harmonious. While the Water Monkey's financial prospects tend to undulate, profits can still be made. An unforeseen windfall is also in the cards.

A colored statue of Ren-Shen Deity

Fortune by the Year

In the Year of the Rat, Monkeys will enjoy booming business and bumper profits. It is a year that is likely to be highly successful and may present opportunities for career advancement. With the support of others and good luck all around, Monkeys should feel free to pursue their endeavors with boldness and courage.

In the Year of the Ox, Monkeys are likely to see smooth sailing in their business pursuits away from home. The beginning of the year may bring along disappointments or minor incidents, while physical ailments and financial outflows may arise at year-end. Health will soon be restored, however, and the year will ultimately pass incident-free.

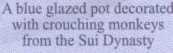

A blue glazed pot decorated with crouching monkeys from the Sui Dynasty

In the Year of the Tiger, Monkeys will face instability and a mixture of ill luck and good fortune. If they decide to pursue

endeavors away from home, Monkeys should be extra cautious and avoid getting caught up in disputes. Marriages are also likely to face difficulties this year.

In the Year of the Rabbit, Monkeys will meet with success on all sides. There is likely to be some trouble or minor adversity, but this should not be cause for alarm. It is also a good year for Monkeys to pursue out-of-town romantic interests.

In the Year of the Dragon, Monkeys will enjoy uninterrupted success and excellent financial prospects, as the efforts of past years finally come to fruition. However, the Monkey should exercise caution when making new friends to circumvent being framed by despicable lowlifes.

In the Year of the Snake, Monkeys are likely to face a serious disease or ailment. By receiving prompt treatment, however, the potential calamity can be deflected.

In the Year of the Horse, Monkeys will be blessed with good luck all around and their lives will overflow with exuberance. Monkeys will also enjoy excellent financial prospects, with investments reaping profits and income coming in from multiple sources.

In the Year of the Sheep, Monkeys are likely to be successful in their business pursuits and enjoy strong returns on their investments.

In the Year of the Monkey, Monkeys will be blessed with familial joy. However, they may find themselves in low spirits or suffering from

THE TWELVE ZODIAC ANIMALS

headaches. They should take extra care to protect their financial assets this year.

In the Year of the Rooster, Monkeys will see their efforts rewarded and their hard work pay dividends. However, they may find themselves mentally exhausted, and are unlikely to make any gains after autumn.

In the Year of the Dog, Monkeys will find themselves down on their luck. They may have difficulty settling down and getting on with their pursuits. However, by exercising due caution, the Monkey's luck is likely to turn around.

In the Year of the Pig, Monkeys are likely to suffer unexpected financial losses, face legal action, and be plagued by headaches or other physical ailments. Fortunately, however, the year will pass with no major calamities.

 ## THE MONKEY AND THE WESTERN ZODIAC

Monkey-Aries:

Monkey-Aries can be characterized as being frank and candid, intelligent and sharp-witted, and possessing patience and fortitude. They have a tendency to gossip and are often willing to do whatever is necessary to reach a goal, but are also able to show understanding and sympathy for others. Monkey Aries are very charming and get along well with others, but often prefer to live a solitary existence. Their keen discriminative skills make them virtually immune to the trickery and deception of others.

Monkey-Taurus:

Monkey-Tauruses have a steady temperament, maintaining vigor even in times of sorrow. Highly introspective by nature, they are unlikely to blame

THE *SHEN* MONKEY HAS SPECIAL PROWESS

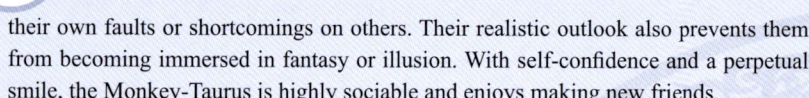

their own faults or shortcomings on others. Their realistic outlook also prevents them from becoming immersed in fantasy or illusion. With self-confidence and a perpetual smile, the Monkey-Taurus is highly sociable and enjoys making new friends.

Monkey-Gemini:
Monkey-Geminis are extremely restless by nature and tend to indulge in exaggeration. They are efficient in their work, not doing something unless it is necessary. With a level of creativity, they also enjoy trying new things and like to ponder that which is new and novel. Monkey-Geminis are independent, have a strong sense of responsibility, and possess their own unique style.

Monkey-Cancer:
Monkey-Cancers are level-headed, resourceful, and liberal in their thinking. Despite being good problem-solvers, they are inclined to give up easily and are often willing to sacrifice themselves for others. Monkey-Cancers also have a tendency to be possessive and oversensitive.

Monkey-Leo:
Monkey-Leos are naturally inquisitive, positive and upbeat, unwavering in their convictions, and unafraid of challenge. They are strong survivalists who like to inquire and explore, and are willing to do anything for their friends. With a down-to-earth personality and preference for orderliness, Monkey-Leos are able to maintain an ideal frame of mind at all times.

Monkey-Virgo:
Monkey-Virgos have an elegant and graceful bearing, and show generosity to others. They also have outstanding vision and foresight, combined with a keen understanding of human nature. As sticklers for detail, Monkey-Virgos often require each and every aspect of a matter to be addressed. They are possessive and controlling by nature, tend to lack a

sense of security, and enjoy prying into the affairs of others.

Monkey-Libra:
Monkey-Librans are naturally gifted in literature and language, and highly expressive and eloquent. They have strong observational skills, but can be indecisive at times and tend to lack confidence. Monkey-Librans gravitate toward a lifestyle of relaxation, comfort and joy.

Monkey-Scorpio:
Monkey-Scorpios are extremely creative, full of vigor,

A jade carving of "the monkey offering the birthday felicitations to an elderly person on his birthday"

The Three Wise Monkeys, a famous pictorial maxim in Japan probably originally came from China. It is similar with the phrase in the *Analects of Confucius*: Look not at what is contrary to propriety; listen not to what is contrary to propriety; speak not what is contrary to propriety.

vivacious and even a bit foolish. They are able to undertake and complete complex tasks, often achieving exceptional results. Resorting to evil tricks when necessary, Monkey-Scorpios are skilled at helping others to escape from difficult predicaments.

Monkey-Sagittarius:
Monkey-Sagittarians are inherently honest, selfless, courageous and resolute. They have the passion to undertake difficult tasks and the ability to delve into the essence of the matter at hand. Their sunny disposition and other positive traits enable them to attract and convince others. With organizational and leadership skills, combined with a penchant for power and profits, Monkey-Sagittarians are well-suited to a career in politics.

THE *SHEN* MONKEY HAS SPECIAL PROWESS

Monkey-Capricorn:

Monkey-Capricorns are naturally gifted, sharp-witted, precise, and self-assured. They prefer order in their lives and are averse to clutter and chaos. Diligent, active, and on the go, they never stop moving forward in their endeavors. The Monkey-Capricorn tends to have a dual personality.

Monkey-Aquarius:

Monkey-Aquarians are strong-minded, agile, gifted and versatile. Placing an emphasis on practical results, they are often able to achieve extraordinary accomplishments. Monkey-Aquarians tend to be indifferent to fame and wealth.

Monkey-Pisces:

Monkey-Piscees have a natural air of mystery and are highly attractive and alluring to others. They are sharp-minded and possess worldly wisdom, but are not snobbish. They tend to be highly calculative and take their own interest into account in everything they do. Despite a tendency sometimes to carry their actions too far, Monkey-Pisceses also know how to restrain themselves when appropriate.

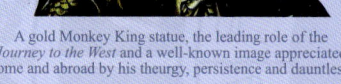

A gold Monkey King statue, the leading role of the *Journey to the West* and a well-known image appreciated home and abroad by his theurgy, persistence and dauntless.

FENGSHUI AND THE MONKEY

The clay sculpture of the Monkey King Making Havoc in Heaven

The quick-witted, lively and cunning personality of monkeys is highly similar to that of humans. Sometimes, a child may be bashful and shy away from contact with the outside world. In this situation, placing a *fengshui* monkey at home (in a place easily discoverable by the child) can serve to gradually transform the child's shy tendency. However, if a child is already highly active

and vivacious, the use of a *fengshui* monkey — whether a painting or a sculpture — is likely to have negative repercussions on the child.

 ## INTERPRETING MONKEY DREAMS

If you dream of a monkey, you will be the victim of deception.

If you dream of a monkey running or jumping, it is a bad omen.

If you dream of a monkey squatting, you will fall ill.

If you dream of monkey viciously attacking you, a disaster will befall your family.

If you dream of a monkey getting angry, you will make enemies with your neighbor, and your reputation will be damaged.

If you dream of a monkey eating something, you will be faced with poverty.

 ## HEALTH SECRETS

People born in the Year of the Monkey often have a nervous temperament. They tend to expend too much physical energy, which may lead to diseases of the trachea. Monkeys should thus learn to practice self-regulation, reduce the pressure of life, exercise more frequently, and engage in more outdoor activities. Only by adopting these measures can they maintain good health.

THE *SHEN* MONKEY HAS SPECIAL PROWESS

THE TWELVE ZODIAC ANIMALS

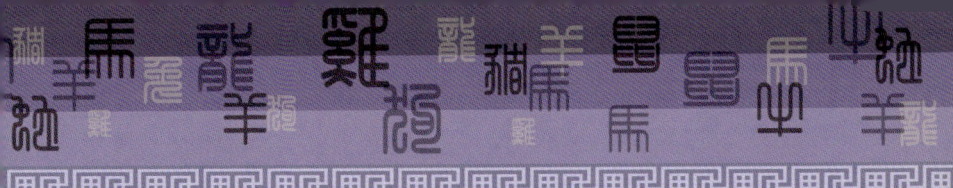

PART 10
THE AUSPICIOUS *YOU* ROOSTER

【ROOSTER】

THE AUSPICIOUS *YOU* ROOSTER

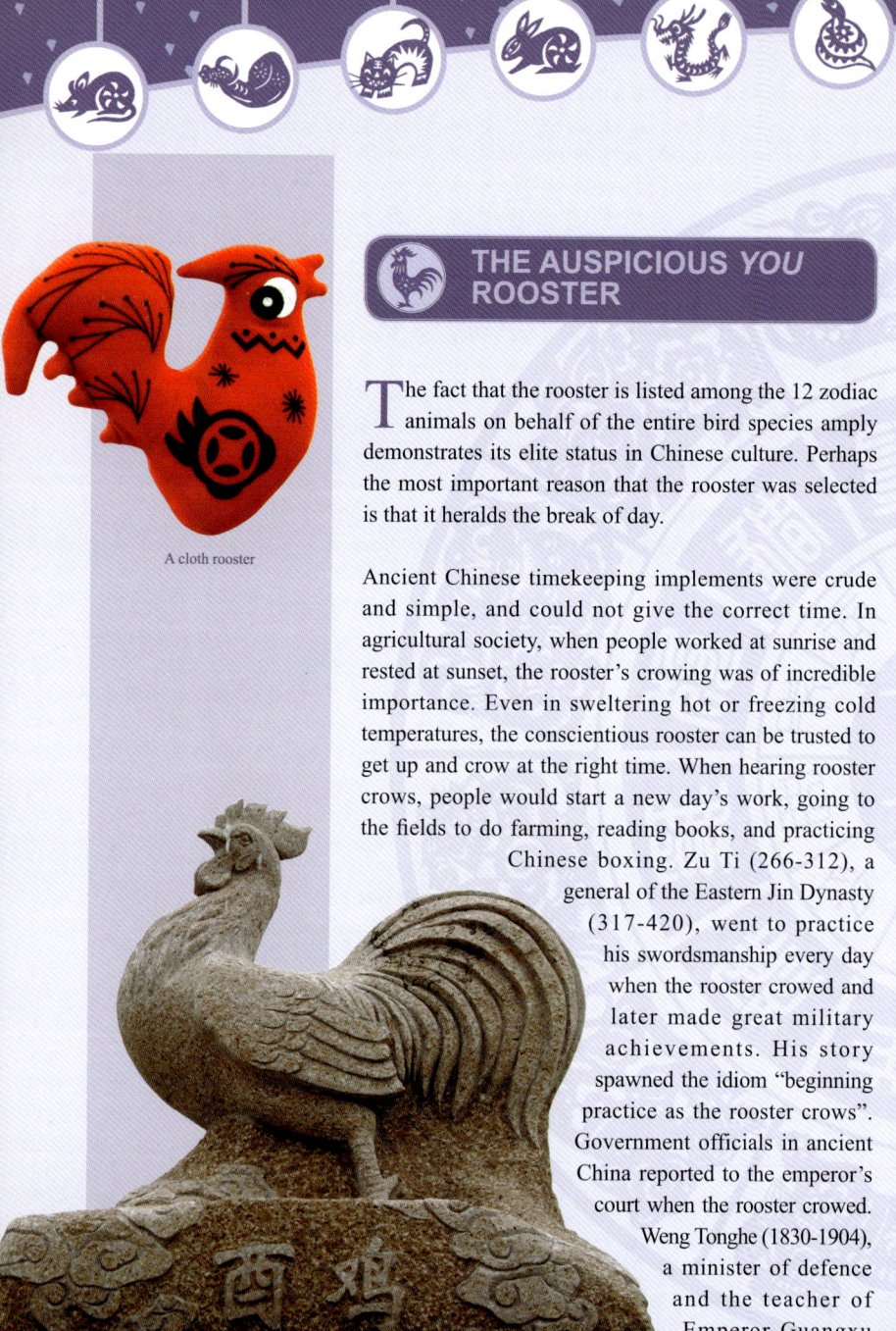

A cloth rooster

The fact that the rooster is listed among the 12 zodiac animals on behalf of the entire bird species amply demonstrates its elite status in Chinese culture. Perhaps the most important reason that the rooster was selected is that it heralds the break of day.

Ancient Chinese timekeeping implements were crude and simple, and could not give the correct time. In agricultural society, when people worked at sunrise and rested at sunset, the rooster's crowing was of incredible importance. Even in sweltering hot or freezing cold temperatures, the conscientious rooster can be trusted to get up and crow at the right time. When hearing rooster crows, people would start a new day's work, going to the fields to do farming, reading books, and practicing Chinese boxing. Zu Ti (266-312), a general of the Eastern Jin Dynasty (317-420), went to practice his swordsmanship every day when the rooster crowed and later made great military achievements. His story spawned the idiom "beginning practice as the rooster crows". Government officials in ancient China reported to the emperor's court when the rooster crowed. Weng Tonghe (1830-1904), a minister of defence and the teacher of Emperor Guangxu (1871-1980) during

the Qing Dynasty, is associated with the phrase "tying the loincloth at the rooster's crowing." In ancient times, the city gate was also opened when the rooster crowed. There is even a classical story about the rooster's crowing. During the Warring States Period, the high reputation of Lord Mengchang of Qi made the King of Qin suspicious and Lord Mengchang was placed under house arrest. Lord Mengchang tried to gain the king's trust by cheating, and then the king set him free. Lord Mengchang was afraid that the king would go back on his words, so he got back to the Qi State day and night. When he arrived at the Hangu Pass in Qin, the city gate was still closed. Lord Mengchang became anxious for fear that soldiers would chase him. At this moment, one of his men who was skilled at ventriloquism started to imitate a rooster crowing, and soon all the roosters in the city began to crow. The stunned gatekeepers opened the city gate, and Lord Mengchang successfully ran for his life. Indeed, the King of Qin regretted his decision, but it was too late to give chase.

The roosters made of the chicken feather

The rooster was so highly valued in ancient times that it was known as the "fowl of five moralities". Its crest symbolizes an official's hat, so it has "cultural morality"; its back claws could be used for fighting, thus it has "military morality"; it can tussle with enemies in front of it, therefore it has the "morality of bravery"; when it has food, it will call out to the other roosters to eat together, so it has the "morality of humanity"; and it never fails to crow at dawn, so it has "morality of good faith". These moralities can be considered the moral laws and ideals of humanity. The fact that the rooster is described by these moral virtues shows the close relationship between the rooster and humankind.

The Chinese character for "rooster" is homophonous

THE AUSPICIOUS YOU ROOSTER

with the character for "auspicious". The rooster is thus a kind of substitute for good luck. In beatific words, patterns, folk-customs and legends, the rooster is used to represent auspiciousness, happiness, and beauty. There are many rooster-related place names in China, such as the famous city of Baoji (literally "Treasure Rooster") in Shaanxi Province. It is said that a mythical rooster once crowed there, which was regarded as an auspicious omen. In Sichuan and Liaoning provinces, there are mountains called the "Crest Mountains", and Xinyang, Henan Province features the "Rooster Mountain". Many hutongs and alleys in Beijing also received their names through shifts in pronunciation. For example, the "Rooster and Duck Market" became "Gather Scholars";

A Qing Dynasty glazed incense burner in the shape of a rooster

"Treasure Rooster Lane" became the "Lane of Assured Luck"; and "Rooster Claws Hutong" (also known as "Rooster Cover Hutong") acquired the name "Lucky Omen Hutong".

After the rooster crows, the sun will rise in the East. The rooster thus is regarded as the one which ousts darkness and brings brightness. In Mao Zedong's poems, there is a famous sentence: "When the rooster crows, the whole world brightens." This sentence shows the bright prospects of the Chinese nation. Many Chinese people also hold the view that the rooster can thwart evil. In the past, every family would paste up rooster paintings or

paper-cuttings on the doors and windows to dispel evil during the Spring Festival. There was also a superstition that on the first day of the tenth lunar month, ghosts would be set free. Because ghosts fear roosters' blood, roosters were to be killed on that day.

There are many interesting folk customs related to the rooster. Hebei and Shandong Province had an ancient wedding custom whereby a rooster was sent as betrothal gift, symbolizing that all will go well. Before the wedding, the bridegroom would prepare a red rooster and the bride would prepare a hen, indicating that she can bring good luck. When getting married, the bride's younger brother would hold the hen, which would come to the bridegroom's home before the rooster crowed. Because the rooster was still sleeping at that time, the waking hen had greater vigor than the rooster. This event indicates that the bride will not be "bullied" by the bridegroom after the two are wedded. The rooster and hen would not be killed, and the two were together known as "long-lived chickens". There is also a custom known as "the rooster kneels down", prevalent in some parts of southeast China, which is a wedding ceremony using a rooster as a substitute for the bridegroom to get married with the bride. If the bridegroom goes fishing that day and suffers storms so that he cannot come back in time for the wedding, the rooster will "substitute" for him. After the wedding ceremony, the roosters are tied with a piece of red cloth and locked in the bridal chamber. It is set free only when the groom returns. The Bai nationality of Yunnan Province has a custom of sending roosters

as gifts when a couple is married, a house is built, or a baby is born. In Shanxi province, a cloth rooster is sewed onto a child's sleeve during the Spring Festival, symbolizing an auspicious new year. In some parts of Zhejiang province, roosters

A commemorative coin issued in Chinese Rooster Year

A stone-carved paper-cutting rooster

THE AUSPICIOUS YOU ROOSTER

are killed on the day of the Magpie Festival. According to legend, the Cowherd and Weaving Maid are reunited that night. If not for the rooster's crow, the two of them would never be apart.

The phoenix is an extremely important mystical animal and auspicious symbol in Chinese culture; only the dragon has a higher status. The rooster — which has a crest, beak and claws similar to those of the phoenix — is also regarded as an important archetype of the phoenix. There is a saying that "a featherless phoenix is not as good as a rooster", which demonstrates the difference between the two creatures. Another saying, "the golden phoenix flies out of the rooster coop", seems to depict their relationship. In the olden days, the rooster was regarded as a mystical bird. The ancient Chinese used the rooster not only for driving out evil spirits and making sacrifices, but also for divining. The Jingpo people of China even used the rooster to judge legal cases. Each of the two parties involved in a lawsuit would carry a living rooster to an arranged place. After the sorcerer had chanted scripture, the two parties

A gold rooster

A phoenix-shaped cover of a Western Zhou Dynasty bronze-ware; the rooster is regarded as an important archetype of the phoenix.

would then set the two roosters free. Judgment on the case would be made according to the roosters' crowing. The party whose rooster crowed first would lose the lawsuit, while the rooster that crowed second would win the lawsuit for its party.

The chicken has always had a close relationship with the lives of the people of China. This bond is reflected in many Chinese idioms and folk adages about roosters and hens. For example, chores are described as "rooster feathers and garlic skins", and the big event of a woman usurping power and confusing policies is compared to "a hen controls morning". Other expressions include "the hen has flown away and the eggs have been broken"; "transfixed as a wooden rooster"; "killing the rooster to get the

eggs"; "a rooster and a dog which went up to heaven"; "like a crane standing among roosters"; "it is not necessary to kill a rooster with a knife for killing ox"; and "better to be a rooster's head than to be an ox's back". Because chicken is rich in nutrition and has tender meat, it is frequently seen on the menus of China's ethnic groups. Since ancient times, chicken has been a must in banquets. A few of the chicken dishes most famous in China are "*guifei* chicken", "beggar's chicken", "baizhan chicken" and "sauteed chicken cubes with chilli and peanuts".

ZODIAC ANIMAL FILE

Earthly Branch: *You*
Years of Birth: 2029, 2017, 2005, 1993, 1981, 1969, 1957, 1945, 1933…
Five Elements: *You* belongs to Metal
Five Constant Virtues: Metal belongs to Righteousness
Auspicious Directions: west, northwest, northeast
Auspicious Colors: gold, brownish yellow, yellow
Lucky Numbers: 7, 5, 8
Lucky Flowers: gladiola, garden balsam, celosia (cockscomb)
Lucky Gemstones: Amber, smoky quartz, rock crystal
Spiritual Protector: acalanatha
Choosing a name: For individuals born in the Year of the Rooster, it is appropriate to select characters with the radicals for rice (米), bean (豆), or insect (虫), signifying happiness, longevity and family prosperity; characters with the radicals for wood (木), grain (禾), jade (玉), or field (田), which embody joy and prosperity; characters with the radicals for moon (月), person (人), or roof (宀), which embody talent and intellect; or characters with the radicals for mountain (山), grass (艹), sun (日), or metal (金), representing intelligence and courage.

A commemorative silver coin issued in Chinese Rooster Year

THE ROOSTER AND PERSONALITY

Strengths:
The Rooster's assets include competence and calmness, diligence and discipline, enthusiasm and generosity, and candor and courage. People of this zodiac sign are trend-savvy, liberal-minded, and highly sociable. They consider matters with care and

THE AUSPICIOUS YOU ROOSTER

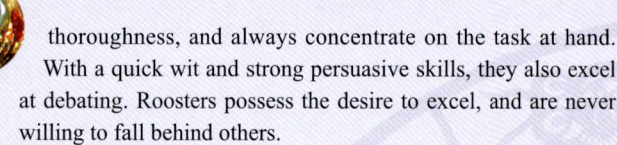

thoroughness, and always concentrate on the task at hand. With a quick wit and strong persuasive skills, they also excel at debating. Roosters possess the desire to excel, and are never willing to fall behind others.

Weaknesses:

The Rooster's limitations include a vain and irascible temperament, arrogance, conceit, as well as narrow-mindedness. People of this zodiac sign place strict demands on others, but are themselves unaccommodating and inflexible. Roosters tend to be emotionally changeable and preoccupied with their own self-interest. In addition, they are often self-complacent and like to blow their own trumpet. They speak unreservedly and without adequate prudence, which can impede their social interactions. Despite reluctance to accept others' counsel, Roosters themselves are only too eager to lecture others.

THE ROOSTER AND BLOOD TYPE

Blood Type A:

Roosters with blood type A are positive and optimistic, cheerful and amicable, diligent and resolute, and energetic and assiduous. Though they have a strong team spirit, their professional drive also instills them with competitiveness. Roosters of this blood type have varying degrees of organizational and leadership skills. They know how to see the overall picture, excel at long-term planning, and are able to see projects through to completion.

Blood Type B:

Roosters with blood type B are liberal and courageous, loyal and sincere, energetic and vigorous, positive and forward-looking,

enterprising and enthusiastic, natural and poised, flexible and adaptable, and gifted and versatile. They possess their own unique style, are resolute and decisive in their problem-solving, and tend to have a vainglorious streak coupled with the tendency to show off. They are highly emotional, distinguish clearly between love and hate, and often wear their hearts on their sleeves.

Blood Type O:
Roosters with blood type O are positive and enterprising; bold and courageous; and stubborn and uncompromising. With outstanding social skills and the ability to handle all affairs with composure and insight, they are destined for success in the business world. Roosters of this blood type know how to dress, and their wardrobe is defined by elegance, style, and stateliness. They are also high in self-confidence but tend to be equally vainglorious.

Blood Type AB:
Roosters with blood type AB are elegant and graceful, cordial and kindhearted, persuasive and convincing in speech, and possess a high IQ and quick wit. Kind and loyal by nature, they make for ideal romantic partners and tend not to get hung up on minor details. They also possess high levels of foresight and aptitude, and are able to apply their skills in daily life. Most Roosters of this blood type capitalize on their talents in a short period of time, earning high praise from others.

THE AUSPICIOUS YOU ROOSTER

THE ROOSTER AND FORTUNE

Lifetime Fortune: Overview

People born in the Year of the Rooster are honest and intelligent, and possess lofty aspirations and good social skills. They are highly resourceful and capable of achieving success. People born in the Year of the Rooster are easily seduced by the opposite sex and, as a result, are likely to have many romantic partners. In each relationship, they become committed and put their heart on the line. Roosters thus need to exercise caution in selecting a companion.

Career:

By focusing their energy and investing their strength, Roosters can attain new levels of success in their work. Young people, by starting to build up their own career, will also have strong prospects for the future.

Financial Luck:

Roosters tend to have good monetary luck as well as a steadily climbing income. To ensure long-term financial stability, however, they need to build up their net wealth. In this respect, the Rooster should exercise due caution when pursuing large business investments or engaging in stock trading.

Romance:

Roosters should try to mitigate potential domestic conflicts which might arise. It is also important that those in a relationship make time to spend with their partner, even if they are busy with work. Roosters also boast a high marriage rate.

Fortune and the Five Elements

Wood Rooster: Born in the Year of *Xin-You* (1981, 1921)

Wood Roosters place a large emphasis on family and are energetic and gentle by nature. They like to joke around and are able to lighten up a tense atmosphere. Though Wood Roosters have good financial prospects, they need to learn to be more independent and proactive in their careers; they should attempt to resolve problems on their own instead of always relying on others.

A colored statue of Gui-You Deity

A colored statue of Ding-You Deity

Fire Rooster: Born in the Year of *Ding-You* (2017, 1957)

Fire Roosters have a keen sense of time. While trustworthy and loyal to their friends, they also tend to have a short temper. Their competitive spirit enables them to achieve success in their careers by middle age. Fire Roosters have excellent money management skills and strong financial prospects, but are likely to face barriers in their love life.

A colored statue of Ji-You Deity

Earth Rooster: Born in the Year of *Ji-You* (1969, 1909)

Earth Roosters have a vivacious personality, and enjoy traveling and making new friends. They strive to build up a good reputation and win over the trust of others. Exhibiting high levels of patience and perseverance, they take a calm and unhurried approach to problem-solving. The Earth Rooster is willing to toil hard and is also blessed with the help of others, leading to a smooth and successful career. The coexistence of wealth creation and wealth retention also leads to solid financial prospects for the Earth Rooster.

A colored statue of Xin-You Deity

Metal Rooster: Born in the Year of *Gui-You* (1993, 1933)

Metal Roosters are level-headed, clear-minded, and demonstrate strong logic in their thinking. They are morally upright, have a clear purpose, and demonstrate both fortitude and perseverance. Despite having difficulty

THE AUSPICIOUS *YOU* ROOSTER

getting along with others in their work, Metal Roosters have strong financial prospects and are able to succeed through their efforts.

Water Rooster: Born in the Year of *Yi-You* (2005, 1945)

Water Roosters tend to be oversensitive but are equally quick-witted, enabling them to readily solve any problem that arises. They gravitate towards beautiful things and have a strong appreciation for art. Though conceited by nature, Water Roosters are kindhearted and not the type to flaunt themselves. In the workplace, they collaborate effectively with colleagues and are likely to receive the support and understanding of superiors. Water Roosters also know how to build up affluence without overworking; by seizing the right opportunities, money will flow in.

A colored statue of Yi-You Deity

Fortune by the Year

In the Year of the Rat, Roosters will see their luck gradually improve. Minor financial losses are inevitable at the beginning of the year, but these will be recovered by year-end. After August, the Rooster should pursue opportunities as they emerge to generate a small surplus.

In the Year of the Ox, Roosters will be unrelenting in their efforts, and are likely to enjoy higher prominence but little economic gain. In spite of the year's lack of stability, Roosters will face no barriers and, ultimately, will stand out among their peers.

In the Year of the Tiger, Roosters will see business thriving and earnings pouring in. Every endeavor pursued will see gratifying returns on investment. Although there are likely to be a few minor ailments and setbacks, the year will pass free of any major obstacles.

In the Year of the Rabbit, Roosters are likely to see the collapse of business operations or capital pools, and they should definitely avoid entering into new partnerships. Fortunately, blessed with the timely assistance of a friend or loved one, the Rooster can get through the year unscathed.

In the Year of the Dragon, Roosters are destined to rule supreme and produce results which others previously thought unattainable. In the process, however, they may find themselves mentally drained and should be cautious to prevent potential illness. Roosters also need to remain vigilant for anyone who might try to plunder their wealth.

In the Year of the Snake, Roosters will be blessed with good fortune but may also face some financial losses, with gains in reputation outpacing profits. However, luck will ultimately turn around, and successes at year-end will leave plenty of food on the table.

In the Year of the Horse, Roosters will meet with both blessing and calamity, as their luck fluctuates back and forth. There will be a mixture of unanticipated joys and sorrows. In general, however, the year is likely to bring an endless stream of happiness.

In the Year of the Sheep, Roosters are destined to enjoy a year of smooth sailing and career advancement. The start of the year will bring good luck, which will stabilize around summertime. Roosters should be cautious in their pursuits toward year-end.

In the Year of the Monkey, Roosters will watch on as their luck slides downhill. They are likely to meet resistance in their endeavors, with earning power limited and efforts going unrewarded. The year may also bring physical and spiritual ailments, as well as disputes and quarrels. The Rooster will ultimately see improvements in fortune, but should be cautious when going out of town.

In the Year of the Rooster, Roosters will face problems in executing their operating plans and business will be limited. Fortunately, low profits can be offset by an enhanced reputation and small gains can be achieved by year-end.

THE AUSPICIOUS YOU ROOSTER

In the Year of the Dog, Roosters are likely to run around in pursuit of fame and gain. Their efforts will not go unrewarded, but it is difficult to know when results will materialize. Though the Rooster is likely to face dejection while away from home, this situation will gradually improve.

In the Year of the Pig, Roosters will find themselves down on their luck as a series of disasters befall. Since it is not an opportune time to seek profits, Roosters may elect to engage in manual labor, but must be careful in all they do.

THE ROOSTER AND THE WESTERN ZODIAC

Rooster-Aries:

Rooster-Aries are gifted and intelligent, frank and outspoken, and never pretentious. Always in happy spirits, they are filled with zeal and vitality and not afraid to try new things. When up against obstacles or adversity, they respond by proactively searching for a solution. They are also highly diligent and carry out their work with both vigor and speed.

Rooster-Taurus:

Rooster-Tauruses are honest, kindhearted, earnest and reliable. Unusually high in aptitude, they are able to run their own business independently and effortlessly. Rooster-Tauruses also show sympathy for the underprivileged and are willing to dig into their own wallets to offer support.

Rooster-Gemini:

Rooster-Geminis are noble, magnificent, tenacious and fortitudinous; the bigger the obstacle they face, the more courageous they are. They embrace a fast-paced lifestyle, pursuing excitement and opting not to lead a dull or ordinary life. Rooster-Geminis have a tendency to impose their ways on others.

Towel Gourd and Two Chickens, by Lou Shibai, a famous painter of China

Rooster-Cancer:

Rooster-Cancers are impulsive and hot-tempered, but equally diligent in their work and always glad to offer their ideas. They are relentless in their pursuit of power and status, paying little attention to trivial matters. Rooster-Cancers are also able to bring happiness to those around them, and enjoy leading a tranquil and traditional family life.

Rooster-Leo:

Rooster-Leos are intelligent and gifted, enjoy dressing up, and overflow with energy and enthusiasm. They are strong-minded, live life somewhere between ideality and reality, and regard money as both a motivator and a source of happiness. Rooster-Leos tend always to be surrounded by a large number of friends.

Rooster-Virgo:

Rooster-Virgos are courageous and fortitudinous, purposeful and resolute, sharp and perceptive, and resourceful and attentive to detail. They are propelled forward by an inner drive but are not lacking in self-restraint. With a kind and genial personality, Rooster-Virgos enjoy harmonious relations with others. They also enjoy travel and have an eye for beauty.

Rooster-Libra:

Rooster-Librans tend to dress casually, paying little attention to their wardrobes. Assiduous and enterprising by nature, they often produce outstanding results and have tremendous artistic potential. They are also gentle and kindhearted, emotionally sensitive, and loyal to others.

Rooster-Scorpio:

Rooster-Scorpios are emotionally loyal, and possess inner strength despite the appearance of weakness. They are direct in speech and never beat around the bush. With the ability to boost their own morale in times of distress, they often

THE AUSPICIOUS YOU ROOSTER

dispel negative emotions by running around and keeping busy. Rooster-Scorpios are idealistic, perfectionistic, and even fastidious at times.

Rooster-Sagittarius:

Rooster-Sagittarians are honest and sincere, have a strong sense of family responsibility, and like to do good deeds and assist the weak and underprivileged. Always willing to work hard and go all-out, they make a deep and lasting impression on others. They are likely to get nervous or excited when faced with new problems, but are able to summon courage quickly and strive forward.

Rooster-Capricorn:

Rooster-Capricorns are sharp-witted and curious; elite and dignified; and polite and courteous. They are cautious in speech, firm in their convictions, and have a strong sense of justice and autonomy. Owing to a stubborn personality, they tend not to accept the ideas of others. Rooster-Capricorns also have a loathing for social conventions and cumbersome procedures.

Rooster-Aquarius:

Rooster-Aquarians are alert and clear-headed, and tend to be somewhat conservative and traditional. Their focus on external circumstances allows them not to be controlled by their own emotions. With the ability to distinguish between the transient and the permanent, Rooster-Aquarians are capable of handling all of life's changes.

Rooster-Pisces:

Rooster-Pisceses are intelligent, adaptable, purposeful, and decisively resolute. Daring and adventurous by nature, they are curious explorers who enjoy traveling the world. Despite being arrogant and conceited, they are also highly loveable. They place high demands on themselves and emphasize practical results in their work. Rooster-Pisceses are likely to face setbacks in their romantic affairs.

FENGSHUI AND THE ROOSTER

From ancient times, the rooster has been charged with the responsibility of crowing to herald daybreak. In the study of *fengshui*, the rooster is equipped with the spiritual

power of raising the spirits of those who suffer from despair or low morale. To ameliorate a dull and lifeless atmosphere, *fengshui* roosters can be placed in the west of one's workplace or the main hall of one's home; they can restore vitality and turn around a declining tendency. The *fengshui* rooster also has an additional aptitude: it can overcome the evil emanations of insects. Whether plagued by borers or any other bug, positioning a *fengshui* rooster to face west will offer some benefit. With respect to selection of material, any material other than plastic would be fine.

INTERPRETING ROOSTER DREAMS

If you dream of a hen hatching a chick, you will have great joy and happiness.

If you dream of rooster in a tree, you will make a fortune.

If a man dreams of a baby chicken, he will become a high-ranking official.

If a businessperson dreams of a baby chicken, revenues will multiply.

If a young boy and girl dream of a baby chicken, they will have a blissful marriage.

If you dream of a strong and healthy chick, it means your superior's words are true.

If you dream of a weak and feeble chick, ill fortune will soon befall you.

HEALTH SECRETS

People born in the Year of the Rooster tend to get nervous easily, often resulting in poor digestion as well as pulmonary or bronchial hypersensitivity. During seasonal changes, Roosters should be careful not to be adversely affected by changes in temperature. It is also important for them to maintain a nutritionally balanced diet.

THE AUSPICIOUS YOU ROOSTER

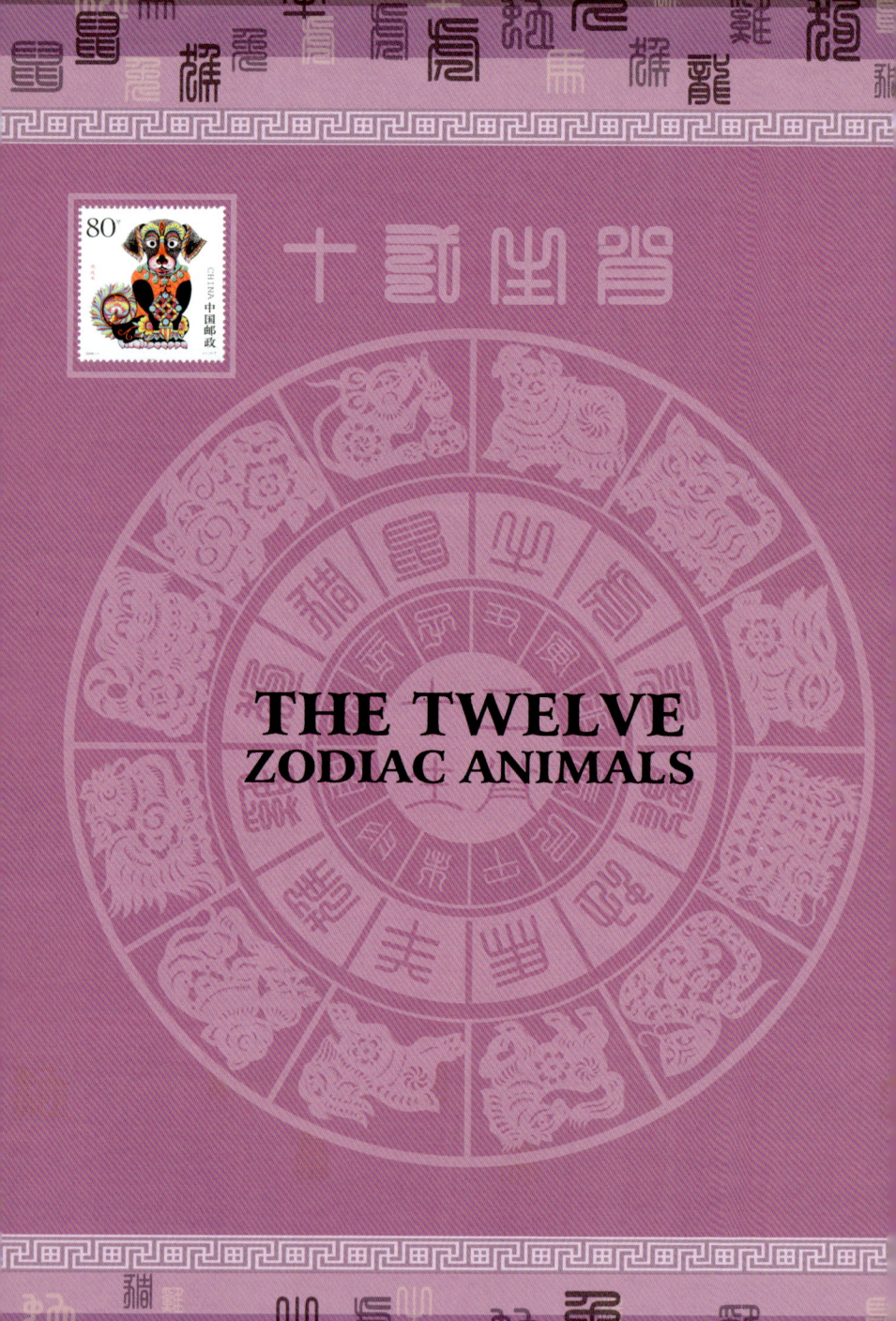

THE TWELVE ZODIAC ANIMALS

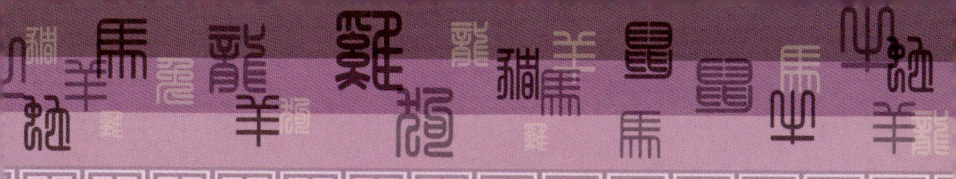

PART 11
THE *XU* DOG BRINGS PROSPEROUS WEALTH

【 DOG 】

THE *XU* DOG BRINGS PROSPEROUS WEALTH

A dog-shaped sachet

For years, the dog — with its sensitive hearing and sense of smell — has guarded the house and protected the yard for the human race. Regardless of whether a dog's owner is wealthy or poor, the dog will never abandon its owner. When a dog's master is in danger, the dog can always bravely step forward to the rescue. The dog is thus honored as humanity's most faithful friend and listed among the 12 zodiac animals.

As the animal domesticated earliest by humankind, the dog — as well as its existence and evolution — bears a complex relationship with the development of human culture. Dog skeletons and the image of a watchdog on unearthed ceramics have been found in archaeological discoveries that date back to the Neolithic Period 10,000 years ago. Since then, the dog has helped people in the realms of hunting, farming, animal husbandry, and guarding the house, and has even served as a means of transport in some areas by pulling sledges or sleds. Even today, the dog can be considered irreplaceable in many respects, and may be thought of as a "speechless friend" to humanity.

China's various ethnic groups each have their own folk customs related to the dog. The Nakhi, Lisu, Lahu, and Pumi peoples all have customs

honoring the dog. It is said that the ancestors of some of China's ethnic groups grew up on dog's milk and thus were forbidden to eat dog meat. Some ethnicities have fables in which the dog is said to have brought grain seeds for them, and so they must feed dogs after ancestor worship. The Buyi people of China hold a dog-worshipping activity when celebrating the Spring Festival. The ancient Mongols had a ceremony called "Shoot the Grass Dog", used to dispel evil forces. In the ceremony, a dog formed of rice straw would be tied and shot with arrows. In parts of Zhejiang, there was once a custom called "Squat Down in a Kennel", used to educate children. After a baby was born, family members put old clothes on the child, and placed it in the kennel for a while. Infant names such as the "Dog Remaining", "Dog Baby", and "Little Dog" may be chosen by parents in hopes that the child will be easy and inexpensive to raise.

A snow-carving of dog

The Chinese people regard the dog as an auspicious animal. If a dog suddenly visited a household, the master would happily adopt it, as the dog signifies that wealth is imminent. This is reflected in the following proverb: "If a pig arrives, poverty will follow; if a dog arrives, wealth will follow; if a cat arrives, mourning (of a deceased loved one) will follow." Many Chinese proverbs praise the dog's high morals. For example, the expression "a dog would not detest a poor family; a child would not dislike his ugly mother" indicates the dog's loyalty to humankind and unconditional love for its master. Countless stories about loyal dogs that requited favors and saved their masters can be found throughout China and around the world. In the past, a family who owned a thin dog would be ashamed that the dog was thin; this led to the saying "if the dog is thin, the master will be ashamed." In the *Classic of Rites*, an important ancient text about decrees and regulations, there were several stipulations related to the dog: "The

THE XU DOG BRINGS PROSPEROUS WEALTH

feudal lord shall not kill the ox without reason; the literary intelligentsia shall not kill the sheep without reason; the soldier shall not kill the dog without reason." It is evident, then, that the ancient Chinese attached great importance to the dog. Emperor Huizong of the Northern Song Dynasty, who was born in the Year of the Dog, issued an imperial decree to forbid people from killing dogs. Upon hearing this news, students at the imperial college gathered in great numbers at the imperial city gate to protest the decree. They argued that Huizong's father was born in the Year of the Rat but that raising cats had not been prohibited. The decree was canceled and the story became a joke.

The dog can defend not only the dwelling but also an entire city, and dogs have played an important role in military history. The dog's sense of hearing and smelling is extremely keen. Especially in the quiet night, the dog will bark as a warning sign at the slightest sign of trouble. The dog thus came to be regarded as the good helper for military vigilance. As early as in the Warring States Period, Mo Zhai, a famous defense expert, used the dog for defense purposes. In his book, he elaborated on the dog's role in defense. If the enemy dug a tunnel outside the city, wells would be dug in the city for guard, and keen-eared and sharp-eyed dogs would be sent to determine the tunnel's location and dig holes to defeat the enemy. If the tunnels were interlinked, the dog would carry on the patrol in the tunnels. If anybody was in the tunnel, the dog would bark. In the *Tongdian* (literally

Comprehensive Institutions), China's first complete work on politics, it is written, "Set the police dog on the city wall, and strengthen the alert where the dog barks." The comprehensive military work *Wu Bei Zhi* (*Treatise on Armament Technology*), written in the Ming Dynasty, also states: "Every 50 steps, a dog is tied under the city besieged at night, and food is set in front of it. Upon hearing the dog's bark, the soldiers on the wall will lift torches to add illumination and enhance preparation." Even today, the dog is still the police officer's trusted partner for criminal investigation, narcotics searches, ground patrol, and fugitive apprehension.

In hunting activity, people caught wild animals with the aid of dogs. During the Han Dynasty (206 BC-220 AD), hunting became a common activity enjoyed by the upper and lower echelons of society alike—from the emperor and the wealthy to the civilians and the servants. In unearthed cultural relics that date back to the Han Dynasty, there are many ceramic dogs, stone portraits and stone bricks that depict hunting. Emperor Kangxi of Qing (1654-1722) even painted a portrait called the *Ten Steed Dogs* of his ten beloved hunting dogs. In a famous poem, Su Shi (1037-1101, also known as Su Dongpo) expresses his lofty ambition of driving out invaders, "Though I am old, I seek the vigor of youth; I pull a yellow hound with my left hand, and hold up a gray falcon in my right hand."

The dog is a good partner of humankind, while the "Celestial Dog" is actually an evil spirit feared by the people. Before a wedding ceremony, the fortune-teller chooses an auspicious day to write out detailed suggestions and tabooed words on a red piece of paper. One of the important items is not to violate the Celestial Dog. Otherwise, the couple will be unable to bear a child. The ancient Chinese also thought that the lunar and solar eclipses were caused by the Celestial Dog, which "swallowed" the

A clay sculpture of dog

moon and the sun. In Chinese mythology, there was a hero who shot the sun and the moon and caused the world to become gloomy. The people thus asked

THE XU DOG BRINGS PROSPEROUS WEALTH

the Celestial Dog to retrieve the sun and moon, and promised to present it with paddy rice. After the Celestial Dog retrieved the sun and moon, however, the people forgot their promise. So when the Celestial Dog is hungry, it will eat the sun or the moon. When this happens, the people make noises and set off firecrackers, frightening the Celestial Dog and causing it to spit out the sun or the moon. This story enabled the ancient Chinese to explain the phenomenon of the eclipse at a time when science was undeveloped.

Although the dog shows loyalty and devotion in taking care of its master, the majority of dog-related idioms and proverbs are actually derogatory. For instance, "a dog that relies on the power of the master" refers to a person who likes to rely on some kind of influence and bully others; "the dog-headed military strategist" refers to someone who likes to offer advice, but whose ideas are unwise; "sell dog meat as mutton" refers to the act of doing something bad or dishonest while pretending otherwise. Other dog phrases and proverbs include "the dog nips Lü Dongbin but it does not know his good will"; "the dog catching mouse is to mind others' business"; "a dog's mouth does not spit ivory"; and "a dog's eyes look down on others". The reason why the dog is represented as a bad animal in these proverbs may be due to the fact that, in the olden days, dogs were typically raised by the wealthy; poor people, therefore, had no choice but to vent their anger on the dog.

There are also exceptions in the way the dog was used in language. In ancient China, a father would use the phrase "dog's son" to refer modestly to his own son. Confucius once was described as "a stray dog", originally referring to someone who scurries about and cannot find a place for shelter when traveling to promote his political opinions. Upon hearing this, Confucius actually

A dough model of dog

thought that the description was quite appropriate. At that time, the great nations of China were busy warring and striving for hegemonic power, while the small nations faced the threat of being annexed. The entire society was thus in a state of turbulence and nobody wanted to listen to Confucius expound his opinions about rituals. As a result, he had no choice but to run around in all directions to drum up support for his ideas. Qing Dynasty painter and calligrapher Zheng Banqiao (1693-1766) was willing to refer to himself as a "running dog" to express his esteem for Xu Wei (1521-1593), who was an outstanding painter, calligrapher and writer. During the Ming Dynasty, hundreds of deceitful officials begged to become the adopted sons of Wei Zhongxian (1568-1627) when he had become a big court eunuch with great power. Among the adopted sons, ten of them were referred to as "ten dogs" — and they took it as an honor. This expression can probably be considered as derogatory.

ZODIAC ANIMAL FILE

Earthly Branch: *Xu*
Years of Birth: 2030, 2018, 2006, 1994, 1982, 1970, 1958, 1946, 1934…
Five Elements: *Xu* belongs to Earth
Five Constant Virtues: earth belongs to Sincerity
Auspicious Directions: east, southeast, south
Auspicious Colors: green, red, purple
Lucky Numbers: 3, 4, 9
Lucky Flowers: rose, oncidium flexuosum, Cymbidium faberi
Lucky Gemstones: ruby, amethyst, rose quartz
Spiritual Protector: Amitabha
Choosing a name: For individuals born in the Year of the Dog, it is appropriate to select characters with the radicals for fish (鱼), bean (豆), or rice (米), signifying ample food and drink, as well as perpetual fame and wealth; characters with the radicals for person (人), roof (宀), or horse (马), which embody peace, happiness, kindness and prosperity; characters with the radicals for metal (金),

THE *XU* DOG BRINGS PROSPEROUS WEALTH

jade (玉), grass (艹), field (田), wood (木), grain (禾), or moon (月), which connote selflessness, intelligence and courage; characters with the person (亻) radical, which embodies integrity, honesty and uprightness; or characters with the fire (火) radical, representing morality and decisiveness.

THE DOG AND PERSONALITY

Strengths:
The Dog's assets include intelligence, agility, and a keen sense of humor. People of this zodiac sign place a high value on friendship, and are loyal, faithful and trustworthy. Dogs are honest, reliable, amicable and kindhearted, and devote their energy to the task at hand. With candor, courage and the ability to discriminate right from wrong, they never hesitate to do what is right or defend others against injustice. People born in the Year of the Dog are highly diligent, possess sharp instincts and a quick wit, and are dedicated to their profession.

Weaknesses:
The Dog's limitations include a hot temper and reliance on others. People of this zodiac sign tend to be stubborn and flaunting. They place a lot of weight on theory, but lack judgment and action in real life. At times, Dogs may fall into a deep silence or seclude themselves seemingly without reason.

A hair embroidery work of dog

THE DOG AND BLOOD TYPE

Blood Type A:
Dogs with blood type A are faithful and honest, smart and careful, and watchful and attentive. They enjoy rest and relaxation, but tend to be relatively silent and rarely take the initiative to engage in conversation with others. Dogs of this blood type are highly agreeable and readily comply with others' wishes.

Blood Type B:
Dogs with blood type B are lively and enthusiastic,

energetic and perceptive, kindhearted and virtuous, just and upright, and natural and poised. Many of them are skilled in sports or the arts but lack a high level expertise. Despite their tendency to act impetuously, Dogs of this blood type show great tolerance and forgiveness, can ascertain others' interests and needs quickly, and know how to enjoy life while at the same time satisfying others.

Blood Type O:
Dogs with blood type O are careful and cautious, competitive and stubborn, and sharp and quick-witted. With strong logic and fairly objective thinking, they are diligent in their studies and work and often highly successful in business. Dogs of this blood type may be relatively quiet on the surface, but are actually extremely eloquent and sociable. However, they are not good at dealing with minor problems in their lives.

Blood Type AB:
Dogs with blood type AB are talented and capable, natural and unrestrained, sharp-witted and sociable, and reasonable and rational. Logical in thought and cautious in speech, they demonstrate efficiency in their endeavors and are able to take the overall situation into account. Dogs of this blood type also have their own unique ways to tackle details, revealing their wisdom and intelligence. They can be expected to attain mastery in any pursuit which interests them.

A green glazed pottery dog from the Eastern Han Dynasty

 ## THE DOG AND FORTUNE

Lifetime Fortune: Overview

People born in the Year of the Dog are sharp, astute, enthusiastic and elegant. However, they are also short-tempered, highly fickle, and have a low level of tolerance. By overcoming these weaknesses, Dogs can naturally improve their overall fortune.

THE *XU* DOG BRINGS PROSPEROUS WEALTH

Career:

Dogs should strive to be prudent and conservative in their careers, but should not feel restrained to challenge themselves if they have the courage to do so. Members of the working class should have an easy time finding a fulfilling job. When considering switching jobs or seeking work away from home, Dogs would be advised not to share these plans with others; otherwise, they are likely to face a series of impediments on the road to success.

Financial Luck:

The Dog's financial luck is less than ideal, with the possibility of a salary cut. Even with revenues coming in, it is often difficult for Dogs to accumulate savings. Large investments should be avoided.

Romance:

If a Dog engages in an extramarital affair, it is likely to cause a scandal. It is common for suspicions to arise between husband and wife; as such, it is important for Dogs to show love and caring to their partners.

A clay sculpture of dog

Fortune and the Five Elements

Wood Dog: Born in the Year of *Wu-Xu* (2018, 1958)

Wood Dogs are honest, reliable and understanding. They are full of gratitude and always seek to return others' kindness. Naturally endowed with a sense of justice, they remonstrate against any action they believe is unjust and rebuke the wrongdoer. They are also highly dedicated to their work; once they have decided something, they will work hard to finish it in spite of any difficulties along the way. Water Dogs can manifest their potential by pursuing work that requires patience and persistence. They are blessed with good and stable luck over the course of their lives.

A colored statue of Wu-Xu Deity

A colored statue of Bing-Xu Deity

A colored statue of Jia-Xu Deity

Fire Dog: Born in the Year of *Jia-Xu* (1994, 1934)

Fire Dogs are gentle, kindhearted, and prudent. With unlimited hopes for the future and a down-to-earth personality, they succeed easily in life and often achieve their ideals. Fire Dogs also know how to put themselves in others' shoes, striving to help others whenever possible. In their work, they tend to be influenced by relations with others; it is especially important that they exercise caution when working with those whom they dislike. Financial prospects are excellent over the course of their lives; if the will and intention to earn money are present, luck will definitely be on the Fire Dog's side.

Earth Dog: Born in the Year of *Bing-Xu* (2006, 1946)

Earth Dogs are highly persevering — always carrying tasks through to the end and never giving up halfway — and have a strong sense of right and wrong. A stubborn streak, however, may present itself at times; when in a bad mood, they are likely to turn a deaf ear to others' advice or consoling. Though Earth Dogs may be willful, they do not intentionally harm anyone, understand how to respect the views of others, and would never force others to accept their opinions. They are not in the habit of interfering in others' lives and, likewise, prefer that others not interfere in their lives. At work, Earth Dogs are always conscientious and meticulous, leading to a high probability of success. Financial prospects, too, are relatively ideal; with their income steadily rising, they are destined to enjoy economic affluence.

Metal Dog: Born in the Year of *Geng-Xu* (1970, 1910)

Metal Dogs are charming and popular, possess a high level of self-esteem, and tend to be cautious and prudent in their pursuits. They take pleasure in lending a helping hand, but are unwilling to rely on others, preferring instead to rely on their own efforts. Metal Dogs never quit until their goals are realized, which leads to solid career prospects; financial luck, however, is mediocre at best.

A colored statue of Geng-Xu Deity

THE *XU* DOG BRINGS PROSPEROUS WEALTH

Water Dog: Born in the Year of *Ren-Xu* (1982, 1922)

Water Dogs are sharp-minded and intelligent, thinking and planning far ahead to lay a solid foundation for the future. They remain strong in the face of obstacles, overcoming difficulties one by one. In the workplace, Water Dogs are conscientious, hard-working, and able to perform their duties well. They also possess strong financial management skills and, despite being unlikely to strike it rich, are able to maintain a stable income.

A colored statue of Ren-Xu Deity

Fortune by the Year

In the Year of the Rat, Dogs will see a mix of joy and suffering, fortune and calamity. While financial prospects are good, there are also likely to be frequent calamities. The Dog should be watchful for sudden incidents which may occur.

In the Year of the Ox, Dogs will be plagued by ill luck and despicable lowlifes who are out to make trouble. Dogs should to be careful to keep their temper in check and be more reserved in speech. By the end of the year, they can turn their luck around with the help of others. The Dog may also be lucky enough to find that special someone.

In the Year of the Tiger, Dogs will find their plans difficult to execute. However, as long as they exercise moderation, avoid extremes, and carry out their duties loyally, they can get through the year safe and sound. During the latter half of the year, the Dog should be on the lookout for opportunities that could be financially rewarding.

In the Year of the Rabbit, Dogs will enjoy great fortune as their lucky star shines high. They should stay on moral high ground by supporting the family, carrying out their professional duties, and doing more good deeds. It is imperative that the Dog avoid licentious behavior, and saving up money for emergency use is also recommended.

In the Year of the Dragon, Dogs will see a coexistence of opportunity and disappointment. Stiff competition for wealth and profits as well as instability on the career front may be unavoidable. On the whole, however, Dogs are destined to have good luck this year, and can expand their ventures by capitalizing on emerging opportunities.

In the Year of the Snake, Dogs will have fairly good luck overall. It is important that they maintain moral integrity and avoid pursuing profits by ill means. The Dog may face a lawsuit during the year but will come out vindicated and victorious. Though it is likely to be an easy year to make money, retaining wealth may prove equally difficult. By maintaining a steady hand in their endeavors and exercising moderation in their pursuits, Dogs can pass the year in peace and good health.

In the Year of the Horse, Dogs will enjoy a year of auspicious fortune. However, they should pay close attention to their health and avoid becoming overworked. The Dog may suffer minor losses this year, or friends or relatives may meet with danger or difficulty.

In the Year of the Sheep, Dogs are afflicted with ill fortune, minimal profits, frequent disputes, and beleaguered health. Fortunately, the Dog's lucky star is shining brightly; as misfortune subsides, Dogs will see their careers stabilize and can make it through the year safe and sound.

In the Year of the Monkey, Dogs will be blessed with affluence and comfort, plenty of delicious food, and some unexpected financial gains.

In the Year of the Rooster, Dogs will have mediocre financial prospects. Despite

THE XU DOG BRINGS PROSPEROUS WEALTH

success on the career front, the mind and body will both suffer. Fortunately, the year will ultimately pass in peace and health.

In the Year of the Dog, Dogs will spend most of their time working to support the family. By watching over their current pursuits, good opportunities will naturally emerge. Dogs are likely to be plagued by the frequent onset of small ailments this year; exercising regularly and making more friends would both prove highly beneficial.

In the Year of the Pig, Dogs should watch over their current business or invest in a new start-up. Only by seizing the year's excellent opportunities can the Dog reach the pinnacle of success.

THE DOG AND THE WESTERN ZODIAC

Dog-Aries:
Dog-Aries are naturally active and enjoy going on outings. They are virtuous, good-natured, innocent and honest by nature, and always look for the good in others. The Dog-Aries is also modest and sincere, and hates being deceived.

Dog-Taurus:
Dog-Tauruses are highly capable and prudent in fulfilling their duties. They are also interested in, and capable of carrying on, many different vocations. Despite possessing both determination and fortitude, they tend to lack self-confidence and suffer from a short temper. With an idealistic approach to life, the Dog-Taurus always demands that things be done better.

Dog-Gemini:
Dog-Geminis are lively and vivacious, and take pleasure in helping others out of embarrassing predicaments or lending a helping hand. They are meticulous in their endeavors, but tend also to be rash and capricious. Dog-Geminis prefer to stay away from anything related to power and money.

🦀 Dog-Cancer:

Dog-Cancers are conscientious, hard-working and down-to-earth, and possess strong intuitive perception as well as high alertness. They are innately sensitive and easily influenced by their surroundings. Generous and big-hearted by nature, Dog-Cancers are kind, considerate, and demonstrate caring for others.

🦁 Dog-Leo:

Dog-Leos have a cheerful and optimistic outlook on life, brim with confidence, and rarely get disappointed by anything. They view their career as a lifetime undertaking, working diligently and often producing extraordinary results. The Dog-Leo is also highly magnanimous, able to forgive the mistakes of others and see things from their point of view.

👧 Dog-Virgo:

Dog-Virgos are sweet and gentle, honest and genuine, and worthy of the trust of others. They have a strong sense of responsibility, and pursue their endeavors with efficiency and thoroughness. Despite being diligent and self-driven, they may occasionally argue over small and trivial details.

⚖️ Dog-Libra:

Dog-Librans are intelligent, clever and deft, possessing the ability to look at things from every angle. With a preference for peace and tranquility, they never get into conflicts or engage in stand-offs with others. They are kindhearted, good-natured, and glad to help and encourage others—sometimes even sacrificing themselves to help others succeed.

🦂 Dog-Scorpio:

Dog-Scorpios possess a spirit of sacrifice, and are warm-hearted, compassionate and sentimental. Wise, farsighted and highly perceptive, they possess keen judgment and are able to get right to the heart of a matter. They are also strong and uncompromising, and tend to be quite talkative as well.

🏹 Dog-Sagittarius:

Dog-Sagittarians are kind, courteous, sincere and cordial, and tend also to

---

THE *XU* DOG BRINGS PROSPEROUS WEALTH

be talkative and impatient. They are willing to respond to challenges and undertake endeavors which others are unwilling to attempt. Well aware of their own preferences, they are also highly selective in making decisions. The Dog-Sagittarian demonstrates creative thinking and has the qualities of a born leader.

Dog-Capricorn: Dog-Capricorns are conservative, eloquent, humorous, and charming. They pursue their own ideals, and often give off an air of mystery and intrigue. Dog-Capricorns are unlikely to get caught up chasing money or power, instead choosing to enjoy the ordinary comforts of life.

Dog-Aquarius: Dog-Aquarians are candid, honest and uncalculating, and readily willing to do favors for others or lend a helping hand. They also excel at consoling others, make excellent listeners, and are glad to offer their own ideas as well. Dog-Aquarians have the tendency to be cynical and detest the world and its ways.

Dog-Pisces: Dog-Pisces are highly gifted and stand out in their profession of choice. They have a strong sense of responsibility, sometimes leading them to feel exhausted or dejected. Despite being serious on the outside, they are sensitive, frank and amiable.

FENGSHUI AND THE DOG

Known affectionately as "man's best friend", the dog makes a loyal and devoted partner to humans. While most people believe that dogs possess a spiritual force, there are also many inelegant or vulgar dog-related phrases. This discrepancy probably relates to the variety of behavioral expressions shown in dogs. In the study of *fengshui*, dogs are classified as neither auspicious nor malevolent creatures; however, they are still regarded as beneficial for their ability to defend people's homes and guard against theft. To utilize a *fengshui* dog for security purposes or even to improve

personal relationships, it would be best to place it in the northwest part of one's home or workplace. If merely to protect against burglary, the *fengshui* dog should be positioned to face the main entrance. Either porcelain or earthenware would make suitable materials. People born in the Year of the Dragon should avoid the use of *fengshui* dogs. In addition, a southeast orientation is to be avoided as it could bring about calamity. In terms of number, it is best to only use one *fengshui* dog; too many *fengshui* dogs could reduce serenity and cause people to feel agitated. Finally, *fengshui* dogs must never be placed behind the door, as this could cause family members to suffer unexpected mishaps.

 ## INTERPRETING DOG DREAMS

If you dream of a rabid dog, an unexpected accident (often a traffic accident) is likely to occur.

If you dream of walking a huge dog, you will enjoy good relationships with others.

If you dream of caressing a puppy, your sense of time will go from bad to worse.

If you dream of two dogs frolicking with each other, your love life will be elevated to a new level.

If you dream of a dog eating some food, you will enjoy smooth sailing and all your wishes will be fulfilled.

If you dream of a dog barking at you, your relationships with friends will sour.

If you dream of a dog sprinting, you will enjoy good financial prospects.

 ## HEALTH SECRETS

People born in the Year of the Dog may be affected by anxiety and depression, and tend to suffer from insomnia and headaches. They are not in the habit of exercising, and often sit around after finishing a meal instead of going for a walk. As a result, many Dogs begin to put on weight after mid-life. By relaxing the mind and exercising regularly, overall health can be improved.

THE *XU* DOG BRINGS PROSPEROUS WEALTH

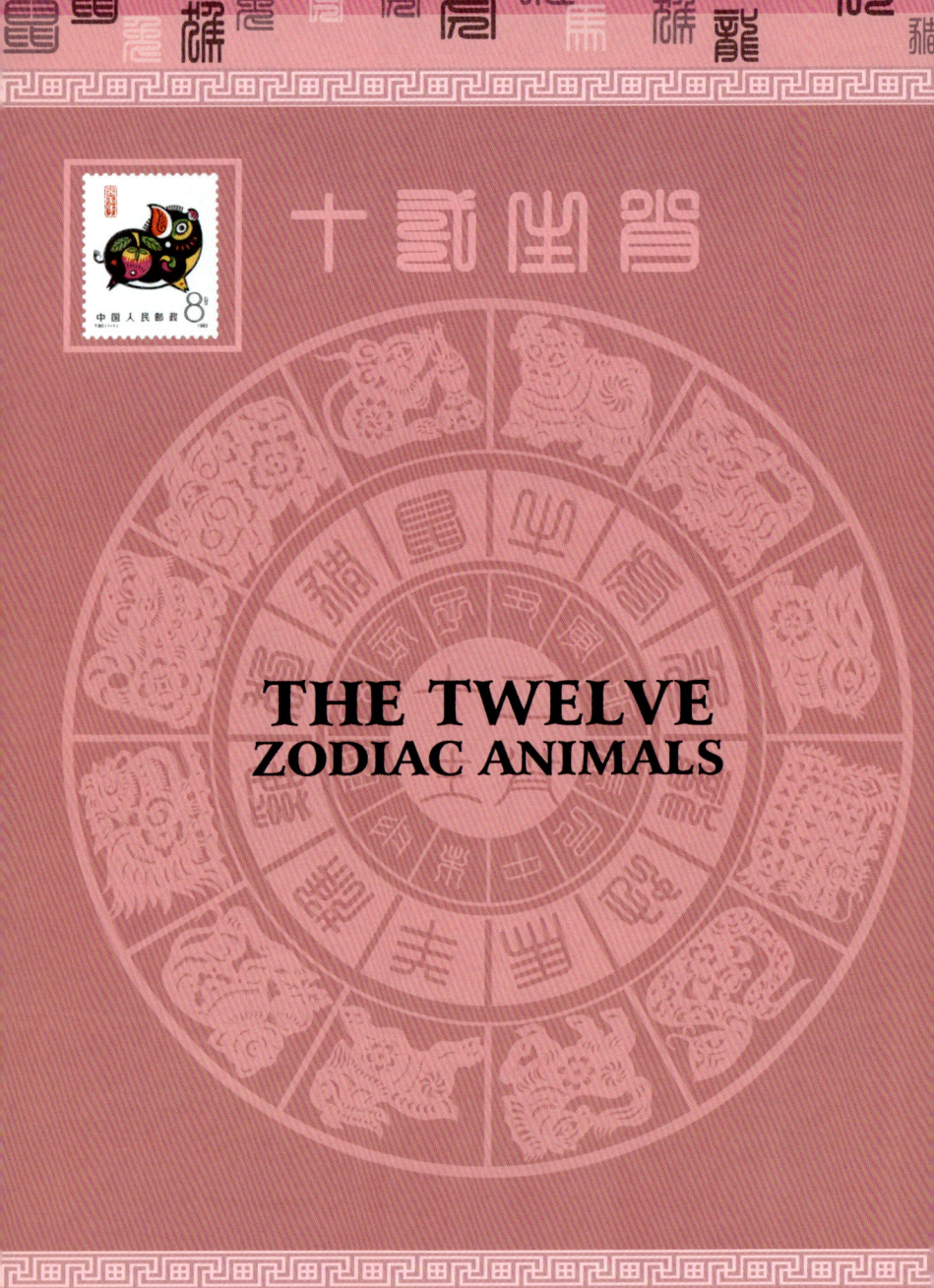

THE TWELVE
ZODIAC ANIMALS

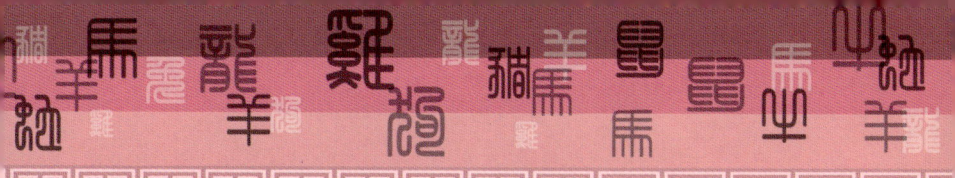

PART 12
THE *HAI* PIG DELIVERS THE LUCK

【 PIG 】

THE *HAI* PIG DELIVERS THE LUCK

The bronze pig head once adorned the Old Summer Palace

The Chinese character for the word "family" (家) depicts a pig (豕) under a roof (宀). One explanation proposed for the structure of this character is that the ancient Chinese thought a family should have a pig in the house. Alternatively, it has been suggested that the roof symbol represented the fences used in ancient times to contain domestic animals or offer sacrifices; in the past, the Chinese word for "family" could also be used to refer to an entire clan. Regardless of which explanation is accurate, it is evident that the pig has an intimate relationship with humankind and plays an important role in people's lives.

Of the 12 zodiac animals, the pig is listed in the final position and paired with the *hai*-hour (9:00pm–11:00pm). One reason put forth for this pairing is that, during this time, the pig eats more food and gains weight

THE TWELVE ZODIAC ANIMALS

A sculpture of pig in the Garden of Twelve Zodiac Animals in Jiangxi Province

most quickly. An alternate explanation is that the world enters into a "chaotic" silence at this time, while the pig's life is one of "chaotic" eating and sleeping, and hence the pig is paired with *hai*. Some people think that the character "亥" (pronounced *hai*) is similar to the character for "pig", and that the two characters are even mutually substitutable. By this line of reasoning, *hai* would have a natural relationship with the pig. The idiom "Lu Yu Hai Shi" (this two pairs of Chinese characters, Lu & Yu, and Hai & Shi, are in shapes but very different in meanings) refers to erroneous characters that appear during the process of writing or engraving.

In China, people began to raise pigs as early as the time of matriarchal society. The pig skeletons unearthed at the site of the Hemudu Neolithic culture in Yuyao, Zhejiang Province, are rich and plentiful. The wild boar has a complete skull and relatively long Proboscis; and the domestic pig has a fairly wide jaw. This indicates that the rudiments of pig domestication had already developed at that time.

The pig is a domestic animal which is familiar to all, and in Chinese folk culture it is known as the head of the "six domestic animals". In ancient times, the working class often viewed the number of domestic animals one possessed as a measure of status and wealth. The pig was precisely one of the earliest domestic animals raised by humankind, and was taken seriously by the ancient Chinese. Over successive dynasties, methods of pig-raising were recorded in several well-known agricultural books, including *Six Domestic Animals* in the Qin Dynasty (221-206 BC), *Essential Techniques for the Peasantry* in the Northern Wei Dynasty (386-534), *Summary of*

THE *HAI* PIG DELIVERS THE LUCK

Farming and Sericulture in the Yuan Dynasty (1206-1368), and the *Encyclopedia of Agricultural Politics* in the Ming Dynasty. Even the *Herbalist's Manual*, written by Li Shizhen, records medicines used in the treatment of sick pigs.

Since ancient times, the pig has been one of the principle sources of meat for most regions of China. Almost every part of its body, from head to toe, is not only edible but also delicious. The pig has played an important role in religious activities as well. In the graves of many ancient people of the Neolithic Age, pigs were offered in sacrifice or included as funerary objects. Pig-shaped pots, ceramic pigs, and pig-shaped decorations, for instance, have been unearthed at the site of the Hemudu Neolithic culture. Some of the pigs in these relics are decorated with plant patterns or rice ears, obviously carrying a special meaning closely tied to agriculture. Scholarly research indicates that the Hemudu pig likely had a relationship with the sorcery of

The jade pig-dragon unearthed in Liaoning Province

praying for rain.

Evidence of the use of pigs to pray for rainfall can be found in later generations' theory of "*yin-yang* and the Five Elements". According to the theory, the pig is paired with *hai*; its position should be in the north; its color should be black; and it should belong to the element of Water. Therefore, the pig was regarded as the "water livestock" by the ancient Chinese. Before Zhu Bajie, one of the major characters in *Journey to the West*, descended to Earth, he commanded the naval units in heaven. Some people have suggested that the pig is one of the dragon's early prototypes. One piece of evidence to support this belief is a Neolithic Hongshan culture relic of a jade pig-dragon, unearthed in Liaoning Province. It has obvious characteristics of the pig: a fat head, big ears, and a flat mouth. There are also obvious wrinkles on the bridge of its nose. This kind of prototype is difficult to find in nature, thus causing it to seem extraordinarily mystical.

The pig belongs to the class Mammalia, the order Artiodactyla, and the family Suidae. The wild boar and domestic pig are relatives, but only the latter is docile. Because it has been tamed for a long time by humankind and is relatively isolated from nature, the pig has lost its natural disposition. The wild boar, however, is fierce and brutal. Since long ago, people thought that the wild boars were the most vicious beasts of all, despite the fact that they do not have horns. The pig (mainly referring to the wild boar) was once worshipped by the Chinese people. Wang Mang of the late Western Han Dynasty (206 BC-25 AD) named his elite troops "brave wild boar" in hopes that his army would be like the fierce wild boar. Wang Lin, a senior general during the Southern and Northern Dynasties (420-589), named his battleship "Wild Boar" to denote bravery and victory.

For the Chinese people, the most familiar image of the pig is that of Zhu Bajie in

Journey to the West. Zhu Bajie was the second disciple of Xuanzang. He was originally the commander-in-chief of the Heavenly Navy Soldiers but, after misbehaving, was banished from Heaven and sent down to Earth to be reincarnated. However, he happened to fall into a pig farm and ended up becoming part-human and part-pig. Zhu Bajie had the skill of "thirty-six transformations", and could soar above the clouds or ride through the mist; he also wielded the weapon of the nine-tooth iron rake. On their way to the West, he is a good helper of the Monkey King. Despite his many

THE *HAI* PIG DELIVERS THE LUCK

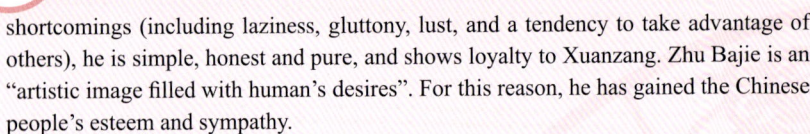

shortcomings (including laziness, gluttony, lust, and a tendency to take advantage of others), he is simple, honest and pure, and shows loyalty to Xuanzang. Zhu Bajie is an "artistic image filled with human's desires". For this reason, he has gained the Chinese people's esteem and sympathy.

In Chinese culture, the pig has many other implications. It is said that during the Tang Dynasty, successful candidates of the highest imperial examination reached an agreement that the one who was appointed as military or political leader should ask

the calligrapher of his classmates to autograph the Wild Goose Pagoda with a red writing brush. Because the Chinese word for "pig" has the same pronunciation as *zhu* (meaning "red"), it became the mascot figure for young scholars who passed the palace examination. Every time someone was going to take this exam, friends and relatives would bestow the red-roast pig's feet to wish him "an autograph with the red writing brush" in advance. Well-boiled pig feet were also bestowed as a gift, to convey wishes that the examinee would "meet with familiar topics on the test." This custom gradually evolved to one in which people gave hams to each other during the Spring Festival, because ham is made by baking the pig's feet.

There is a Chinese proverb that when "the pig enters the door, abundant happiness will arrive." Therefore, images of "the fat pig arching around the door" or "the pig carrying a treasure vase on its back" have been passed down for generations in Chinese New Year's paintings, paper-cuttings, embroidery, and folk arts. In Tianjin and Hebei, there is a festival involving the use of paper-cutting window decorations that depict a fat pig arching around the door. The design, which shows a pig carrying

a treasure vase on its back, is cut out of glazed black paper. The paper-cuttings are then pasted on the left and right sides of the front door to symbolize wealth and prosperity. The fat pig seems to have become a "messenger" who transmits or brings good fortune. This role is captured in the following Chinese proverb: "The pig is a family's treasure, and excrement is the earth's gold."

Numerous customs related to the pig are prevalent in China. In one part of Shaanxi Province, there is a wedding custom of bestowing and returning the pig's feet; this symbolizes that social relationships will become more intimate. The Bulang people of Xishuangbanna (in Yunnan Province) also have a pig-related custom. On the day of a wedding ceremony, the families of the bride and groom kill a pig, slice the pork into small pieces, skewer it on bamboo rods, and send it to families throughout the village to symbolize "proximity of blood." The Wa people of Yunnan have a divining custom called "divination of the pig's gallbladder". After killing a pig, a judgment of good or

bad fortune is made according to the pig's gallbladder. If the gallbladder is relatively moist and has a vertical grain, it is an auspicious sign; if the gallbladder's grain is horizontal and the gallbladder is relatively dry, it is regarded as a "hidden symbol." This divining custom, conducted by the sorcerer, is generally used for activities of great importance.

ZODIAC ANIMAL FILE

Earthly Branch: *Hai*
Years of Birth: 2031, 2019, 2007, 1995, 1983, 1971, 1959, 1947, 1935…
Five Elements: *Hai* belongs to Water
Five Constant Virtues: Water belongs to Wisdom
Auspicious Directions: west, northeast
Auspicious Colors: yellow, gray, gold
Lucky Numbers: 2, 8, 5

THE *HAI* PIG DELIVERS THE LUCK

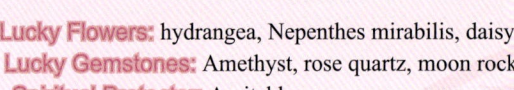

Lucky Flowers: hydrangea, Nepenthes mirabilis, daisy
Lucky Gemstones: Amethyst, rose quartz, moon rock
Spiritual Protector: Amitabha
Choosing a name: For individuals born in the Year of the Pig, it is appropriate to select characters with the radicals for bean (豆), rice (米), or fish (鱼), signifying joy, prosperity, honor and honesty; characters with the radicals for water (氵), metal (金), or jade (玉), which embody geniality and virtue; characters with the radicals for moon (月), wood (木), or grain (禾), which embody flourishing offspring; or characters with the radicals for person (亻), mountain (山), earth (土), or grass (艹), representing a strong sense of loyalty and duty.

 THE PIG AND PERSONALITY

Strengths:

The Pig's assets include optimism, honesty, integrity, and candor. People of this sign are generous, direct and straightforward. They carry out affairs conscientiously, while not being punctilious. Simple and guileless by nature and never willing to argue over trivial details, they enjoy excellent relations with others and take good care of their friends. The Pig is also able to make ends meet without having to overwork.

Weaknesses:

Pigs are rarely suspicious or skeptical of others, making them easy targets for the enemy's deception. In addition, they often have a sharp temper, get excited easily, and lack the mind to communicate or coordinate with others.

 **THE PIG AND BLOOD TYPE**

Blood Type A:

Pigs with blood type A are kindhearted and tolerant, magnanimous and open-minded, and honest and diligent. They are naturally helpful, work hard without complaint, and are always willing to give others a chance to rectify their mistakes. Pigs of this blood type may sometimes acquiesce to their romantic partner without hesitation, causing

them to lose some of their individuality.

Blood Type B:
Pigs with blood type B are extroverted and energetic, romantic and amorous, enterprising and spirited, kindhearted and enthusiastic, and multi-talented and down-to-earth. They tend to have strong social skills, and are likely to have many friends and enjoy good relations with others. Pigs of this blood type, however, often hold stubbornly to their opinion, and may carry a hidden sorrow deep in their heart.

Blood Type O:
Pigs with blood type O are optimists in a world of realists, yet manage to handle matters objectively and neutrally. With dedication, motivation, an earnest attitude and strong social skills, Pigs of this blood type are likely to succeed in the business world. Despite a propensity to seek material things and pursue their own interests, they are also eager to help those less fortunate than themselves.

Blood Type AB:
Pigs with blood type AB are optimistic, serious, magnanimous and pragmatic. They demonstrate shrewdness, mental agility, and wisdom in all their endeavors, and possess the ability to endure pressure and difficulties. Pigs of this blood type show high tolerance, often choosing to forgive and forget. They are also kindhearted and easily

THE PIG AND FORTUNE

Lifetime Fortune: Overview

People born in the Year of the Pig tend to be resolute and steadfast. However, they also have a tendency to rely on others, and lack tolerance and social skills. Pigs should avoid being overly righteous to prevent the occurrence of social disputes.

THE *HAI* PIG DELIVERS THE LUCK

Career:

Pigs typically have a solid career plan which they are able to bring into full play. They should certainly take advantage of any opportunities on the horizon to bring their desires to fruition. Whether as business owners or members of the working class, Pigs are full of vigor and destined to receive the support of others, ensuring them victory and success in their work.

Financial Luck:

Pigs are blessed with optimal financial luck and a steadily growing fortune. In addition to making capital investments, it would also be wise to invest in financial management to ensure stable and sustained economic growth.

Romance:

The Pig's love life can de described as smooth sailing all the way. Married persons of this zodiac sign will enjoy a blissful and harmonious family life, while those who are still single are destined to encounter special someone in due time.

Fortune and the Five Elements

Wood Pig: Born in the Year of *Ji-Hai* (2019, 1959)

Wood Pigs are lovable, good-natured, and like to laugh and enjoy life. Despite having a short temper, they are high in endurance and not easily defeated by setbacks. Their easy-going and plainspoken demeanor allows them to sustain harmonious relations with others. With respect to romance, the Wood Pig is likely to enjoy a stable and fulfilling love life. As soon as Wood Pigs come into money, they tend to spend freely and recklessly; even if they are broke, they seem not to care. To be prepared for contingencies, the Wood Pig should try to get into the habit of saving.

A colored statue of Yi-Hai Deity

Fire Pig: Born in the Year of *Yi-Hai* (1995, 1935)

Fire Pigs possess high ambitions and an entrepreneurial drive, and are highly suited to conducting professional research. Tending to rely on others, it may be best for them to work together as part of a team. Fire Pigs enjoy harmonious relationships and are always ready to accept the suggestions of friends. Their love life tends to be smooth

sailing, with deep feelings and a strong bond. Those who are still single are likely to encounter that "special someone"; as long as they persevere in their love conquests, that romantic connection can definitely be made. Fire Pigs are also blessed with superlative financial prospects.

A colored statue of Ji-Hai Deity A colored statue of Ding-Hai Deity

Earth Pig: Born in the Year of *Ding-Hai* (2007, 1947)

Earth Pigs possess exceptional social skills and have a keen sense of time. They also have a strong sense of responsibility; any task entrusted to them will be handled properly and with care. Money management skills, too, are strong, with sound financial prospects over the course of their life. Earth Pigs tend to toil hard in their youth, leading to a lucrative income from mid-life onwards and a life of affluence in old age. Overall, the Earth Pig is blessed with very good fortune.

Metal Pig: Born in the Year of *Xin-Hai* (1971, 1911)

Metal Pigs are broadminded, pleasant and loyal, and take very good care of their friends. They take pleasure in helping others and always seek to return a favor. With a tendency to be overaggressive at work, Metal Pigs can achieve great success by exercising a bit more prudence. They are good at expressing their own feelings and can enjoy a stable and healthy marriage. Financial prospects are mediocre, as the Metal Pig often spends extravagantly; it would be wise to get into the habit of tracking expenditures.

A colored statue of Xin-Hai Deity

Water Pig: Born in the Year of *Gui-Hai* (1983, 1923)

Water Pigs are highly conscientious, but tend to be inflexible once a decision has been made and often insist on doing things their way. They also have a dual personality, and are easily influenced by others. In romance, they are able to comply with their partners' wishes. Water Pigs enjoy good financial luck and may have the opportunity to strike it rich. However, they should watch out for a possible economic crisis, and maintain a steady and prudent approach to resolving any problem that may arise.

A colored statue of Gui-Hai Deity

THE *HAI* PIG DELIVERS THE LUCK

Fortune by the Year

In the Year of the Rat, Pigs will have difficulty turning a profit. Fortunately, their guardian angel will come to the rescue during these times of turmoil and Pigs will be blessed in their romantic affairs. However, they should remain vigilant, as elation may soon be frustrated by ill luck.

In the Year of the Ox, Pigs are likely to see time move in their favor. As business booms and opportunities appear

one after the next, large profits will flow in and the Pig's wealth will accumulate. Some mid-year financial losses may occur, but the year will pass free of any major obstacles.

In the Year of the Tiger, Pigs will be afflicted by unforeseen adversity, with their efforts often proving fruitless. Fortunately, luck will pick up again and the Pig will make unexpected gains.

In the Year of the Rabbit, Pigs will see all misfortune washed away, leaving behind hefty profits and chances for career advancement or promotion. As year-end approaches, Pigs should be careful not to be implicated by troublemakers who seek to do evil.

In the Year of the Dragon, Pigs are blessed with a surplus of joy and jubilance.

However, unforeseen ailments and expenses will be unavoidable, and the Pig's generosity and liberal spending may leave behind a good reputation but an empty wallet.

In the Year of the Snake, Pigs are likely to see a change of direction in their career. By exploiting opportunities as they emerge, healthy profits will naturally follow. However, the Pig should remain vigilant for scoundrels who may be lurking in the darkness.

In the Year of the Horse, Pigs will be blessed with enviable financial luck, copious profits, and an endless stream of good luck.

In the Year of the Sheep, Pigs will enjoy smooth sailing, a myriad of opportunities, and the fulfillment of their goals. By striving forward and putting their words into action, they can ensure that the year is one of success and merriment.

In the Year of the Monkey, Pigs are likely to meet with bad luck early on, as their efforts are continually frustrated. At this juncture, Pigs would be advised to bide their time. Over the course of the year, frequent disputes and career setbacks may be inevitable. By year-end, however, luck will turn around and the Pig's hard work will be rewarded.

In the Year of the Rooster, Pigs will experience turbulence and adversity, financial losses, and disappointment on the business front. While it is an inopportune time to seek profits, luck may be slightly better for officials and bureaucrats. To achieve their goals, Pigs should wait for the right opportunity to arrive and, in the meantime, make more friends with the elite.

In the Year of the Dog, Pigs will enjoy good luck and solid success. However, the only way to ensure financial profits this year will be to endure hardship. Pigs should thus build up their courage and confidence, and avoid indolence at all costs.

In the Year of the Pig, Pigs will see instability in their careers and

THE *HAI* PIG DELIVERS THE LUCK

breakdowns in strategic planning. It is not an optimal time to pursue earnings or to make new friends. In addition, it is imperative that the Pig not undertake any major investments.

THE PIG AND THE WESTERN ZODIAC

Pig-Aries:
Pig-Aries are natural and graceful, simple and honest, generous and helpful, and well-liked by others. They have unlimited enthusiasm for their work, and are especially suited to careers of a creative or cultural nature. Pig-Aries often have a short fuse, and are likely to face setbacks in their love life.

Pig-Taurus:
Pig-Tauruses are generous and kindhearted, unpretentious, and highly appealing to others. They tend to pursue wealth and status, and sometimes behave as if they were the boss. Diligent in their work and highly capable, they are unlikely to meet with any problem which they are unable to solve.

Pig-Gemini:
Pig-Geminis are gifted and multi-talented, positive and cheerful, strong and courageous, and cautious and prudent. In spite of being lazy and stubborn, they are quick-witted and able to solve problems quickly. Pig-Geminis are also endowed with management and organizational skills; they are often able to succeed in starting a business from scratch, without the assistance of others.

Zhu Bajie (left) and the Monkey King (right)

A facial make-up of Zhu Bajie in Beijing Opera

THE TWELVE ZODIAC ANIMALS

🦀 Pig-Cancer:

Pig-Cancers tend to be highly religious and traditional, resolutely abiding by their own ideals and ways. They often engage in self-denial and may suffer from feelings of gloom and depression. Because of their negative and pessimistic view of the world, combined with extreme sensitivity, they get disappointed easily and have a hard time seeing the positive side of things.

🦁 Pig-Leo:

Pig-Leos are plain and honest, modest and studious, and generous and hospitable. Their keen wit and sense of humor often bring smiles to the faces of others. They are willing to toil hard to enjoy the finer things in life or to enhance their material environment. Although Pig-Leos tend to put their family above all else, they are also able to create miracles in their career pursuits.

🌾 Pig-Virgo:

Pig-Virgos are extremely innocent and kindhearted. They tend to place their complete trust in other people and sometimes lack the ability to discern good and bad in others, putting themselves in a vulnerable position. Though they are often obsessed with reputation and pursuing a life of opulence and pleasure, they wouldn't hesitate to sacrifice it all for the one they love. The Pig-Virgo also has the ability to get right down to work, and is well-suited to a career in the arts.

⚖️ Pig-Libra:

Pig-Librans regard love as everything in life and show extremely devotion to their companion. Despite indulging in fantasy and being highly emotional, they have lofty ambitions and are able to achieve phenomenal results in their career pursuits. Pig-Librans also excel at performing household duties and managing family affairs.

🦂 Pig-Scorpio:

Pig-Scorpios are energetic and ambitious, have exquisite taste, and are good at dressing up. Despite their charm and appeal, they are also loud-mouthed and like to rush others. They also have a fiery temper, get jealous easily, and are

THE *HAI* PIG DELIVERS THE LUCK

narrow-minded and conservative. Though Pig-Scorpios have strong willpower, they sometimes make compromises to pursue their own interest.

Pig-Sagittarius:

Pig-Sagittarians are meticulous in their endeavors and possess strong observational skills. Despite being stubborn and inflexible, they are equally honest, faithful and generous. They enjoy being close to nature and often choose to lead a simple country life.

Pig-Capricorn:

Pig-Capricorns are gifted and intelligent, ambitious and inspired, polite and courteous, and confident and clear-headed. With a diligent, conscientious attitude and a strong sense of responsibility, they show dedication to both their career and family. They always abide by the rules and tend to be a bit stubborn and old-fashioned.

Pig-Aquarius:

Pig-Aquarians are optimistic, courageous, and able to rise to the occasion. They also have a strong mind and excellent debating skills. Despite being aggressive, conceited and even a bit foolish, Pig-Aquarians know how to gain the adoration of others and thus have many friends. They are highly charming, able to forgive others, and come across as kind and friendly.

Pig-Pisces:

Pig-Pisceses are gentle, kindhearted, and unwavering in their loyalty. However, they also have a tendency to suppress their own sorrow or anger, and lack the ability to communicate these feelings to others. Pig-Pisceses also suffer from high pressure as well as hyper-vigilance.

THE TWELVE ZODIAC ANIMALS

FENGSHUI AND THE PIG

With their obese and rotund shape, pigs are traditionally held as a symbol of affluence and good fortune. In the study of *fengshui*, pigs possess the spiritual power of generating wealth. Pigs usually appear as part of sacrificial worship; at home or in the workplace, too, *fengshui* pigs can be used to enhance financial inflows. Fengshui pigs can be placed in any room or location other than lavatories and bathrooms; ideally, they should be placed somewhere auspicious. Since their primary use is to beget riches, only *fengshui* pigs made of gold can give full play to the pig's spiritual force of wealth creation. Another way to harness this mystical power is to deposit small change into a piggy bank on a daily basis; however, the piggy bank must not be moved from its original location. Since the earthly branches *Si* and *Hai* are mutually conflicting, the use of *fengshui* pigs by people born in the Year of the Snake would be ineffectual.

INTERPRETING PIG DREAMS

If you dream of killing a pig, it is a good omen.

If you dream of a dead pig, it is a bad omen.

If you dream of a pig turning into a human, you will soon become an official.

If you dream of a pig and sheep scratching their itches, an argument will break out.

HEALTH SECRETS

People born in the Year of the Pig should try to eat smaller portions, and drink alcohol in moderation if at all. They should be vigilant against diseases of the kidney. Staying up all night or overeating at a single meal could be especially damaging to their health. It is also important that they adjust their mental state as necessary, and try to look on the bright side of things. Pigs may refuse to eat when something is weighing on their mind. This kind of self-starvation should be avoided, as it could adversely affect the stomach and intestines and cause gastrointestinal disorders.

THE *HAI* PIG DELIVERS THE LUCK

Appendix

A Comparison Table Between Chinese Zodiac Calendar and Western Calendar

Zi Rat	Chou Ox	Yin Tiger	Mao Rabbit	Chen Dragon	Si Snake	Wu Horse	Wei Sheep	Shen Monkey	You Rooster	Xu Dog	Hai Pig
1900	1901	1902	1903	1904	1905	1906	1907	1908	1909	1910	1911
1912	1913	1914	1915	1916	1917	1918	1919	1920	1921	1922	1923
1924	1925	1926	1927	1928	1929	1930	1931	1932	1933	1934	1935
1936	1937	1938	1939	1940	1941	1942	1943	1944	1945	1946	1947
1948	1949	1950	1951	1952	1953	1954	1955	1956	1957	1958	1959
1960	1961	1962	1963	1964	1965	1966	1967	1968	1969	1970	1971
1972	1973	1974	1975	1976	1977	1978	1979	1980	1981	1982	1983
1984	1985	1986	1987	1988	1989	1990	1991	1992	1993	1994	1995
1996	1997	1998	1999	2000	2001	2002	2003	2004	2005	2006	2007
2008	2009	2010	2011	2012	2013	2014	2015	2016	2017	2018	2019
2020	2021	2022	2023	2024	2025	2026	2027	2028	2029	2030	2031
2032	2033	2034	2035	2036	2037	2038	2039	2040	2041	2042	2043
2044	2045	2046	2047	2048	2049	2050	2051	2052	2053	2054	2055
2056	2057	2058	2059	2060	2061	2062	2063	2064	2065	2066	2067
2068	2069	2070	2071	2072	2073	2074	2075	2076	2077	2078	2079
2080	2081	2082	2083	2084	2085	2086	2087	2088	2089	2090	2091
2092	2093	2094	2095	2096	2097	2098	2099	2100	2101	2102	2103
2104	2105	2106	2107	2108	2109	2110	2111	2112	2113	2114	2115
2116	2117	2118	2119	2120	2121	2122	2123	2124	2125	2126	2127

Chinese Zodiac Signs Compatibility Chart

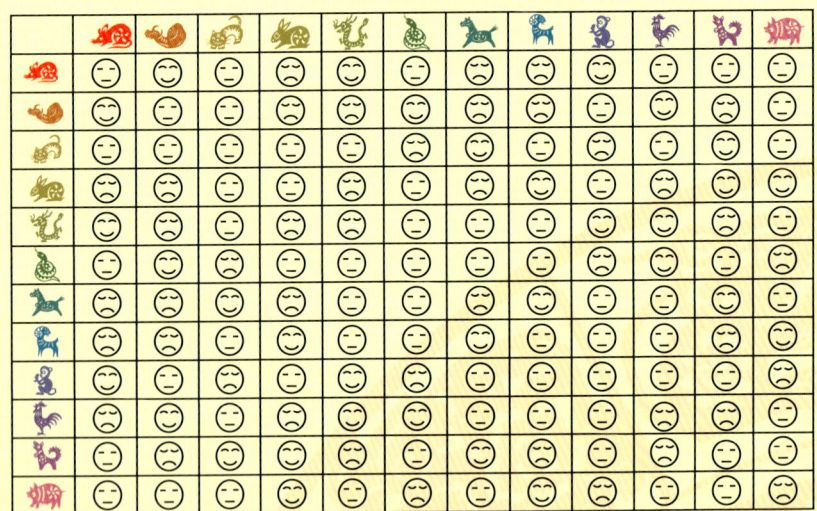

A Comparison Table of the Twelve Zodiac Animals, Five Elements, and Heavenly Stems and Earthly Branches

No.	The twelve zodiac animals	Five Elements	Heavenly Stems and Earthly Branches	No.	The twelve zodiac animals	Five Elements	Heavenly Stems and Earthly Branches
1	Rat	Metal	Jia-Zi	31	Horse	Metal	Jia-Wu
2	Ox	Metal	Yi-Chou	32	Sheep	Metal	Yi-Wei
3	Tiger	Fire	Bing-Yin	33	Monkey	Fire	Bing-Shen
4	Rabbit	Fire	Ding-Mao	34	Rooster	Fire	Ding-You
5	Dragon	Wood	Wu-Chen	35	Dog	Wood	Wu-Xu
6	Snake	Wood	Ji-Si	36	Pig	Wood	Ji-Hai
7	Horse	Earth	Geng-Wu	37	Rat	Earth	Geng-Zi
8	Sheep	Earth	Xin-Wei	38	Ox	Earth	Xin-Chou
9	Monkey	Metal	Ren-Shen	39	Tiger	Metal	Ren-Yin
10	Rooster	Metal	Gui-You	40	Rabbit	Metal	Gui-Mao
11	Dog	Fire	Jia-Xu	41	Dragon	Fire	Jia-Chen
12	Pig	Fire	Yi-Hai	42	Snake	Fire	Yi-Si
13	Rat	Water	Bing-Zi	43	Horse	Water	Bing-Wu
14	Ox	Water	Ding-Chou	44	Sheep	Water	Ding-Wei
15	Tiger	Earth	Wu-Yin	45	Monkey	Earth	Wu-Shen
16	Rabbit	Earth	Ji-Mao	46	Rooster	Earth	Ji-You
17	Dragon	Metal	Geng-Chen	47	Dog	Metal	Geng-Xu
18	Snake	Metal	Xin-Si	48	Pig	Metal	Xin-Hai
19	Horse	Wood	Ren-Wu	49	Rat	Wood	Ren-Zi
20	Sheep	Wood	Gui-Wei	50	Ox	Wood	Gui-Chou
21	Monkey	Water	Jia-Shen	51	Tiger	Water	Jia-Yin
22	Rooster	Water	Yi-You	52	Rabbit	Water	Yi-Mao
23	Dog	Earth	Bing-Xu	53	Dragon	Earth	Bing-Chen
24	Pig	Earth	Ding-Hai	54	Snake	Earth	Ding-Si
25	Rat	Fire	Wu-Zi	55	Horse	Fire	Wu-Wu
26	Ox	Fire	Ji-Chou	56	Sheep	Fire	Ji-Wei
27	Tiger	Wood	Geng-Yin	57	Monkey	Wood	Geng-Shen
28	Rabbit	Wood	Xin-Mao	58	Rooster	Wood	Xin-You
29	Dragon	Water	Ren-Chen	59	Dog	Water	Ren-Xu
30	Snake	Water	Gui-Si	60	Pig	Water	Gui-Hai

The Twelve Constellations and Corresponding Twelve Chinese Zodiac Animals

Constellations	Corresponding Zodiac animals	Constellations	Corresponding Zodiac animals
Aquarius ♒	Rat	Leo ♌	Horse
Capricorn ♑	Ox	Cancer ♋	Sheep
Sagittarius ♐	Tiger	Gemini ♊	Monkey
Scorpio ♏	Rabbit	Taurus ♉	Rooster
Libra ♎	Dragon	Aries ♈	Dog
Virgo ♍	Snake	Pisces ♓	Pig

THE TWELVE ZODIAC ANIMALS

十二生肖 THE TWELVE

EPILOGUE

The twelve zodiac animals are an important symbol of Chinese folk culture. Over the course of two thousand years of development and distillation, the culture of the Chinese zodiac, with its profound and abundant content, has deeply penetrated every realm of societal life, even impacting spiritual beliefs and notions of fate. As of today, the zodiac animals have become a cultural symbol — a sparkling gemstone in the treasury of Chinese culture.

China is a large family comprising 56 ethnic groups. The culture of the zodiac animals not only prevails among the Han nationality; it is also universally seen among the numerous ethnic minorities of China. Some ethnic groups, including the Mongols and Zhuangs, have a zodiac culture which is essentially consistent with that of the Hans. Other ethnic groups, however, selected animals to correlate with their respective living environments and predominant species. To some extent, this has enhanced the diversity of China's zodiac culture. For example, in the 12 zodiac animals of Xinjiang's Kyrgyz people, the dragon is replaced by the fish, and the monkey is replaced by the fox. In contrast, the Yi people of the Ailao Mountains replaced the dragon with the pangolin. There are also some differences in zodiac-related folk customs, the sequence of the zodiac, and the way in which it was used to record time. In general, however, these different zodiacs all originate from the same source. The culture of the Chinese zodiac animals is a crystal of collective wisdom; at the same time, the different versions prevalent among each of China's ethnic groups offer added color, richness and variety.

ZODIAC ANIMALS

Culture knows no boundaries. As of today, the impact of the shengxiao and its surrounding culture has reached far beyond China's borders. The Chinese zodiac animals are well-known and widely used by the peoples of North and South Korea, Vietnam, and Japan. As Chinese communities spread around the world, the Chinese zodiac was carried and transmitted to regions and countries far and wide. The Chinese zodiac animals have since become a shared cultural treasure of humankind. More and more nations have issued stamp sets or commemorative coins of the twelve zodiac animals and organized thematic activities related to the zodiac culture. Indeed, the culture of the Chinese zodiac can be thought of a contribution of the ancient Chinese people to world culture.

This book is intended to serve as a vehicle for cultural exchange. By selecting widely influential Han customs as its main content and using a combination of engaging text and colorful illustrations, it presents an account of the rich and varied culture of the Chinese zodiac. In addition to introducing the legends and folk customs associated with each of the zodiac animals, the book also presents related information on "lifetime fortune", fortune telling, and the interpretation of dreams. Although the culture of the Chinese zodiac animals has been passed on through successive dynasties, changing social systems, and countless generations, it has endured over this vast span of time and, even today, is still as popular as ever. The reason that this culture possesses such vitality and endurance is that the zodiac animals, through the symbolic meanings which they have been endowed, manifest the Chinese people's search for destiny as well as the universal aspiration toward a beautiful and fulfilling life.

图书在版编目（CIP）数据

十二生肖：汉英对照 / 旅舜主编. —北京：研究出版社，2009.3
ISBN 978-7-80168-461-5
Ⅰ. 十⋯
Ⅱ. 旅⋯
Ⅲ. 十二生肖—通俗读物—汉、英
Ⅳ. K892.21-49
中国版本图书馆CIP数据核字（2009）第 028593号

旅 舜：主 编	Editor in Chief: Lü Shun
之 眉 黄慎如：责任编辑	Managing Editor: Zhi Mei Huang Shenru
余泯然 赵伟玉：执行编辑	Executive Editor: Yu Minran Zhao Weiyu
罗 童 马 特：英文翻译	Translators: Luo Tong Matthew Trueman
王 磊 等：摄 影	Photographers: Wang Lei etc
帅 芸：装帧设计	Art Designer: Shuai Yun

本书部分图片由cnsphoto 和phototime.cn 提供

《十二生肖》
The Twelve Zodiac Animals

出版：研究出版社
编者：北京精典博雅旅游图书有限公司
开本：889 × 1194 mm 32开
印张：7.5
印数：1-3000
版次：2009年4月第一版第一次印刷
书号：ISBN 978-7-80168-461-5
http://www.旅游图书.cn

Published by Yan Jiu Publishing House
Edited by Beijing Jingdian Boya Traveling Book Co., Ltd
Format: 889 × 1194 mm 1/32
Printed Sheet: 7.5
Impression: 3,000
Printed Order: First Impression & First Edition in April, 2009
ISBN: 978-7-80168-461-5
http://www.jdbybook.com

0012800

如发现质量问题，请致电 010-6711 8480 联系调换
版权所有　　盗版必究